Competition and
Entrepreneurship

ISRAEL M. KIRZNER

Competition and Entrepreneurship

THE
UNIVERSITY OF CHICAGO
PRESS

CHICAGO AND LONDON

B'Ezras Hashem

The University of Chicago Press, Chicago 60637
The University of Chicago Press, Ltd., London
© 1973 by The University of Chicago
All rights reserved. Published 1973
Second Impression 1974
Printed in the United States of America
International Standard Book Number: 0-226-43775-2
Library of Congress Catalog Card Number: 72-95424

Contents

Contents

Contents

6

COMPETITION, WELFARE, AND COORDINATION

212

Preface

RECENT YEARS HAVE WITNESSED A REVIVAL OF INTEREST IN microeconomic aspects of economic systems. The theory of price has once again become the core of economic analysis. For the most part, however, contemporary price theory has continued to be presented within an equilibrium framework. This not only has diverted attention away from the market process and toward equilibrium, but has led to virtual exclusion of the entrepreneurial role from economic theory.

Thoughtful critics of contemporary price theory have very recently begun to draw attention to these shortcomings. Some of the writings of Abbott, Baumol, Brozen, Dewey, Leibenstein, McNulty, and D. McCord Wright, despite the wide differences among them, reflect a common concern with the failure of contemporary microeconomics to grapple with the market process. What has been generally overlooked, however, is the existence throughout this century of at least one tradition of economic thought in which these shortcomings have never been permitted to appear. While the Anglo-American tradition deriving from neoclassical price theory has remained frozen within the equilibrium framework, the writers who took their origin from the Austrians have consistently worked along lines in which entrepreneurship and market processes received their proper due. This book can be viewed as a critique of contemporary price theory from an "Austrian" perspective; or it may be viewed as an essay on the theory of entrepreneurship, or on the theory of competition. Its purpose is in fact to show that these views coincide. Besides its emphasis on entrepreneurship, the book offers a new perspective on quality competition, on selling effort, and on the fundamental weakness of contemporary welfare economics.

Among those with whom conversation or correspondence has proved helpful I gratefully recall J. Buchanan, R. Coase, D. Dewey, L. Lachmann, H. Demsetz, G. Tullock, and A. Zabarkes. Above all I owe whatever understanding I have of the market process to almost two decades of study under L. Mises, whose ideas as expounded in a lifetime's work are only now beginning to be properly appreciated. I acknowledge with gratitude the generous research support I received from the New York University Schools of Business Research Office and from the Relm Foundation. Of course responsibility for any inadequacies in this book rests with me alone.

]1[
Market Process versus Market Equilibrium

THIS BOOK IS AN ATTEMPT TOWARD A THEORY OF THE MARKET and of the price system that differs in significant respects from the orthodox theory of price. In this introductory chapter I will briefly survey the range of problems we will be dealing with and outline the salient points of difference that will set my own approach apart from the standard approach to microeconomic theory. As we will discover, the most important of these differences finds expression as dissatisfaction with the usual emphasis on *equilibrium analysis*, and in an attempt to replace this emphasis by a fuller understanding of the operation of the market as a *process*. Much of this chapter will therefore be devoted to this issue.

THE MARKET SYSTEM AND THE THEORY OF THE MARKET

The theory of the market — more usually but less felicitously known as the theory of price or as microeconomic theory — is founded on the basic insight that market phenomena can be "understood" as the manifestations of systematic relationships. The observable phenomena of the market — the prices at which commodities are exchanged, the kinds and qualities of commodities produced, the quantities exchanged, the methods of production employed, the prices of the factors of production used, the structure of the various markets, and the like — are seen not as masses of isolated, irreducible data but as the

1

outcomes of determinate processes that can, in principle, be grasped and understood.

This fundamental insight has been explored and exploited by the many theorists who have contributed over many decades to the edifice of price theory. They have studied ways in which market phenomena depend on one another, developing theories of consumer demands, of production, and of market prices for commodities and factors that indicate the chains of causation that link together the basic data of the market — the arrays of tastes, technological possibilities, and resource availabilities — with the observable phenomena of the market system.

From this intensive intellectual activity over the years there has emerged an imposing structure that constitutes a well-recognized body of theoretical knowledge, the theory of price. The theory as it is presented in the textbooks and taught in the classroom is rather well established. There were many lively — sometimes furious — controversies during the history of price theory; and there were on occasion complete "revolutions" involving drastic reworking of the entire corpus of theory. There is still much activity, and original work is still being done on particular pieces of the structure; there have been repeated strong expressions of dissatisfaction with particular parts of the theory; and there is, has always been, and probably always will be sharp criticism, of the entire approach taken by price theory, of its assumptions, its method, and the relevance and validity of its conclusions. But, granting all this, it yet remains true that "orthodox" price theory as standardly presented is less controversial and in less of a ferment than other parts of economics.

The dominant "orthodoxy" in Anglo-American price theory has clearly visible roots in the earliest divergent schools of economic thought. The major element is clearly Marshallian in origin, modified by the Robinson-Chamberlin innovations of the thirties, perhaps enriched here by the infusion of Walrasian general-equilibrium insights and there by the absorption of Austrian ideas on cost, and rendered more sophisticated throughout by more refined geometrical techniques and more rigorous by increased dependence on mathematics as a language. Contemporary price theorists will generally argue, with some justification, that little that was valuable in any of the opposing views aired in past controversies is absent from the widely shared corpus of modern price theory.

The position that I will take diverges in several significant respects from this generally approving view of the contemporary theory of price. I will argue that the direction in which the dominant stream of microeconomic thought has flowed must be judged, on several counts, to be an unfortunate one; that some of the less sophisticated views of participants in earlier controversies, views which have *not* found their way into the modern theory, reflected more penetrating and useful insights into the operation of the market than the modern theory possesses. I will argue that the dominant theory not only suffers from serious weaknesses as a vehicle for economic understanding, but has also, as a result, led to grievously faulty conclusions for economic policy. Our position will call for reconsidering very substantial portions of the theory of price, and I will attempt to point to the lines along which a reconstructed theory of the market may be built.

As the reader will discover, there is little I will say that has not been said somewhere by someone. The position taken up in this essay does not, in its main features, set out to be an original one; but there does seem to be an urgent need to set down systematically what I feel is the more useful approach to understanding the operation of the market, and to contrast it carefully, point by point, with relevant portions of the dominant contemporary theory of price.

THE TASK OF PRICE THEORY: TWO VIEWS

The crucial issue separating the dominant theory of price from the approach to be put forward here can perhaps best be described as involving a disagreement about what to look for in a theory of price. This in turn has caused the two approaches to emphasize different aspects of the market. I will thus argue that the dominant theory, by emphasizing certain features of the market to the exclusion of others, has constructed a mental picture of the market that has virtually left out a number of elements that are of critical importance to a full understanding of its operation.

In the theory of price as generally expounded, the function of price is perceived to be something as follows. In a market system the activities of market participants consist of choosing the quantities and qualities of commodities and factors to be bought and sold and the prices at which these transactions are to be carried out. Only definite values of these quantity and price variables are consistent with equilibrium in the price system. In other words, given the basic data (tastes, technological possibilities, and resource endowments), there is only one set of planned activities that permits all of them to be carried out as planned. A theory of price is seen as explaining the determination of this unique pattern of activities, permitting the assignment, in principle, of definite values for the price and quantity variables. The theory of price approaches this task by analyzing how decisions are made by the various market participants — consumers, producers, and factor owners — and examining the interrelations between these decisions under various possible patterns of market structure. In this way the price theorists may, in principle, deduce the constellation of prices and quantities consistent with all of these decisions. (At a more ambitious level the theory may, it is true, aim at understanding not only the equilibrium pattern of prices and quantities, but also paths over time of prices and quantities. At this level of analysis the task of theory is to develop functional relationships, not only between the prices and quantities prevailing at the instant of equilibrium, but also between each of these variables at each instant along the path to equilibrium.

4

This function of price theory, it must be pointed out, is distinctly subordinate to that of the equilibrium analysis. In most treatments of contemporary microtheory, in fact, this function is omitted entirely. Where it is at all seriously treated, its main purpose is seen as the investigation of the stability of equilibrium.)

The focus of attention, in this view of the task of price theory, is thus on the *values of the price and quantity variables,* and in particular on the set of values consistent with *equilibrium* conditions. In investigating the consequences of a particular market structure, this approach examines the associated pattern of equilibrium prices, costs, and outputs. In investigating the consequences of a particular change in taste, or technology and the like, it examines the equilibrium conditions after the change, comparing them with those before the change. The very efficiency of the market system as an allocator of society's resources is appraised by examining the allocation of resources at equilibrium. In investigating the desirability of particular government policies, this approach appraises the effects of the changes these policies will bring about in the equilibrium situation. In all this the emphasis is on the *prices* and *quantities* and, in particular, on these prices and quantities as they would emerge under *equilibrium* conditions.

By contrast, the approach to the theory of price underlying this book perceives its task in a significantly different way. The market is still, of course, seen as made up of the activities of the market participants — the consumers, producers, and factor owners. Their activities result from decisions to produce, to buy, and to sell commodities and resources. And once again there exists a pattern of decisions which are mutually consistent, so that all planned activities can be carried out without disappointment. Furthermore, this pattern of decisions is recognized as of very special interest because it makes up the state of equilibrium. *But it is not this equilibrium situation which is the focus of attention.* The task of price theory is not seen as primarily concerned with the configuration of prices and quantities that satisfies the conditions for equilibrium. The important insights which familiarity with the theory of price promises to confer are not seen as consisting in any exclusive or even predominant way of an understanding of the requirements for equilibrium or of the ability to state and solve, whether in words or in algebra, the equations that must be simultaneously satisfied in order for all plans to be carried out. Moreover, in this approach it is never the values of the price and quantity variables which are themselves the object of theoretical interest. It is not the relationship between equilibrium prices and quantities or the relationships over time of disequilibrium prices and quantities which represents the *quaesita* of a theory of price.

Rather, in the approach to price theory underlying this book, we look to price theory to help us understand how the decisions of individual participants in the market interact to generate the market forces which compel *changes* in prices, in outputs, and in methods of production and the allocation of resources. We look to price theory to elucidate the nature of the mutual influence exercised by decisions so that we may understand how changes in these decisions, or in the data which underlie them, systematically set into motion further alterations elsewhere in the market. The object of our scientific interest is these alterations themselves, not (except as a matter of subsidiary, intermediate, or even incidental interest) the relationships governing prices and quantities in the equilibrium situation.

From the normative point of view, too, the approach to price theory adopted here sees its function in a way that is not related in any essential manner to the state of affairs at equilibrium. The efficiency of the price system, in this approach, does not depend upon the optimality (or absence of it) of the resource allocation pattern at equilibrium; rather, it depends on the degree of success with which market forces can be relied upon to generate spontaneous corrections in the allocation patterns prevailing at times of disequilibrium.

As we will discover, this difference in the conceptions of the task and purpose of price theory has far-reaching implications for the methods and the substantive content of the alternative approaches. However, my position here is not that these conflicting views on the function of price theory have (for either of the approaches) served explicitly as the logical starting points and foundations for the alternative theories. Rather, I am suggesting that after the alternative theories are examined, the difference between them is seen to be best interpreted as reflecting the (perhaps unconscious) assignment of different functions and roles to the theories. It may well be that many writers have not attempted to set forth explicitly the purposes for which a theory of price is to be constructed. Nonetheless, the many important differences in analysis that separate the dominant approach from that underlying this book are most neatly summed up as reflecting disagreement (possibly only implicit disagreement) concerning the aim of price theory in general. In introducing the substantive matters on which this essay will express dissenting views, therefore, it is useful to emphasize, as I have done, that aspect of our approach to price theory which seems to set it apart most fundamentally from the alternative orthodoxy. With these basic considerations concerning the purpose of price theory in mind, let us survey the major theoretical issues that will occupy us in later chapters. Thereafter, we will return to further development of the contrast between a theory of equilibrium prices and a theory of the market process.

COMPETITION AND ENTREPRENEURSHIP

Much of our discussion will revolve around two notions crucial to an understanding of the market and central to its theory — *competition* and *entrepreneurship*. Both terms are widely used in the everyday speech of laymen concerning economic and business affairs. During the history of economics a great deal has been written about these notions, and the first of the two has become the subject of an enormous literature. In current presentations of the theory of price, entrepreneurship is discussed in connection with the theory of distribution (especially with the theory of profits), and to some extent in connection with the theory of production and the theory of the firm. I will maintain that, despite a number of highly perceptive contributions, the proper role of the entrepreneur in the market system is not typically presented in its true light, or with adequate recognition for its being the driving force for the entire market process. And I will argue further that the role of the entrepreneur in relation to competition has been virtually ignored.

Competition, as many writers have told us, is a term that has been used in innumerable senses. Economists have worked with many different models, each marked with one form or another of the competitive label. Still central to much of contemporary price theory is the model of perfect competition. Despite all the criticisms showered on this model during the past forty years, it still occupies the center of the stage, both in positive and in normative discussions. The dissatisfaction with perfectly competitive theory produced new models dealing with various imperfectly competitive market structures, but these have not succeeded in dislodging the perfectly competitive model from its preeminent position. Much of the discussion here will have to do with all of these models. My position will be not only that the model of perfect competition fails to help us understand the market process, but that the models of imperfect competition developed to replace it are little more helpful. I will maintain that the theorists who developed these models of imperfectly competitive markets failed to recognize the really important shortcomings of the perfect competition theory. As a result they were unable to perceive the direction in which a genuine rehabilitation of price theory must be developed and proceeded instead to construct models which suffer from the very defects which invalidate the perfectly competitive model.

As was noted above, a feature common to all these competitive models to which I will be taking exception is their exclusion of the entrepreneurial element from the analysis. We will find that a useful understanding of the market process requires a notion of competition that is analytically inseparable from the exercise of entrepreneurship. This will have powerful consequences for the analysis of such problems as *selling costs*, *advertising*, and *monopoly*. The notion of competition we will find essential for understanding the market process will lead us toward a fresh way of "seeing" selling costs and evaluating their role in the market economy. At the same time, our notions of competition and entrepreneurship will lead us to a quite unorthodox view of the nature of monopoly in a market. The fact that entrepreneurship may be a step toward monopoly power will call for a new evaluation of both the allegedly harmful effects of monopoly and the reputedly beneficial effects of entrepreneurship. It will be useful at this point to outline the picture of the market process which incorporates our views on competition and entrepreneurship, contrasting it briefly with the dominant concept of the market. This outline will serve as an overview of the position to be put forward at greater length in subsequent chapters.

THE MARKET PROCESS

We see the market as made up, during any period of time, of the interacting decisions of consumers, entrepreneur-producers, and resource owners. Not all the decisions in a given period can be carried out, since many of them may erroneously anticipate and depend upon other decisions which are in fact not being made. Again, many of the decisions which are successfully carried out in a given period may not turn out to have been the best possible courses of action. Had the decision-makers been aware of the choices others were making during the same period, they would have perceived opportunities for more attractive courses of market action than those actually adopted. In short, ignorance of the decisions which others are in fact about to make may cause decision-makers to make unfortunate plans — either plans that are doomed to disappointment or plans which fail to exploit existing market opportunities.

During the given period of time, exposure to the decisions of others communicates some of the information these decision-makers originally lacked. If they find that their plans cannot be carried out, this teaches them that their anticipations concerning the decisions of others were overly optimistic. Or they may learn that their undue pessimism has caused them to pass up attractive market opportunities. This newly acquired information concerning the plans of others can be expected to generate, for the succeeding period of time, *a revised set of decisions*. The overambitious plans of one period will be replaced by more realistic ones; market opportunities overlooked in one period will be exploited in the next. In other words, even without changes in the basic data of the market (i.e., in consumer tastes, technological possibilities, and resource availabilities), the decisions made in one period of time generate systematic alterations in the corresponding decisions for the succeeding period. Taken over time, this series of systematic changes in the interconnected network of market decisions constitutes the market process.

The market process, then, is set in motion by the results of the initial market-ignorance of the participants. The process itself consists of the systematic plan changes generated by the flow of market information released by market participation — that is, by the testing of plans in the market. As a matter of considerable theoretical interest we may investigate the possibility of a state of affairs in which *no* market ignorance is present. We would then have a pattern of perfectly dovetailing decisions. No decision made will fail to be carried out, and no opportunity will fail to be exploited. Each market participant will have correctly forecast all the relevant decisions of others; he will have laid his plans fully cognizant of what he will be unable to do in the market, but at the same time fully awake to what he *is* able to do in the market. Clearly, with such a state of affairs the market *process* must immediately cease. Without autonomous change in tastes, or in technological possibilities, or in the availability of resources, no one can have any interest in altering his plans for the succeeding periods. The market is in equilibrium; the pattern of market activity will continue without change period after period.

As was indicated earlier, the thrust of our analysis will be primarily toward understanding the market process, not toward specifying the conditions required for the state of equilibrium, the situation in which the market process has ceased. Let me now draw attention to the competitive character of the market process.

COMPETITION IN THE MARKET PROCESS

We have seen the market during any period of time as made up of decisions of market participants. These decisions, I said, presupposed corresponding decisions on the part of others. Consumers' decisions to buy depend on the decisions of entrepreneur-producers to sell. Decisions by resource owners to sell depend on the decisions of entrepreneur-producers to buy — and vice versa. Each pair of dovetailing decisions (each market transaction completed) constitutes a case in which each party is being offered an opportunity which, to the best of his knowledge, is the best being offered to him in the market. Each market participant is therefore aware at all times that he can expect to carry out his plans only if these plans do in fact offer others the best opportunity available, as far as they know. This is simply saying that each market participant, in laying his buying or selling plans, must pay careful heed not only to the prospective decisions of those to whom he hopes to sell or from whom he hopes to buy, but — as an implication of the

11

latter — also to the prospective decisions of others whose decisions to sell or to buy may compete with his own.

And as the market process unfolds, with one period of market ignorance followed by another in which ignorance has been somewhat reduced, each buyer or seller revises his bids and offers in the light of his newly acquired knowledge of the alternative opportunities which those to whom he may wish to sell, or from whom he may wish to buy, can expect to find available elsewhere in the market. In this sense the market process is inherently *competitive*. The systematic alteration in decisions between each period and the succeeding one renders each opportunity offered to the market more competitive than that offered in the preceding period — that is, it is offered with fuller awareness of the other opportunities being made available, against which it is necessary to compete.

We should observe that awareness of competing opportunities implies something more than that a decision-maker knows that no decision can be carried out if it creates less attractive opportunities for the market than those offered by his competitors. It also implies that he knows he must offer opportunities *more* attractive than those of his competitors. So in the course of the market process the participants are continually testing their competitors. Each inches ahead by offering opportunities a little more attractive than theirs. His competitors, in turn, once they become aware of what *they* are competing against, are forced to sweeten still further the opportunities they make available to the market; and so on. In this struggle to keep ahead of one's competitors (but at the same time to avoid creating opportunities more attractive than necessary), market participants are thus forced by the competitive market process to gravitate closer and closer to the limits of their ability to participate gainfully in the market. Competition among consumers for a given commodity may, for example, tend to force its price upward; each consumer is careful not to consume beyond the point where the marginal purchase is just worthwhile; during the process, those who are less eager consumers of marginal units drop out of the race earlier. Competition among the owners of a particular resource may tend to force its price downwards; those owners for whom its sale involves the greater sacrifices will tend to drop out of the race as the falling price makes it worthwhile for them to sell only fewer and fewer units of the resource.

Were this competitive process to run its course to completion — in other words, were all decisions to become fully dovetailed — each participant would no longer be under pressure to improve the opportunities he is currently offering to the market, since no one else is offering more attractive opportunities. So with fully dovetailed decisions it is entirely possible for participants to continue offering parallel opportunities to the rest of the market, period after period. It is unnecessary, under these circumstances, for any participant to inch ahead of his competitors (in the attractiveness of opportunities offered), since all current plans can be carried out in the market without disappointment. This situation of market equilibrium is surely one in which competition is no longer an active force. The cessation of the market process which we have already seen as characteristic of the equilibrium state is the cessation of a *competitive* process. It is against the background of this notion of competition, in which competition is inseparable from the market process itself, that I will later criticize the usefulness of notions that confine competition to the situation in which the market process has ceased — the state of equilibrium. Let me now make clear the crucial role the entrepreneur plays in the market process.

ENTREPRENEURSHIP IN THE MARKET PROCESS

Essential to the notion of the market process as I have described it is the acquisition of market information through the experience of market participation. The systematic pattern of adjustments in market plans which makes up the market process

13

arises, as we have seen, from the market participants' discovery that their anticipations were overly optimistic or unduly pessimistic. It can be shown that our confidence in the market's ability to learn and to harness the continuous flow of market information to generate the market process depends crucially on our belief in the benign presence of the entrepreneurial element.

To see this, let us imagine a market in which all those currently participating are in fact *unable* to learn from their market experience. Would-be buyers who have been returning home empty-handed (because they have not been offering sufficiently high prices) have *not* learned that it is necessary to outbid other buyers; would-be sellers who return home with unsold goods or resources (because they have been asking prices that are too high) have *not* learned that they must, if they wish to sell, be satisfied with lower prices. Buyers who have paid high prices do not discover that they could have obtained the same goods at lower prices; sellers who have sold for low prices do not discover that they could have obtained higher prices. Into this imaginary world of men unable to learn from their market experience let us now introduce a group of outsiders who are themselves neither would-be sellers nor would-be buyers, but who *are* able to perceive opportunities for entrepreneurial profits; that is, they are able to see where a good can be sold at a price higher than that for which it can be bought. This group of entrepreneurs would, in our imaginary world, immediately notice profit opportunities *that exist because of the initial ignorance of the original market participants* and that have persisted because of their inability to learn from experience. They would move to buy at low prices from those sellers who have not discovered that some buyers are paying high prices. And they would then sell these goods at high prices to those buyers who have not discovered that some sellers have been selling for low prices.

It is easy to perceive that so long as this group of entrepreneurs is active in the market, and so long as they are alert to the changing prices their own activity brings about, the market process can proceed in an entirely normal fashion. These entrepreneurs will communicate to the other market participants the market information which these other participants are themselves unable to obtain. The competition between the various entrepreneurs will move them to offer to buy from the low-price sellers, at prices higher than these sellers had thought possible; entrepreneurs in competition with one another will also sell to high-price buyers at prices lower than these buyers had thought possible. Gradually, competition between the entrepreneurs as buyers, and again as sellers, will succeed in communicating to market participants a correct estimate of the other market participants' eagerness to buy and to sell. Prices will move in exactly the same way as they would move in a world in which buyers and sellers *were* able to learn from their market experience.

Clearly then, it is not *necessary* for us, in constructing the analytical model of a market in process, to postulate such a rigid compartmentation of roles. Instead of one group of market participants who do not learn from experience and another (entrepreneurial) group who do, we can work with market participants who *are* alert to changing buying and selling possibilities. The *process* will still remain an essentially entrepreneurial one, but instead of working with a group of "pure" entrepreneurs, we could simply recognize an entrepreneurial aspect to the activities of each market participant.

The outcome is always the same: the competitive market process is essentially entrepreneurial. The pattern of decisions in any period differs from the pattern in the preceding period as market participants become aware of new opportunities. As they exploit these opportunities, their competition pushes prices in directions which gradually squeeze out opportunities for further profit-making. The entrepreneurial element in the economic behavior of market participants consists, as we will later discover in detail, in their alertness to previously unnoticed changes in circumstances which may make it possible to get far more in exchange for whatever they have to offer than was hitherto possible.

Our insights into the competitive character of the market process and its entrepreneurial character teach us that the two notions of competition and entrepreneurship are, at least in the sense used here, analytically inseparable. (And regardless of *which* terms one chooses to use, these two notions *must* be recognized, and must be perceived as being at all times merely two sides of the same coin.) The key point is that *pure* entrepreneurship is exercised only in the *absence* of an initially owned asset. Other market roles invariably involve a search for the best exchange opportunities for translating an initially owned asset into something more eagerly desired. The "pure" entrepreneur observes the opportunity to sell something at a price higher than that at which he can buy it. It follows that *anyone* is a potential entrepreneur, since the purely entrepreneurial role presupposes no special initial good fortune in the form of valuable assets. Therefore, whereas the market participation of asset owners is always to *some* extent protected (by the peculiar qualities of the assets possessed), the market activity of the entrepreneur is *never* protected in any way. The opportunity offered in the market by an asset owner cannot be freely duplicated or surpassed by just anyone; it can be duplicated only by another owner of a similar asset. In a world in which no two assets are exactly the same, no opportunity offered by an asset owner can be exactly duplicated. But if an entrepreneur perceives the possibility of gaining profit by offering to buy at a price attractive to sellers and by offering to sell at a price attractive to buyers, the opportunities he thus offers to the market can in principle be made available by anyone. The entrepreneur's activity is essentially competitive. And thus competition is inherent in the nature of the entrepreneurial market process. Or, to put it the other way around, entrepreneurship is inherent in the competitive market process.

THE PRODUCER AND THE MARKET PROCESS

The considerations outlined above are rather general. They would apply to a world in which no production is possible at all — a pure exchange economy — and they apply with equal validity to a world in which nature-given raw materials and labor are converted through production into consumer goods (both in a capital-goods-using economy and in a hypothetical world that employs no capital goods). But it will be useful, especially in respect to future discussions on monopoly and on selling costs, to explain a little more specifically how the market process operates in a world of production.

Production involves converting resources into commodities. Therefore the market in a world of production is most simply seen as a network of decisions in which resource owners make plans to sell resources to producers, producers make plans to buy resources from resource owners in order to sell them (in the form of produced commodities) to consumers, and consumers make plans to buy commodities from producers. The producer, it turns out, need not initially be an asset owner. He may simply be an entrepreneur who perceives the opportunity to buy resources at a total cost lower than the revenue he can obtain from the sale of output. Even if the producer happens to be a resource owner, he is to be considered an entrepreneur with respect to the other resources he needs for production. And it is convenient to consider him as an entrepreneur even with respect to the resource he owns (in the sense that, in using it for his own production process, rather than selling it at its market price to other producers, he is "buying" it at an implicit cost).

An interesting observation is relevant to this way of seeing the market in a world of production. I said in the preceding section that the market process is essentially entrepreneurial; that

17

it can proceed either on the basis of the entrepreneurial element present in the activity of all market participants or on the
basis of a hypothetical group of entrepreneurs operating in a
market in which the other market participants are not alert to
new opportunities and merely react passively to the changing
opportunities directly offered them. It turns out now that in
the world of production we find ourselves endowed, as it were,
with a built-in group of entrepreneurs — the producers. We
have just seen that production involves a necessarily entrepreneurial type of market activity. It thus becomes highly convenient to view the market, in a world of production, *as if all*
entrepreneurial activity were in fact carried on by producers;
in other words, it now becomes convenient to think of resource
owners and consumers as passive price-takers, exercising no entrepreneurial judgment of their own and simply reacting passively to the opportunities to sell and buy which the producer-
entrepreneurs hold out to them directly. Of course this is only
an analytical convenience, but it will simplify much of the discussion and will help lay bare the inner workings of the market
in the complex world of production.

We see the producer, then, as one who perceives profit opportunities in the market, consisting in the availability of sellers
who ask less than what buyers are willing to pay somewhere
else in the market. In the production context, of course, what
can be bought are resources, and what can be sold are products;
but to the entrepreneur the profit opportunity is still an arbitrage possibility. (The time duration of a production process
does not, except by introducing the uncertainties involved in an
unknown future, alter its entrepreneurial aspect.)

In searching out these opportunities and exploiting them the
producer is thus performing the entrepreneurial role in the
market process. In this process the plans of consumers and of
resource owners are gradually brought into greater and greater
consistency with one another. Consumers' initial ignorance of
the kinds of commodities technologically possible with cur-

rently available resources and of the relative prices at which these commodities can in principle be produced gradually diminishes. Resource owners' initial ignorance of the kinds of commodities consumers will buy and of the relative prices which can in principle be obtained for these commodities gradually diminishes. The new knowledge is acquired through changes in the prices of resources and of products, brought about by the bids and offers of the entrepreneur-producers who are eagerly competing for the profits to be won by discovering where resource owners and consumers have (in effect) underestimated each other's eagerness to buy or to sell. This process of bringing the plans of market participants into dovetailing patterns is, as we have seen, competitive. No one producer — in his role of entrepreneur — can ignore the possibility that a profit opportunity may be grabbed by another entrepreneur. After all, an entrepreneur needs no assets to engage in profitable market participation. A producer need not own any resources in order to engage in production; he merely has to know where to buy resources at a price that will make it worthwhile to produce and sell the product at its attainable price. Since, then, anyone can, at least in principle, be a producer (since no special natural or other endowment is necessary), the market process, which is channeled through the activities of the producers, is competitive. The question then arises, What are economists referring to when they talk of "monopolistic markets"? And, in particular, What is to be understood by the term "monopolistic producer"? Have we not seen that producers are entrepreneurs who can *never* be immune from the forces of competition?

MONOPOLY AND THE MARKET PROCESS

Perhaps the central purpose of this book is to offer a satisfactory answer to the questions just posed, while adhering consistently to the framework of discussion which raised these questions in the first place. This framework has, first of all, identified the market process in general as a *competitive* one (in the sense that it proceeds by the successive efforts of profit-seeking entrepreneurs to outstrip one another in providing attractive buying and selling opportunities to the market). Further, we have emphasized the entrepreneurial role filled by the *producer*, so that the productive efforts of producers turned out to be of the very same pattern as the competitive activities of entrepreneurs in general. Being entrepreneurs, producers are engaged in the very competitive-entrepreneurial process which is at the heart of the market process itself.

A competitive process, I have said, proceeds because participants are engaged in an incessant race to get or to keep ahead of one another (where, as always, "to be ahead" means "to be offering the most attractive opportunities to other market participants"). Clearly, then, any circumstances which render a market participant immune from the necessity to keep ahead would not merely hamper competition, but also impede the course of the market process. But (and here was the apparent cause of difficulty) we have seen that entrepreneurship can *never* be immune from the competitive pressure. It thus *seems* that competition can never be absent from the market, and so the market process can never be impeded by its absence. Is there no possibility of an absence of competition? Is there no possibility of monopoly?

The answer must be that, in the sense in which we have used the term "competition" (a sense which, although sharply divergent from the terminology of the dominant theory of price, is entirely consistent with everyday business usage), the market process is indeed always competitive, so long as there is freedom to buy and sell in the market. Nonetheless, there remains a definite place for monopoly within the framework of analysis we have developed. Entrepreneurship is necessarily open to all who wish to deal in the market; hence production, involving the purchase of resources and the sale of products, is necessarily competitive. But *resource ownership* may well be monopolistic in character, and where a resource is owned by a monopolist, this may have important implications for the course of production. It is as a result of resource monopoly that those important cases arise which in the language of the layman, the economist, and the antitrust lawyer are called monopolistic production. Our own position will be to insist on the crucial distinction between the possibility of a monopolist producer qua producer (which, in our terminology, is ruled out almost by definition) and the possibility of a monopolist producer qua resource owner (which is very real and significant).

If nature has endowed a particular market participant with *all* the current endowment of a certain resource, he is in the fortunate position of being a monopolist resource owner. This may sharply affect the price of this resource and, as a further result, may affect the prices of other resources and products, as well as the entire pattern of production. But it is important to observe that the competitive character of the market process *has not been affected in the slightest*. The final equilibrium position toward which the market is tending may be drastically affected by monopoly resource ownership, but the process of bringing the decisions of market participants into more closely dovetailing patterns remains unchanged. All this does not at all mean that monopoly, within our framework of discussion, has become less potentially dangerous or less important. But it does mean that in analyzing the effects of what appears to be clear cases of monopoly, we know where to look for the source of the problem. Most important, this way of looking at things teaches us that if a producer controls the production of a given commodity he is a monopolist — if he is such — not by virtue of any entrepreneurial role, but as a result of a resource monopoly. As an immediate implication of this we distinguish very sharply between a producer who is the sole source of supply for a particular commodity because he has unique access to a necessary resource and one who is the sole source of supply as a result of his entrepreneurial activities (which can easily be duplicated by his competitors, if they choose). During the course of the market process the competitive efforts of a particular producer-entrepreneur may lead him to offer something to the market which no one else is currently producing. In our theory this is simply an example of the *competitive* process at work. It has nothing in common with cases in which a particular producer, by acquiring monopoly control over a resource, is able to maintain his position as sole source of supply indefinitely. The one case is an example of competitive entrepreneurship; the other is one of monopolistic resource ownership. Nonetheless, a very important possibility must be considered in which a monopolist producer has acquired monopoly control over one of his factors of production *by means of his entrepreneurial activities.*

THE ENTREPRENEUR AS MONOPOLIST

This possibility may arise very simply. A market participant with no initial assets perceives the possibility of making large profits by buying up *all* the available supply of a given resource, and then establishing himself as the monopolist producer of a particular commodity. His role, taking the long-range perspective, is clearly entrepreneurial (he had no initial assets), and thus competitive. (Since he had no initial asset endowment, anyone else could have done what he did; again, he was able to do what he did only because in so doing he was offering both to those from whom he bought and to those to whom he sells opportunities more attractive than those offered by others.) And yet, once his entrepreneurial resource purchase has been made, he is in the position of a producer who is a monopolist by virtue of being a resource owner. It seems, then, that not only may an entrepreneur-producer be a monopolist because he *happens* at the same time to be a monopolist resource owner, he may be a monopolist because he has made himself a monopolist resource owner *in the course of his entrepreneurial activities.*

If we recognize this possibility we may gain much valuable

22

insight into the complex forces acting in the real world. Many real-world cases of what appears to be monopoly in production can be disentangled and understood in the light of the theoretical possibilities being examined here. In a later chapter we will return to a more thorough investigation of this kind of situation. Here it is enough for us to notice its possible existence and to draw attention to the highly interesting combination of competition and monopoly. When one looks merely at the situation *after* the resource has been monopolized by the entrepreneurial skill of the producer, one sees only a monopolist producer — exempt from competition to the extent his resource monopoly permits. When one takes a longer-run view of the monopoly situation, one sees that it was won *by* competition, and that it represents, as such (and as far as it goes), a step forward in the entrepreneurial process of the market. This entrepreneur's capture of his monopoly position was a step toward eliminating the inconsistencies between the decisions of consumers and those of the earlier resource owners. The profits won by the producer, which in the short run view seem clearly a monopoly rent attributible to the monopolized resource, turn out to be, in the long run view, the profits of competitive entrepreneurship. This insight will be of great value in the normative analysis of monopoly situations.

THE PRODUCER AND HIS CHOICE OF PRODUCT

Up till now our discussion has been couched in terms of "opportunities" offered to the market by entrepreneur-producers. We have talked generally of "more attractive opportunities" and of "less attractive opportunities," but we have not considered the kinds of alteration in an "opportunity" that might make it more attractive in the eyes of the consumers.[1] In a monetary economy one opportunity is better than a second if

1. This section is phrased in terms of the opportunities offered to consumers. Corresponding observations apply with respect to the opportunities producers offer to resource owners. See further below, pp. 180–86.

it offers consumers the same product at a lower price; so entrepreneurial competition among producers may take the form of attempting to offer products at lower prices. But one opportunity is also better than a second if it offers consumers a more desirable product at the same price; so entrepreneurial competition among producers may also take the form of attempting to make more desirable products available to consumers. In fact, producers are at all times under competitive pressure to offer more and more desirable products at lower and lower prices. It is important to notice that "a more desirable product" may mean a superior quality of what is generally considered to be the "same" product, or it may mean an entirely different product. In theory, of course, any difference which makes one commodity more desirable to a consumer than another makes it "different." In the theory of the *firm* the entrepreneur-producer has acquired certain resources which may now commit him, to an extent, to the production of a particular product. For the firm, therefore, quality competition often means the attempt to improve the quality of a *particular* commodity, broadly defined. But in the long run quality competition always involves the attempt to offer a better product, without commitment to any one commodity class, at a lower price.

As will be discussed at greater length in a later chapter, it may not be possible for an external observer to know independently whether one product or quality of product is more desirable to consumers than another. Only the choices of the consumers can prove the superiority of the more desirable item. But again, where the application of additional resources has made a commodity more eagerly sought after by consumers, it may not be possible to ascertain objectively whether the additional resources have "really improved" the product or whether they have "educated" the consumer to prefer the "same" product. It follows that no distinction can, as a matter of science, be made between "production costs" and "selling costs." Such a distinction can, of course, still be made on the basis of arbitrary judgment of value (which may declare that a given expenditure has, in the opinion of the observer, left a commodity unchanged). All this will have very important implications for the analysis of "selling costs."

In particular our discussion has taught us that even where the entrepreneurial outlays qualify (on whatever grounds) as genuine selling costs, and even where the impact of these outlays is to *differentiate* the products of one producer from those of his competitors, the result cannot be immediately stamped as partaking of monopoly. Our discussion has shown that so long as the resources used by producers are accessible to all, all their activities are entrepreneurial-competitive. That one producer has expended resources in order to educate or manipulate consumer tastes may perhaps offend the ethical values of some observers of the market, and it is not a simple matter, on strictly scientific terms, to evaluate the effect of this kind of activity. But so long as no resources used in "selling" or in producing are owned monopolistically, we are forced to conclude that this activity is essentially competitive and cannot result in any kind of monopolistic control over production or any impairment of the competitive process.

The fact that at any given moment only one producer is making a particular product is not by itself an impairment of the competitive process. It may simply mean that at this moment only one entrepreneur had taken the step of presenting this particular opportunity to the market. If the step was a wise one, it will tend to attract others to do even better in this regard. If it proves to have been a mistake this entrepreneur himself will be under market pressure to abandon this line of production. Insofar as our interest is in the market process and its competitive character, we should no more be surprised that only one producer is making a product at a particular time than that of many producers of a particular product one is charging a price which no other producer is asking. Both possibilities may simply be evidence that the market process has not yet run its course.

Much of this discussion diverges sharply from the terminology and doctrines of the theory of monopolistic competition. Later I will take up in greater detail the points of contact and contrast between the approach underlying this essay and that embodied in the theory of monopolistic competition. At this point I will attempt to show briefly how it was only to be expected that emphasis on equilibrium conditions — an emphasis which we have seen characterizes the dominant approach to price theory — should deflect attention from the way of looking at the market that I have described.

EQUILIBRIUM ECONOMICS, ENTREPRENEURSHIP, AND COMPETITION

We have already noticed earlier in this chapter [2] that our disagreement with the dominant theory of price centers in particular on its unsatisfactory treatment of entrepreneurship and competition. In the preceding sections I have outlined the way I believe the notions of entrepreneurship and of competition are to be employed in constructing a helpful theory of the market process. The failure of the dominant approach in this respect seems a direct implication of its stress on equilibrium situations and its view of price theory as explaining the conditions for equilibrium.

In equilibrium there is no room for the entrepreneur. When the decisions of all market participants dovetail completely, so that each plan correctly assumes the corresponding plans of the other participants and no possibility exists for any altered plans that would be simultaneously preferred by the relevant participants, there is nothing left for the entrepreneur to do. He will be unable to discover possibilities of buying from those who underestimated the eagerness of potential buyers and of then selling to these eager buyers (who might in turn have un-

2. See above, pp. 7–9.

derestimated the eagerness of the sellers). Thus he cann(
tribute to a reallocation of resources or products that wi
come inefficiencies and lack of coordination generated by
market ignorance, since no such ignorance and lack of coordination exist in equilibrium.

An economics that emphasizes equilibrium tends, therefore,
to overlook the role of the entrepreneur. His role becomes
somehow identified with movements from one equilibrium position to another, with "innovations," and with dynamic changes,
but *not* with the dynamics of the equilibrating process itself.
Instead of the entrepreneur, the dominant theory of price has
dealt with the firm, placing the emphasis heavily on its profit-
maximizing aspects. In fact, this emphasis has misled many
students of price theory to understand the notion of the entrepreneur as nothing more than the locus of profit-maximizing
decision-making within the firm. They have completely overlooked the role of the entrepreneur in exploiting superior awareness of price discrepancies within the economic system.

Emphasis on the firm (which in our view is to be seen as a
combination of entrepreneur and resource owner) also led to
a failure to recognize the significance of pure resource ownership in securing monopoly positions in production. Monopoly
came to be associated with the firm and thus, most unfortunately, with the entrepreneur.

At the same time, the emphasis on equilibrium hampered
any possible appreciation of the notion of competition which
we have seen to be the outstanding characteristic of the market
process. By definition, a state of equilibrium does not permit
activity designed *to outstrip* the efforts of others in catering to
the wishes of the market. Thus, whatever the laymen might
mean by the term "competition," the equilibrium theorist came
to use it to connote a market in which each participant is too
weak to effect any change in price. This is entirely understandable. If the attention of the theorist is focused upon a particular state of affairs — equilibrium — rather than upon the market

process, the adjective "competitive" cannot be used in the sense of the characteristic of a process. And yet, because the equilibrium theorists intended their models to be helpful in understanding the real world — in which the force of competition is too obvious to be overlooked — the equilibrium model itself came to be described as either competitive or otherwise. But clearly, if a state of affairs is to be labeled competitive, and if this label is to bear *any* relation to the layman's use of the term, the term must mean either a state of affairs from which competitive activity (in the layman's sense) is to be expected or a state of affairs that is the consequence of competitive activity. Both possible uses of the term are clearly sharply different from the layman's use (which we have seen refers to an essential feature of the market process); it is most unfortunate that of these two possible uses the one which came to be adopted is *furthest* from that of the layman. Competition, to the equilibrium price theorist, turned out to refer to a state of affairs into which so many competing participants have already entered that no room remains for *additional* entry (or other modification of existing market conditions). The most unfortunate aspect of this use of the term "competition" is of course that, by referring to the situation in which no room remains for further steps in the competitive market process, the word has come to be understood as the *very opposite* of the kind of activity of which that process consists. Thus, as we shall discover, any real-world departure from equilibrium conditions came to be stamped as the opposite of "competitive" and hence, by simple extension, as actually "monopolistic."

All this has led to the confusion in the theory and terminology of competition and monopoly which this essay attempts to help disperse. The amazing extent of this confusion can be gauged from the course taken by the "revolution" in price theory that occurred in the mid-thirties. The theories of monopolistic competition and of imperfect competition emerged as a result of extensive dissatisfaction with the Marshallian theory of price as it had developed until the twenties. The shortcomings of the model of the market used in this theory were seen, in large measure, in its failure to correspond with any degree of neatness to many apparently omnipresent features of the real economic world.[3] And yet the habits of thought associated with the existing theory had become so entrenched that the authors of the new theory failed entirely to correctly identify the source of its unrealistic character. Instead of attacking the equilibrium emphasis in the theory of pure competition, these authors introduced *different* equilibrium theories.

All this had most unfortunate consequences for the recognition of the power of the theory I have outlined in this chapter. The new theories failed to perceive that the characteristic features of the real world (to which nothing in the perfectly competitive model corresponds) are simply the manifestations of entrepreneurial competition, a process in which would-be buyers and sellers gropingly seek to discover each other's supply and demand curves. The new theories merely fashioned new equilibrium configurations — based, as was the theory of perfect competition, on *given* and known demand and supply curves — differing from the earlier theory only in the *shapes* assigned to these curves. In the course of attempting to account for such market phenomena as quality differentiation, advertising, or markets in which few producers are to be found, the new theories were led to conclusions which grossly misinterpret the significance of these phenomena.

3. See E. H. Chamberlin, *The Theory of Monopolistic Competition*, 7th ed. (Cambridge: Harvard University Press, 1956), p. 10.

]2[
The Entrepreneur

THE PRECEDING CHAPTER HAS PROVIDED AN OVERALL VIEW OF
the position I will develop in greater detail in the course of
this book. In this and the remaining chapters I will take up
different aspects of this position for more thorough examination and exposition. It is entirely appropriate to devote the first
of these chapters to the role of the entrepreneur in the price
system. Not only does the entrepreneur play, in our view, the
crucial role in the market process, but this role has been — especially in recent decades — almost invariably ignored.[1] And this
hiatus exists not merely with respect to the understanding of
the vital part entrepreneurship plays in the equilibrating process,
but even with respect to an appreciation of the very nature of
entrepreneurship.

THE NATURE OF ENTREPRENEURSHIP

The entrepreneurial role in the market is an elusive one. This
is demonstrated in the virtual elimination of this role from
most contemporary expositions of price theory, as well as in
the multiplicity of careful attempts by earlier writers to define
the entrepreneur and to distinguish his role from that of the

1. For recent recognition of this see, for example, W. J. Baumol, "Entrepreneurship in Economic Theory," *American Economic Review* 58
(May 1968): 72.

capitalist or of the hired manager. These attempts reflect the desire to identify with precision something whose presence is undoubtedly sensed, but which lends itself superficially only to vague definition. In my view it is possible to pin down the elusive element of entrepreneurship in a satisfactory way. I further believe that to do so is of the utmost importance to understanding the market process. One distinction between the theory of the market subscribed to here and the one that dominates the contemporary price theory textbooks is the latter's lack of an adequate appreciation of the nature and function of entrepreneurship in the market system.

A preliminary outline of my position on the nature of entrepreneurship may be helpful. I will argue that there is present in all human action an element which, although crucial to economizing activity in general, cannot itself be analyzed in terms of economizing, maximizing, or efficiency criteria. I will label this, for reasons to be made apparent, the entrepreneurial element. I will argue further that the entrepreneurial role in the market can best be understood by analogy from what I have labeled as the entrepreneurial element in individual human action. Resource allocation through the impersonal forces of the market is frequently compared with the allocative decision-making of the individual. It is this which provides the basis for the analogy I have referred to. Just as efficiency criteria by themselves are insufficient for the comprehension of individual human action, since a crucial factor for the emergence of economizing individual activity is the "extraeconomic" entrepreneurial element, so too the allocative role of the market process cannot be understood in terms of the interaction of individual maximizing activities alone. A market consisting exclusively of economizing, maximizing individuals does not generate the market process we seek to understand. For the market process to emerge, we require in addition an element which is itself not comprehensible within the narrow conceptual limits of economizing behavior. This element in the market, I will main-

31

tain, is best identified as entrepreneurship; it occupies precisely the same logical relationship to the more narrow "economizing" elements in the market that, in individual action, is occupied by the entrepreneurial elements in relation to the efficiency aspects of decision-making. Let us turn now to more detailed elaboration of the way of looking at entrepreneurship that I have here outlined.

DECISION-MAKING AND ECONOMIZING

Price theory as it has developed during the past four decades operates by referring all market phenomena back to individual decisions. As "microtheory," it sees the determination of prices, of product qualities and quantities, and of methods of production as being achieved by the interaction of the economizing activities of the individual market participants. It seeks to understand the changing phenomena of the market by analyzing the reactions to changes in exogenous market data (tastes, techniques of production, and the availability of resources) of the individual market participants. The basis of the economic analysis of individual decision-making is found in its economic aspect. Since the classic discussion by Lord Robbins (*An Essay on the Nature and Significance of Economic Science*, 1932), the economic aspect of individual activity has been understood in terms of the allocation of scarce means among competing ends. Each individual is seen as confronted with an "economic problem" — the problem of selecting those courses of action, with respect to given means, that will secure the fulfillment of as many of his goals (in order of their significance) as possible. This problem is sometimes expressed as that of securing efficiency, or as "maximizing" goal satisfaction. The common feature of all Robbinsian formulations of the problem is the need to achieve the pattern of manipulation of given means that will correspond most faithfully to the given hierarchy of ends.

It is my position that this analytical vision of economizing, maximizing, or efficiency-intent individual market participants is, in significant respects, misleadingly incomplete. It has led to a view of the market as made up of a multitude of economizing individuals, each making his decisions with respect to *given* series of ends and means. And in my opinion this view of the market is responsible for the harmful exclusive emphasis upon equilibrium situations already discussed. A multitude of economizing individuals each choosing with respect to given ends and means cannot, without the introduction of further exogenous elements, generate a market process (which involves systematically *changing* series of means available to market participants.)

Instead of economizing, I maintain, it will prove extremely helpful to emphasize the broader Misesian notion of *human action*. As developed by Mises, the concept of *homo agens* is capable of all that can be achieved by using the notions of economizing and of the drive for efficiency. But the human-action concept, unlike that of allocation and economizing, does not confine the decision-maker (or the economic analysis of his decisions) to a framework of *given* ends and means. Human action, in the sense developed by Mises, involves courses of action taken by the human being "to remove uneasiness" and to make himself "better off." Being broader than the notion of economizing, the concept of human action does not restrict analysis of the decision to the allocation problem posed by the juxtaposition of scarce means and multiple ends. The decision, in the framework of the human-action approach, is not arrived at merely by mechanical computation of the solution to the maximization problem implicit in the configuration of the given ends and means. It reflects not merely the manipulation of given means to correspond faithfully with the hierarchy of given ends, but also *the very perception of the ends-mean framework* within which allocation and economizing is to take place.

Robbins's economizing man is endowed with the propensity to mold given means to suit given ends. The very concept presupposes some given image of ends and of means; without such an image economizing cannot begin at all. Mises's *homo agens*, on the other hand, is endowed not only with the propensity to pursue goals efficiently, once ends and means are clearly identified, but also with the drive and alertness needed to identify which ends to strive for and which means are available. Human action encompasses the efficiency-seeking behavior typical of Robbinsian economizers, but it also embraces an element which is by definition absent from economizing. Economizing behavior — or, more accurately, its analysis — necessarily skips the task of identifying ends and means. The economizing notion by definition presupposes that this task (and its analysis) has been completed elsewhere. Human action treats both tasks — that of identifying the relevant ends-means framework and that of seeking efficiency with respect to it — as a single, integrated human activity. To the extent that we can identify the ends-means framework which *homo agens* perceives as relevant, we can analyze his decision in orthodox Robbinsian allocation-economizing terms. But whereas with the narrower economizing notion no explanation is available for why this particular ends-means framework is held to be relevant and of what might render it no longer relevant, such insight is available through the broader human-action concept — it is built into the propensity for alertness toward fresh goals and the discovery of hitherto unknown resources with which *homo agens* is endowed. (It is of course true that the Robbinsian notion of economizing may quite adequately explain the deliberate, cost-conscious search for information. Economizing man may indeed be seen as allocating guessed-at quantities of means among alternative research projects [with guessed-at potentialities]. But to the extent that this search *can* be subsumed within the economizing framework, it clearly *presupposes some* envisaged ends-means background. And the point here is that the economizing notion *must* exclude from its purview the explanation of the relevance of this particular background.)

Decision-Making and Economizing

Now I choose (for reasons that will shortly be made clear) to label that element of alertness to possibly newly worthwhile goals and to possibly newly available resources — which we have seen is absent from the notion of economizing but very much present in that of human action — the *entrepreneurial* element in human decision-making. It is this entrepreneurial element that is responsible for our understanding of human action as active, creative, and human rather than as passive, automatic, and mechanical.[2] Once the entrepreneurial element in human action is perceived, one can no longer interpret the decision as merely calculative — capable in principle of being yielded by mechanical manipulation of the "data" or already *completely implied* in these data. One must now recognize that the human decision cannot be explained purely in terms of maximization, of "passive" reaction that takes the form of adopting the "best" course of action as marked out by the circumstances. Once the theorist has identified the circumstances the decision-maker believed were relevant, he may indeed explain the decision in terms of calculative optimization. But explicit recognition of the entrepreneurial element in decision-making carries with it the recognition that such an allocative explanation is at best only partial; that such an explanation presupposes one's ability to identify unambiguously an ends-means framework perceived unambiguously, in turn, by the decision-maker himself *before* his decision; and that the psychology of decision-making in situations lacking such a prior perception of any ends-means framework by the decision-maker may

2. A number of writers have drawn attention to the passivity of the Robbinsian type of decision-maker who dominates contemporary microeconomic theory. See especially G. L. S. Shackle, *The Nature of Economic Thought, Selected Papers 1955–64* (New York: Cambridge University Press, 1966), p. 130. For a brief discussion of the difference between Shackle's approach and my own, see I. M. Kirzner, "Methodological Individualism, Market Equilibrium, and Market Process," *Il Politico* 32 (1967): 787–99. See also I. M. Kirzner, *The Economic Point of View* (Princeton, N.J.: Van Nostrand, 1960), pp. 121 ff.

altogether invalidate such allocative explanation, except as a heuristic device with no pretensions to realism.

But recognition of the entrepreneurial element in decision-making does not bring with it merely the awareness of the limited realism of allocative explanations of the human decision. Such recognition opens up the way for fruitful insights not otherwise available. In particular, recognizing this entrepreneurial element may make it possible to view a succession of different decisions by the same individual as a logically unified *sequence*, with each decision comprehensible as the logical outcome of the prior decision. In other words, once we become sensitive to the decision-makers' alertness to new possibly worthwhile ends and newly available means, it may be possible to explain the pattern of change in an individual's decisions as the outcome of a learning process generated by the unfolding experience of the decisions themselves. An analysis confined to allocative explanations must fail entirely to perceive such continuity in any sequence of decisions, since each decision is comprehended purely in terms of its own relevant end-means framework. With purely allocative explanations, no earlier decision can be used to explain later decisions on the basis of learning; if the pattern of ends-means held relevant by the individual at the later decision differs from that held relevant earlier, then there is, with the "economizing framework," nothing but a discontinuity. Such exogenous change has simply wiped out one decision-making situation and replaced it with a different one. There is nothing *in the formulation of the economizing view of the decision* that tells us how, in the absence of unexplained exogenous changes, one pattern of relevant ends-means comes to be replaced by another. We must recognize what I have called the entrepreneurial element in order to perceive that the changing patterns of ends-means held relevant to successive decisions are the possibly understandable outcome of a process of experience in which the decision-maker's alertness to relevant new information has generated a continuously changing sequence of decisions.[3]

THE ENTREPRENEUR IN THE MARKET

The preceding section presented a view of the individual decision which emphasized the alertness that human beings always display toward potentially worthwhile goals hitherto unnoticed, as well as toward unnoticed potentially valuable, available resources. Recognizing this element in individual decision-making, an element I have labeled "entrepreneurial," will help us to understand the role of the entrepreneur in the market and to see what sets the analysis of this role apart from the analysis of the roles of other participants.

We have seen that, where a clearly identifiable framework of ends and means is held relevant by a decision-maker before his decision, we may explain his decision quite satisfactorily as yielded mechanically by calculation with the ends-means data. In other words, where the circumstances of a decision are believed to be certainly known to the decision-maker, we can "predict" what form that decision will take merely by identifying the optimum course of action relevant to the known circumstances. Now this "mechanical" interpretation of decision-making would be entirely acceptable for a world of perfect knowledge and prediction. In such a world there would be no scope for the entrepreneurial element. If each individual knows with certainty what to expect, his plans can be completely explained in terms of economizing, of optimal allocation, and of maximizing — in other words, his plans can be shown to be in principle implicit in the data which constitutes his knowledge of all the present and future circumstances relevant to his situation.[4] But of course we know that human beings do not oper-

---

3. On this point see further below, pp. 70–72.
4. In a world of perfect knowledge the only scope for decision-making relates to opportunities for exchanging — either with man or with nature — something one values relatively little for something one values more highly. In a world of imperfect knowledge, there may exist at any given time some-

ate in a world of perfect knowledge, and it was this that led us to emphasize the importance of the alertness individuals display toward new information.

To the extent, therefore, that economic theory is concerned with the world of perfect knowledge, it is entirely appropriate to analyze market phenomena solely in terms of Robbinsian economizers or maximizers. There is no need and, indeed, no possibility in the theory of such a world to introduce entrepreneurship as such or to draw attention to any entrepreneurial element in individual decision-making; the assumption of perfect knowledge automatically eliminates all such elements. The entrepreneurial element in the individual decision makes its entry only when this assumption is dropped. But when we shift our attention from a world in complete equilibrium, in which knowledge is perfect, toward the disequilibrium world, in which knowledge is far from perfect, we can no longer conduct our investigations purely through the analysis of Robbinsian economizers. We must then grapple with explaining how the market process supplies new information to the participants — how the decision-makers revise their view of the ends-means framework relevant to their situations. And here is where the notion of entrepreneurship enters — in one or both of two distinct ways.

First, of course, the decision-makers, the market participants,

---

thing selling at more than one price in the market. Once this price difference is noticed, once some *knows* it, a profit opportunity has been discovered. It is probably of dubious value to separate the discovery of such an opportunity from its exploitation. If one does make such a separation, however, it should be observed that the "decision" to capture an opportunity for profit, once the opportunity has been discovered with sufficient certainty, may be considered for our purposes a "Robbinsian" decision. It is yielded unambiguously by the data (and is in fact similar to the special Robbinsian case where the economizer has only a single end and, of course, simply applies all available means single-mindedly toward it). No entrepreneurial element is required for this "decision." Entrepreneurship is required for the *discovery* of the profit opportunity; once one has chosen to artificially separate the discovery of the opportunity from its actual exploitation, one must recognize that the latter decision is purely Robbinsian (despite the fact that no "allocation" is involved).

become visible not merely as mechanical Robbinsian maximizers and economizers, but as human beings engaged in Misesian human action, that is, displaying what I have labeled the entrepreneurial element in individual decision-making. "In any real and living economy every actor is always an entrepreneur."[5] The analysis of market processes is able to exploit the insight that participants do not merely react to given market data, but rather display entrepreneurial alertness to possible changes in these data — an alertness which can be used to explain how such changes can occur in general.

Second (and for the purposes of this section more important), when we extend economic analysis to a world of imperfect knowledge it becomes possible to find place for an entirely new economic role, one which was by definition excluded from the world of perfect knowledge. It becomes possible to introduce a market participant whose decisions are *entirely incapable* of being subsumed under the category of Robbinsian economizing. We can now introduce into the analysis the device of the *pure entrepreneur*, that is, a decision-maker whose *entire* role arises out of his alertness to hitherto unnoticed opportunities.[6] Some clarification and explanation is in order here.

The entrepreneurial element, we have seen, also finds a place in the decisions of market participants whose roles do *not* depend on the imperfection of knowledge. Thus the consumer, whom we can without any difficulty envisage as operating in strictly Robbinsian fashion in a perfect-knowledge environment, can be seen to exercise the element of entrepreneurship as soon as we place him in a setting of imperfect knowledge. Similarly, the resource owner selling his resources in the factor market may be viewed, in the setting of imperfect information,

5. L. Mises, *Human Action* (New Haven: Yale University Press, 1949), p. 253.

6. "Economics, in speaking of entrepreneurs, has in view not men, but a definite function. This function . . . is inherent in every action. . . . *In embodying this function in an imaginary figure*, we resort to a methodological makeshift." Mises, *Human Action*, pp. 253–54 (italics added).

as exercising a measure of entrepreneurship, whereas in the equilibrium world of perfect knowledge his activities would be reduced to nothing but pure economizing. What characterizes these cases is that the decision-maker starts out with given means (money income for the consumer, resources for the resource owner). Thus in these cases it is possible to discuss how these means can best be exploited to further the goals of the decision-maker. With these goals given, and with market prices (of products and of resources) known with certainty, this "best way" can in principle be obtained by mechanical calculation. With the decision-maker aware of the possibility that better prices, say, may be lurking around the corner, this "best way" is no longer purely a matter of calculating or economizing; its determination also depends crucially on the entrepreneurial quality of the decision-maker — on his propensity to sense what prices are realistically available to him.

What the introduction of the *pure entrepreneur* means, however, is that for our analysis we create a decision-maker who starts out *without any means whatsoever*.[7] Thus, in a world of perfect knowledge, that is, in a world in which unexploited opportunities for gain have been excluded by definition, such a decision-maker simply has nothing to do — has no scope for the exercise of *any* decision-making, Robbinsian or otherwise. Without means there are simply no courses of action available. But introducing a decision-maker without means into the analy-

7. Although I point out that pure entrepreneurship requires that we view the decision-maker as starting out without means, it does not follow that all decision-making made without initial means must necessarily be entrepreneurial. We have already noticed (see chap. 2, n. 4) that where we choose to imagine, in a world of imperfect knowledge, an entrepreneur who has *already discovered* the existence of a pure profit opportunity, his subsequent decision to exploit this opportunity is to be considered as already implied in the data — as not being in any way entrepreneurial. (In fact, it would almost be permissible to consider the profit opportunity, once we artificially imagine it to have been discovered with sufficient certainty — *apart from* the act of its exploitation — as being a *means* now available to the entrepreneur, who has, in this way of looking at things, exhausted his entrepreneurial role and become a full-fledged Robbinsian economizer with only a single end.) See further below, p. 46.

sis of the world *without* perfect knowledge is an entirely different matter. Because the participants in this market are less than omniscient, there are likely to exist, at any given time, a multitude of opportunities that have not yet been taken advantage of. Sellers may have sold for prices lower than the prices which were in fact obtainable (in particular, resources may have been sold for the production of products less urgently needed by consumers than other products obtainable from the same resources). Buyers may have bought for prices higher than the lowest prices needed to secure what they are buying (in particular, consumers may be buying commodities produced with resources that are more costly than other resources capable of yielding comparable commodities). The existence of these unexploited opportunities opens up a scope for decision-making that does not depend, in principle, upon Robbinsian economizing *at all*. What our decision-maker without means needs to arrive at the best decision is simply to know where these unexploited opportunities exist. All he needs is to discover where buyers have been paying too much and where sellers have been receiving too little and to bridge the gap by offering to buy for a little more and to sell for a little less. To discover these unexploited opportunities requires alertness. Calculation will not help, and economizing and optimizing will not of themselves yield this knowledge. Thus the decision of our new decision-maker is not at all capable, even in principle, of being simply "read off" from the data; it is not at all implied in the circumstances in which he is placed.

The analytical device of speaking in terms of pure entrepreneurs permits a simplification of market theory that has not always been appreciated. Once we have introduced the pure entrepreneur into our analysis of the market process, *it becomes possible to speak of a market in which all other market participants are pure Robbinsian economizers, without any element of entrepreneurship whatsoever.* It is possible to construct a theory of the market process explaining how market prices, as well as quantities and qualities of inputs and outputs, change as a result of the interaction of individual plans, while assuming that all decision-makers (except the pure entrepreneurs) are passive price-takers, simply optimizing against the background of assumed data. All changes in prices, quantities, and qualities of input used and outputs produced can be fully explained by referring them to the activity of the pure entrepreneurs, who contain no element of Robbinsian economizing in their makeup. An analytical world in which no entrepreneurship at all is permitted to exist (either in the form of a distinct market role or as an element in the makeup of market participants with other primary roles) can explain nothing but the pattern of equilibrium; it completely lacks the power to explain how prices, quantities, and qualities of inputs and outputs are systematically changed during the market process. But in order to grapple with these latter problems it is not, it now turns out, necessary to complicate the analysis of the decisions of *all* market participants by altering them from passive, Robbinsian economizers and price-takers into active, Misesian "entrepreneurial" actors. It is possible to continue the analysis of consumer decisions, and of resource-owner decisions, exactly as this analysis proceeds in a strictly equilibrium context; these participants in the market can continue to be envisaged as passively reacting no longer to *actual* equilibrium market prices, but to the prices they believe, probably erroneously, to be the equilibrium prices. Errors in the information these Robbinsian market participants believe to be relevant will then yield opportunities for profitable activity on the part of the pure entrepreneurs. The activity of these pure entrepreneurs can then explain how prices and input and output quantities and qualities change.[8]

Nor need we view this simplification of price theory, whereby

8. See, however, below pp. 147–49, for further discussion of how one must envisage the market model in which all but the pure entrepreneurs are purely Robbinsian economizers.

market participants are seen either as pure Robbinsian economizers or as pure entrepreneurs (with no scope at all for Robbinsian economizing), as an artificial model which, however adequate it may be as a heuristic device, nonetheless fails as a satisfying explanation of the real world (in which *all* decision-makers are endowed with the entrepreneurial element, at least to some degree). All this simplification means is that, although each human being acts in a wholly integrated manner which we may *analyze* into two separate components, Robbinsian economizing on the one hand, and the entrepreneur type of activity on the other, it is analytically expedient to treat him as if he represented two entirely separate decision-makers, one a passive economizer, the other a pure entrepreneur. (This is not greatly different, after all, from what we do when we discuss, say, "consumer decision" — although we know perfectly well that many decisions to buy consumer goods are activated by motives most accurately described as those of the producer or investor. And the same is true when we analyze the rug purchased for a businessman's office into one component viewed as an input invested in the business, and another component viewed as a consumer product.)[9]

THE PRODUCER AS ENTREPRENEUR

This discussion of entrepreneurship, and this explanation of the role of the pure entrepreneur in the analysis of the market process, helps clarify the nature of the "producer's" role and the extent to which his role overlaps that of the entrepreneur. To the extent that the producer himself contributes a necessary resource (let us say his ability to organize a smoothly working production team out of an array of uncoordinated factors of production), he is clearly just another resource owner. And

9. Cf. Schumpeter's example of the "distinction between a workman and a landowner, who may also happen to form a composite economic personality called a farmer." J. A. Schumpeter, *Business Cycles* (New York: McGraw-Hill, 1964), p. 77.

even when we consider the producer as contributing the resources required to successfully carry through the market transactions needed to assemble the (other) inputs for the productive process and to get the product sold to consumers, it is still *possible* to view him simply as a resource owner. In a world in equilibrium he would still be present, contributing his bit week after week toward translating resources in the hands of resource owners into products in the market baskets of the consumers.

But once we see the producer as buying resources and selling products it is difficult to avoid recognizing that one of the most crucial junctures in the entire market where pure entrepreneurship is likely to be called for is precisely this point of contact between the resource market and the product market. In other words, many of the unnoticed opportunities for more efficient use of resources are likely to be in the form of imperfect coordination between the transactions in the resource markets and those in product markets. Owners of resources may be selling their resources to industries or producers who are making products less urgently needed by consumers than are other products that could be made with these resources. Buyers may be purchasing products produced with resources more costly than others capable of yielding these same products. This absence of coordination will express itself in price differences — differences between the sum of prices on the resource markets of a bundle of factors able to produce a product and the price of that output on the product market. The profit opportunities represented by such price differences open up a dimension for purely entrepreneurial activity which requires the entrepreneur to contribute *no* resources whatsoever. This activity will consist *exclusively* in buying resources and selling products. (By temporarily assuming that production is instantaneous, we avoid for the moment the need to endow the entrepreneur with finance capital.) It is here that the temptation to identify the "producer" with the "entrepreneur" becomes very strong indeed. And from a strictly formal point of view there need be no objection to this. We may indeed view the producer as an entrepreneur. But we must not forget that if we wish to view him as a *pure* entrepreneur, we must free our notion of the producer from the responsibility of contributing any resources whatsoever to the productive process. If our producer is to be a pure entrepreneur we must view him as *hiring* all the talent needed to organize factors of production into a smoothly working team and as *buying* all the resources needed to effectively complete the transactions which his entrepreneurship suggests he enter into.

What all this means is that if we wish to apply price theory to the world of production, the producer's decisions are most easily handled by viewing him in two distinct roles: that of pure entrepreneur and that of a resource owner. As resource owner we view the producer as contributing his own managerial or other services to the enterprise, and we insist, as economists, on recognizing the implicit cost to the enterprise of these services.[10] But to the extent that we view the producer as a resource owner, we need not endow him with any entrepreneurial element in his makeup. We can see him "maximizing" the return from his resources on exclusively price-taking lines. Moreover, a large part of what is usually discussed under the heading "theory of production" can be understood without reference to any entrepreneurship whatsoever. The choice of the optimum input mix is comprehensible on strictly Robbinsian lines — and this is so because when we contemplate the producer as a user of inputs we are viewing him as beginning with inputs which he must use most effectively in the light of the technological courses of action available.

But when we view the producer in his other role, as a pure

10. See H. T. Koplin, "The Profit Maximization Assumption," *Oxford Economic Papers* 15 (July 1963): 130–39.

entrepreneur, we are seeing him from an entirely different perspective, which sees him commencing his decision-making with *no* resources whatever to contribute to the process of production. We are, in this respect, viewing him before he has acquired the inputs from which products are to be obtained. His decisions as pure entrepreneur display no trace at all of Robbinsian economizing; there is nothing at all to be allocated. As pure entrepreneur he is seen displaying nothing but alertness to the existence of price differences between inputs and outputs.

It is important to realize that the typical theory of profit-maximizing enterprise in price theory, especially as cast in the usual diagrams, tends to completely mask this purely entrepreneurial function of the producer. The analysis of profit-maximization usually operates with *known* revenue and cost functions; in fact, these functions are *shown* to us very explicitly as curves in the diagram. Once we have assumed these functions to be already known, the rest is "merely" a matter of calculation; the optimum decision is already implied in the revenue and cost data. By assuming that all the revenue and cost information is already in the possession of the producer we have, so to speak, already placed the maximum profit obtainable in his grasp. No matter how complicated the procedure of determining the profit-maximizing output-price combination may seem to undergraduates, the solution is already embedded in the data; its discovery involves nothing we may not demand from a passive, Robbinsian maximizer. In the typical theory, no element of entrepreneurship is visible at all.[11]

11. On this see chap. 2, n. 4 and n. 7. Views very similar in many respects to those stated here have been expressed by H. Leibenstein in a series of papers. Especially in his "Allocation Efficiency vs. 'X-Efficiency,' " *American Economic Review* 56 (June 1966): 392–415, and "Entrepreneurship and Development," *American Economic Review* 58 (May 1968): 72–83, Leibenstein emphasizes the limitations of orthodox price theory in treating only allocative efficiency — in its theory of the firm assuming the production function to be "clearly defined, fully specified, and completely

Entrepreneurial Profits

When we wish to focus our attention on the producer as entrepreneur, we must not inquire into how the least-cost input combination, or even the profit-maximizing output-quantity-price combination, is to be determined from given revenue and cost data. We must inquire into what revenue functions and what cost functions (reflecting not merely technological efficiency but, most important, relevant output and input price judgments) the entrepreneur-producer will believe to be relevant for him in general. Entrepreneurship does not consist of grasping a free ten-dollar bill which one has already discovered to be resting in one's hand; it consists in realizing that it is in one's hand and that it is available for the grasping.

ENTREPRENEURIAL PROFITS

An important point which has emerged from the preceding discussion is that ownership and entrepreneurship are to be viewed as completely separate functions. Once we have adopted the convention of concentrating all elements of entrepreneurship into the hands of pure entrepreneurs, we have automatically excluded the asset owner from an entrepreneurial role. Purely entrepreneurial decisions are by definition reserved for decision-makers who own nothing at all. To the extent that an individual is being viewed as an asset owner, his decisions must be analyzed, if the above convention is to be adhered to with consistency, in purely Robbinsian terms. (And to the extent that we wish to consider him in his entrepreneurial role, an individual who does own assets must, as we saw in the case of the producer, be viewed as "purchasing" the services of these

known," and assuming "that the complete set of inputs are specified and known to all actual or potential firms in the industry." For Leibenstein, scope for entrepreneurship arises, in large measure, from the unrealism of these assumptions. Among the differences separating Leibenstein's approach from my own is, perhaps most important, the following: For Leibenstein entrepreneurship and the "x-inefficiency" which provides scope for entrepreneurship are important neglected aspects of the market. For me, entrepreneurship and the imperfection of knowledge which provides the scope for entrepreneurship are the essential elements in the market process in general. See further below, p. 223.

assets from himself.) All this becomes extremely important in the precise definition of pure entrepreneurial profits and their analytical separation from other receipts.

An owner of assets proceeds, as a Robbinsian economizer, to translate his asset bundle into the most desirable form possible, in light of the terms of exchange made available to him by the market or by nature or both. Thus a laborer sells his labor for the highest wages he can discover, and a consumer uses his money income to buy the most desirable basket of consumer products he can find. The better position which results from the owners' decisions has been obtained by taking advantage of the available avenues for exchanging initially owned assets. Something goes into the economizing process, and something more desirable comes out of it.

The pure entrepreneur, on the other hand, proceeds by his alertness to discover and exploit situations in which he is able to sell for high prices that which he can buy for low prices. Pure entrepreneurial profit is the difference between the two sets of prices. It is not yielded by exchanging something the entrepreneur values less for something he values more highly. It comes from discovering sellers and buyers of something for which the latter will pay more than the former demand. The discovery of a profit opportunity *means the discovery of something obtainable for nothing at all.* No investment at all is required; the free ten-dollar bill is discovered to be already within one's grasp.

Of course, many of the hitherto unnoticed opportunities for entrepreneurial profit may involve time-consuming processes of one kind or another. A resource which is capable of producing an urgently desired consumer product happens to be employed in an industry producing a much less valued commodity; the difference between the low resource cost and the high commodity revenue the resource can make possible presents a profit opportunity. But if the production of the highly valued commodity takes time, the high selling price may not be available at the time when the low buying price must be paid. The profit opportunity requires the investment of capital. But it is still correct to insist that the entrepreneur qua entrepreneur requires no investment of any kind. If the surplus (representing the difference between selling price and buying price) is sufficient to enable the entrepreneur to offer an interest payment attractive enough to persuade someone to advance the necessary funds, it is still true that the entrepreneur has discovered a way of obtaining pure profit, without the need to invest anything at all. The capitalist role, needed to make entrepreneurial profit possible in this case of time-consuming production, is filled by resource owners who find the interest payment sufficiently attractive so they are willing to sell resources under an agreement which promises them revenue only at some later date. (In a monetary economy the capitalist role need not be filled by resource owners willing to wait for their payment until production has been completed. The capitalist role may be fulfilled by "lending" money capital — with which the wages of currently employed resources may be paid — but the underlying economics of the case still involves the "sale" of current assets in exchange for the promise of revenue in the future.) And of course an entrepreneur may happen to own resources (or money) himself and find it worthwhile to finance his own entrepreneurial ventures. In other words, the same individual may be both entrepreneur and capitalist, just as the same individual may be both entrepreneur and resource owner. (As we have seen, the capitalist role may be considered, in an important sense, as a special kind of resource-ownership role.) The important point is that analytically the purely entrepreneurial role does not overlap that of the capitalist, even though, in a world in which almost all production processes are more or less time-consuming, entrepreneurial profit opportunities typically require capital. The distinction between pure entrepreneurial profits and pure interest is now well es-

tablished in economic theory; here I have merely sought to
show how the distinction emerges with exceptional clarity
within the framework of the system developed in this chapter.

Although I have emphasized that pure entrepreneurial
profits are captured by entrepreneurs, never by owners, an
explanatory observation may be necessary to avoid my being
misunderstood. Suppose an entrepreneur buys something at
one date (let us say, a resource service) in order to sell it (or
its resulting product) at a higher price at some later date.
Now at the time of sale, that is, at the later date, the transaction may look like nothing but a sale of something owned. If
the profits won by this entrepreneurial venture are calculated
(by subtracting the price paid at the earlier date from the
present selling price), it might appear that these profits have
been won by an owner who has made a profitable sale. But, I
must insist, this is not the case. To the extent that we wish to
view the entire venture as an entrepreneurial one, we must
focus attention on the *entrepreneurial decision* responsible for
the venture. This decision was made *before* the original act of
purchase; in fact it was a decision to buy in order to sell subsequently. When we ask ourselves what the outcome of *that*
decision has been, we may indeed answer that at the conclusion of the entire venture it has become evident that the
original entrepreneurial decision was profitable. The surplus
of selling price over buying price is indeed pure profit *if it is
related back to the original entrepreneurial decision.* This surplus, however, is *not* to be viewed as entrepreneurial profit if
we confine our attention solely to the *later* decision, the decision to sell at the later date. At the time of the sale, the
owner-entrepreneur is free to abandon the originally formulated entrepreneurial plan, which called for selling at the present time. His final decision to sell, therefore, is made quite
independently of the original plan to sell; this later decision
is then the decision made by an *owner.* If we inquire concerning this decision, then (as long as we follow the convention of

classifying decisions as *either* purely entrepreneurial *or* purely Robbinsian) we are not able to relate it to entrepreneurial profit at all. This is simply an owner's decision to sell at the market price. Only when we relate the entire sequence of buying and selling transactions back to the original entrepreneurial plan can we talk of profit.

It thus turns out that the final sale in this venture *has* yielded entrepreneurial profit, if we are referring it back to the original entrepreneurial decision, and yet this gain is being pocketed by an *owner*. Clearly, then, in insisting on the insight that entrepreneurial profit is never captured by owners, we are at the same time insisting that where the receipt of a given amount of money is described as a winning of pure profits this does not mean that this *same* receipt cannot at the same time be viewed equally correctly as something other than profits. In other words, the correct theoretical characterization of a particular receipt depends on the character of the decision responsible for that receipt. And where, as is frequently the case, a particular receipt is the consequence of *more* than one decision, each of which was required before the receipt could materialize, then the economic character of the receipt itself depends, for the purpose of any given discussion, upon which of the contributing decisions it happens to be referred to in that discussion. Thus in our example the surplus yielded by the final sale over the original purchase price can be seen as the successful outcome of the original entrepreneurial decision; as such it is pure profit. On the other hand, all the revenue received by this final sale has resulted from the final decision to sell (and this final decision, although *planned* at the time of the original decision to buy, was not at all *assured* until actually made); as such this revenue is simply the proceeds of the sale of an asset, and no part of it is viewed as pure profit. At all times entrepreneurial profits are to be identified only when related to a purely entrepreneurial decision. Thus the fact that this very receipt is being pocketed by an owner and can indeed even be viewed, taking a different perspective, as the consequence of an owner's decision does not at all weaken our insistence that what is being seen as entrepreneurial profit can never be referred back to the exercise of any ownership role. All this will be of help to us when we turn to examine the nature of the firm and its relationship to the entrepreneur.

The "firm" has become a standard term in both pure and applied price theory. A significant portion of price theory, in fact, is often presented under the title "theory of the firm." The position usually taken is that one of the important loci of decision-making in the market economy is within "the firm," and that an important part of microeconomic theory should be devoted to investigating exactly who, within "the firm," makes its decisions and what considerations are taken into account in making these decisions. It is from this point of view that such problems are discussed as the effect of the "separation of ownership from control" upon the decisions of the corporate firm.

However, the truth is that in analysis the firm ought to be recognized as a complex entity. As Papandreou has pointed out, the firm emerges only when "the owners of productive services sell them to an entrepreneur."[12] The firm, then, is not at all the same thing as the pure entrepreneur. It is that which results *after* the entrepreneur has completed some entrepreneurial decision-making, specifically the purchase of certain resources. Once the entrepreneur has acquired some of the resources necessary to produce some commodity he is, so to speak, in business. He is committed (to a degree that depends on the specificity and mobility of the resources already

12. A. G. Papandreou, "Some Basic Problems in the Theory of the Firm," in *A Survey of Contemporary Economics*, ed. B. F. Haley (Homewood, Ill.: Richard Irwin, 1952), 2:183.

acquired) to a particular branch of industry, and he is able now, by acquiring the necessary additional resources, to take advantage of his earlier acquisitions. The particular entrepreneur is no longer only a pure entrepreneur; he has become, as a result of earlier entrepreneurial decisions, an owner of resources.

Thus when, in conventional price theory, statements are made concerning the profit-maximizing decisions of the firm, we must not lose sight of the complexity of the situation. In an important sense the notion of entrepreneurial profit may simply not be relevant here. Even if we mean, when we say that the firm seeks to maximize its profits, that the *entrepreneur* running the firm seeks to maximize *his* profits, we must realize that to the extent that the entrepreneur is the *owner* of the firm (and thus no longer visible as a "pure" entrepreneur at all), what he is seeking to maximize may really be *not* entrepreneurial profit but rather the quasi-rents to be derived from the ownership of the already-acquired resources. It is true that, when we relate the profits of the firm to the *earlier* entrepreneurial decisions to purchase the initial resources needed to get the firm started, we must recognize that, to the extent that the flow of current quasi-rents (appropriately discounted and summed to the date of the original purchases) exceeds the purchase costs, true entrepreneurial profits are present. And, moreover, in his continuing operation of the business the entrepreneur-owner may exploit opportunities for deploying the firm's resources in exceptionally profitable ventures. (In such cases the entrepreneur who happens to own the firm has, in his entrepreneurial alertness, discovered ways of deploying the firm's resources so as to yield a pure surplus in revenue over the market value of all required resources — including the market value for the quasi-rents derived from the already-acquired resources of the firm. Thus we view him as a pure entrepreneur "purchasing" the firm's initial resources [at their low market value] and turning them to profitable account in ventures which other firms have not realized are attractive.) These latter profits, it must be emphasized, do not accrue to the entrepreneur in his capacity as owner of the firm. He could make the *same* profits by hiring (at the low market value) the complex of resources making up someone else's firm and then proceeding to deploy these resources in the new lucrative ventures he has discovered (hiring whatever additional current inputs might be needed).[13]

We have already noticed [14] that the conventional theory of the firm tends to mask the purely entrepreneurial element in the decision-making of producers. Yet the fact that the firm is assumed to make decisions which maximize "profits" tends to promote the misunderstanding that it is indeed entrepreneurship that is at the core of the theory of the firm. On the other hand, it has become the fashion to identify the urge to maximize profits not with entrepreneurship but with *ownership*! [15] In fact, probably the most serious criticism leveled at price theory in general by its detractors depends on the charge that the institutional realities of the modern corporate firm render the profit-maximization assumption irrelevant, because ownership (to which is alone attributed the incentive

13. On these points cf. R. Triffin, *Monopolistic Competition and General Equilibrium Theory* (Cambridge: Harvard University Press, 1940), pp. 172–77, 181–84.

14. Above, p. 46.

15. For a recent example of this see A. A. Alchian, "Corporate Management and Property Rights," in *Economic Policy and the Regulation of Corporate Securities*, ed. H. G. Manne (Washington, D.C.: American Enterprise Institute, 1969), pp. 342–43. The discussions in this and the preceding sections will have made clear the only sense in which it may be argued that profits accrue only to owners. Where an entrepreneur acquired assets for a low price and is able to secure from their subsequent sale (or from the sale of products produced by these assets) a revenue that exceeds his original purchase outlay, he has captured profits. It is indeed his ownership of these assets that enables him now to secure these excess receipts. However, we have seen, these receipts become visible as entrepreneurial profits only when traced back to the decision — made before ownership was established — to purchase the assets.

to maximize profits) is in actuality separated from entrepreneurship (thought of loosely as the focus of control governing the firm's profit-winning operations). All this reflects confusions which we are now in a position to dispel.

OWNERSHIP, ENTREPRENEURSHIP, AND THE CORPORATE FIRM

In the large literature appraising the relevance of orthodox price theory in light of the contemporary dominance of the corporate firm, surprisingly little serious effort has been made to "locate" the corporate firm in terms of the fundamental categories of the theory. This discussion of entrepreneurship and its relation to ownership in the firm may prove helpful. Stripped to essentials, the corporation is nominally owned by its stockholders, who hire managers to run the business. Let us attempt to ignore the legal facade and identify (*a*) the capitalists and (*b*) the entrepreneurs as *economic* categories.

Apart from the bondholders, who are clearly capitalists, it is well recognized that stockholders too are capitalists. Without prejudging at this point the question whether stockholders are to be considered entrepreneurs, it is clear that when a stockholder buys a newly issued share of stock he is providing capital to the enterprise. (If we wish to consider him as an entrepreneur as well, we will have to consider him as borrowing capital from himself.) The fact that the stockholder is a part *owner* of the firm does not affect what has just been stated. He is in the position of one who has borrowed capital from himself in order to buy resources; he owns the resources but is nonetheless also a capitalist, since he has "lent" the capital invested.

When a stockholder receives "profits," he is sometimes described as an "owner" receiving "his" entrepreneurial profits. But of course ownership has nothing to do with entrepreneurial profits. Insofar as the stockholder is viewed as a capitalist, what he receives is implicit interest; insofar as he is being viewed as an owner, what he receives is quasi-rent. If the stockholder is an entrepreneur, then any entrepreneurial profits that may be discovered can be ascribed neither to his role as capitalist nor to his role as owner.

Something of this was perceived, not in entirely satisfactory fashion, by R. A. Gordon in a paper published in 1936.[16] After reviewing various theories of entrepreneurial profit, Gordon rejects them because they identify entrepreneurial profits with ownership income. Consideration of divorced control in the corporation, Gordon argues, shows that ownership need not coincide with entrepreneurship. He identifies entrepreneurship as the "guiding, integrating, and initiating force" — in a word, "control" — for production. Since in Gordon's view control over the corporation is exercised by managers, not by stockholders, it is the former who are entrepreneurs, not the latter. Entrepreneurial profit must therefore be defined and explained in such a way that none of it can be won by the stockholders. Any residual, noncontractual receipts by stockholders may be explained in any way one pleases — reward for risk-bearing, a result of friction, or whatever — but must not be identified as entrepreneurial income.

The discussion in this chapter supports Gordon in his conclusion that entrepreneurial profit not be viewed as going to owners qua owners. But for us this follows simply from the definitions of the relevant analytical categories; in no way do we rely for this conclusion on his hardly satisfactory definition of entrepreneurship as "control,"[17] or on the equally dubious basis that stockholders are in *no* way to be consid-

16. R. A. Gordon, "Enterprise, Profits, and the Modern Corporation," in *Explorations in Economics* (New York: McGraw-Hill, 1936), reprinted in Fellner and Haley, eds, *Readings in the Theory of Income Distribution* (New York: Blakiston, 1949), pp. 558 ff. See also S. Peterson, "Corporate Control and Capitalism," *Quarterly Journal of Economics* 79 (February 1965): 1–24; and O. E. Williamson, "Corporate Control and the Theory of the Firm," and A. A. Alchian, "Corporate Management and Property Rights," both in *Economic Policy and the Regulation of Corporate Securities*, ed. H. G. Manne (Washington, D.C.: American Enterprise Institute, 1969).

17. However, see further below, pp. 83–84.

ered entrepreneurs. (On the contrary, to the extent that stock-holders promoted the corporation in the first place, at least a part of their receipts from the corporation must unquestionably be viewed as entrepreneurial profits, when referred back to their original *entrepreneurial* decisions to start the firm.)

The truth is that the temptation to define entrepreneur-ship simply as *control* may be responsible for some of the confusion surrounding the location of entrepreneurship in the corporate firm. The position taken is that the ongoing activities of the corporate firm are clearly under the control of some group of persons. Since casual empiricism (based on such "evidence" as stockholders' attendance at corporate meetings and the like) suggests that it is the managers rather than the stockholders who are "in control," entrepreneur-ship is ascribed to the managers. For us, mere control is by no means sufficient to establish entrepreneurship: Robbin-sian economizers, after all, may be "in control" of their rele-vant spheres of decision-making. Nor, in identifying the "long-run" entrepreneurship which initiated a firm, is *current* control even a necessary condition for entrepreneurship. For us the crucial question concerns whose vision and alertness to hitherto unnoticed opportunities is responsible for the effec-tive decisions of the corporate firm. Clearly it is impossible to give an a priori answer to this question, but careful thought can clarify the alternatives and point to some of their impli-cations — which appear to have frequently been overlooked. We will proceed by examining a simple hypothetical example.

A HYPOTHETICAL EXAMPLE

Let us imagine an economy in which the high price of meat makes hunting appear likely, in A's judgment, to be a gainful enterprise (for which only a gun and the services of a hunter are required). Let us suppose that A thereupon decides to go into the hunting business and purchases or rents a gun (at the going market price). Clearly this purchase is an entrepreneurial one. And if a week's "profit" — that is, the week's hunting revenue minus the wages of the hunter — exceeds the rental cost of the gun, then this excess is of course pure entrepreneurial profit attributed to the purchase of the gun. Once others realize the profitability of hunting, other hunting "firms" will spring up, raising the cost of guns and lowering the market value of meat until this kind of pure entrepreneurial profit disappears for prospective new firms. The weekly rental cost of a gun, together with the weekly wage of the hunter, will exhaust the total weekly hunting revenue.

An important case is that where A has not only been ahead of the other businessmen in setting up his hunting firm, but is also more alert in his ability to sense where the best opportunities for hunting exists, so that he sends his hunter on expeditions which yield greater hunting revenue per week (than the expeditions sent out by other firms with hunters of equal skill). Then A will be winning entrepreneurial profits also, in that the weekly rental cost of his gun and the weekly wage of the hunter do *not* exhaust the total weekly hunting revenue.

But for our purposes it will be most useful to consider yet another case. Suppose that A is *not* a more alert entrepreneur than other firms are, in sensing better opportunities for hunting expeditions. But let us instead suppose that he has hired a hunter, B, and that although in the actual labor of hunting for which he is hired B is no better than the other hunters, he happens at the same time to be exceptionally alert to possibilities for unusually valuable hunting expeditions. To B, the labor he expends on the more valuable expedition is no greater than that required for an average expedition; so his employer A *may* find that he still ends up with a surplus after deducting (from gross weekly hunting revenue) the weekly rental of the gun and the regular hunter wage which B is receiving. This surplus we will presumably describe as entrepreneurial profit, ascribed to A's perception (or good luck) in hiring B rather than other hunters. In fact, it seems almost natural to view the ability to hunt as inseparable from alertness to the relative merits of alternative hunting possibilities — to describe B simply as a superior hunter and to predict that the market price for B's services will, as a result of employer competition, gradually be driven up until A's surplus disappears. But let us persist for the moment with the notion that we *can* divide B's abilities into two distinct parts: the ability to use a gun where he is told to shoot (in which ability he is not superior to other hunters); and the ability to sense unsuspectedly good places to shoot in (in which he is superior to others). Then we must ask exactly what it is that B is being hired to do, at regular hunter's wages. If B is only being hired to shoot *where he is told to*, then of course B will not have the opportunity to exercise his second ability at all, his employer will reap no profits, and his wages will not rise. If B is told to shoot wherever *he* chooses, but is not charged with the responsibility to discover the *best* place for shooting, it will be only by chance that B will produce more hunting revenue than others. If B is hired to shoot wherever he thinks it best to shoot, then, we are tempted to say, B is being hired to exercise *both* abilities, while as a result of general market unawareness of his second special ability his wage is no more than that paid to other hunters having only the first ability. Thus it once again seems that we ought to expect competition among employers interested in using *both* of B's abilities to tend to force up his total wages. But before we uncritically accept this, let us pause to analyze the case we have in hand.

The heart of the matter concerns the degree to which it is possible to describe an employer, A, as hiring B's ability to be alert to hitherto unnoticed opportunities for unusually successful hunting expeditions. Suppose for the moment we accept such a description as valid. This would mean that in return for a fixed wage B has committed himself to bend his exceptional abilities (in respect of alertness) to A's ends. If

B faithfully fulfills his side of the arrangement, we could quite accurately describe A, too, as possessing superior alertness toward exceptional hunting possibilities (since after all it was A who had the alertness to secure B's alertness, for his [A's] own ends). We can indeed expect A's competition to gradually follow A and eventually force up B's wages, wiping out A's profit. At the same time we are compelled to ask why, assuming that he knows himself to be superior (in alertness to exceptional hunting possibilities) B does not set up his own hunting firm and reap the entrepreneurial profits for himself. The answer to this question must, on our assumptions, be that whatever alertness B possess, it is for one reason or another not *entrepreneurial* alertness; that is, B's awareness of superior opportunities is sufficient for him to sell his services for a wage, but is not *sufficiently convincing to himself* to inspire him to go after the profits he suspects he perceives. If this answer is correct, then our conclusion must be that *only* A has shown so far that he possesses the superior alertness toward exceptional hunting possibilities that makes the entrepreneur. A is the *only* entrepreneur in his firm; B exercises abilities of different kinds, he is a *better hunter* by virtue of these abilities, but he is *not* an entrepreneur.

But what if B does *not* faithfully fulfill his side of the arrangement? What if B discovers scope for somehow exploiting his superior alertness toward hunting possibilities for his personal enrichment? What if B's ethics (or lack of ethics) lead him to enrich himself, instead of his employer, to reap prestige for himself, to command comforts for himself (both at home and while at work), instead of adding to the profits of his employer? And what if the circumstances of the situation make A powerless to force B to fulfill the arrangement faithfully (or perhaps even to detect that he is not so fulfilling it)? Here A reaps no entrepreneurial profits from B's superior abilities; he has not been able to get B to bend these abilities to his (A's) own ends. A has certainly not displayed entrepreneurship in this regard: he has discovered no way of putting his gun to work that is superior to the methods used by other firms. A has not succeeded in hiring B's ability to be alert. And of course we have no reason in this case to ask why B does not set up his own firm and so reap the entrepreneurial profits of his own alertness for himself. He *is* reaping these profits for himself, through using A's gun in the best possible way (as reflected in consumer willingness to pay greater revenues), right where he is. In fact, if he is doing so, then B is indeed acting entrepreneurially *in his present position.* Whether his actions in this regard are unethical in light of his employment agreement with A may be an important question. But if B's conscience does not disturb him, and if A is powerless to interfere, then the situation is as we have described it. A, who acted entrepreneurially in originally securing the gun, is now simply putting the gun to work in the best way known to him (which is to hire a standard hunter at standard wages); his present day-to-day decisions (to continue hiring B), yield no entrepreneurial profit. B, who knows how to put a gun to work in exceptionally valuable ways (ways unknown to A and to other hunting firms), finds that in order to reap the entrepreneurial profits which he perceives to be there for the grasping it is not necessary for him to rent a gun and start his own firm. He can capture these profits by hiring himself out as a hunter at standard wages, then turning in to his employer a standard week's hunting revenue and pocketing the additional revenue which he alone is able to secure with a gun.

Entrepreneurial competition would apply, of course, regardless of how B went after profits. Others would learn of the opportunities that B knows about first, and the market prices of guns or meat or both would move to eliminate entrepreneurial profit. What our example has shown is that where B possesses exceptional alertness we may have either (but not both) of two situations. Either A has succeeded in hiring this alertness of B — in which case A is the only entrepreneur in the picture and B's alertness is not entrepreneurial at all — or A does *not* succeed in hiring this alertness of B, and B himself captures the opportunities he perceives — in which case B's alertness is indeed entrepreneurial, and A is not an entrepreneur at all in respect to B's alertness. In all cases profits go to the entrepreneur. If A gets the profits he is acting as an entrepreneur, not as a mere owner. If B gets the profits he is acting as an entrepreneur for himself, not as a mere hired factor.

This example has also shown that the exercise of pure entrepreneurship need not involve the purchase of *all* the factors of production. The entrepreneur (B) may acquire one factor of production (say, labor), *sell* it to another entrepreneur (A) who has acquired a second factor of production (say, a gun), and thus be in a position to reap the profits he perceives are available (by utilizing the complex of inputs in ways others have not noticed). If guns are not monopolized by A's firm, B's profits will eventually be eroded through competition. (Even if A's firm monopolizes guns, B's profits will still be lessened as other entrepreneurs acquire labor and compete for B's job with A's firm. As I will show in the following chapter, pure entrepreneurship is by definition never monopolized.) Let us now apply what our example has taught us to the corporate firm.

THE CORPORATE FIRM ONCE AGAIN

The example has shown us that if the institutional environment of the corporate firm is such that managers, in controlling the firm's operations, are able to reap private benefit for themselves, we may indeed ascribe entrepreneurship to them — not in the sense of "control" but in the sense of putting resources to use in superior (and "profitable") opportunities as yet unnoticed by others. Nothing in the example suggests that this need represent any serious departure from the scheme of the private-enterprise economy envisaged in orthodox price theory.

The casual observer may not be able to easily identify the elements within the complex corporate firm which correspond to the simple categories used in price theory, with its simple vision of the profit-maximizing enterprise. But we have seen that no matter how complicated the corporate firm may be, no matter how complex the "political," "organizational," or "sociological" aspects of the stockholder-management relationship, the presence of entrepreneurship at several possible levels and of the consequent winning of profits by alert decision-makers can be discerned without difficulty. Nothing in all this suggests that in a market-economy characterized by corporate firms decisions on utilizing resources will be actuated by any motives other than *to put them to work in the most lucrative way known to the relevant decision-makers.*[18] To be sure, if we focus attention on the corporate firm as a single integrated economic unit we will not necessarily find that the decisions made within the firms are such as to maximize stockholder "profits," but this should be no cause for concern. In our hypothetical hunting example we saw that in order for B to use A's gun to provide the most and the best meat for consumers, it was not at all necessary that the decisions made by B be calculated to maximize A's profits. And it must of course be conceded that to the extent that management is able to enrich itself only in *non*pecuniary ways, it will no longer be true that the maximization of *money* profit assumption can be used uncritically.[19] But the general proposition that the profit motive governs in-

18. See H. G. Manne, *Insider Trading and the Stock Market* (New York: Free Press, 1966), for a pioneering demonstration of the insight that "insider profits" won by corporate executives are pure entrepreneurial profits.

19. For one thoughtful approach to the problem of incorporating nonpecuniary emoluments into the usual profit-maximization hypothesis, see H. T. Koplin, "The Profit Maximization Assumption," *Oxford Economic Papers* 15 (July 1963): 130–39.

dividual decision-making in the market economy, and especially the welfare implications of this proposition, can be entirely valid for an economy in which stockholder ownership and managerial control are entirely divorced from one another.[20]

The objection may perhaps be raised that the ability of a corporate manager to feather his own nest in the course of operating the firm may not at all be the expression of his exceptional entreprencurial alertness in putting the firms' resources to work in ways valuable to consumers. Perhaps his ability to feather his nest is simply his skill in robbing the stockholders while performing at no better than standard managerial performance levels. Perhaps B's ability to enrich himself through the use of A's gun does not stem from his use of the gun in superior opportunities but from his ability to withhold some of the revenue which average, run-of-the-mill use of the gun might yield. If this were so, then the gun (and the corporation resources) would indeed be being used in ways not at all in accord with profit-maximizing assumptions.

Consideration of our hypothetical hunting example should enlighten us on the score. If B's propensity to pocket a part of the firm's revenues does *not* reflect any entrepreneurial superiority in utilizing the firm's gun, A may soon find that his weekly revenue is not sufficient to cover B's standard wages and the standard (implicit) weekly rental cost of the gun. In any event, it will soon be apparent that B's usefulness to the firm is less than that of the hunter with similar wages and without B's disturbing propensities. We need have no fear (ethics and police protection aside) that hunters with B's propensity to raid the till will persist long in their jobs. But what, one may object, if the power which B, as incumbent hunter, possesses within A's firm is such as to ensure him permanent tenure? What if stockholders lack the effec-

20. On this see Triffin, *Monopolistic Competition*, p. 186.

tive power to fire management? Then indeed we are assuming that competitive forces among hunters and among management personnel are for some unspecified reason impotent to ensure profit-maximizing decision-making. The validity of this assumption is of course a question of institutional fact, not to be decided by a priori reasoning. (If valid, it implies that mere incumbency confers a degree of monopoly upon the incumbent manager.) And, again, if this assumption *is* valid, then at least in the long-run people such as A will know that in buying a gun and setting up a hunting firm one of the prospective hazards is the likelihood that his hunters will raid the till regularly. If in light of this known cost of doing business by setting up a firm A persists in doing so, we must conclude that in his *entrepreneurial* judgment the cost is worthwhile.

Let us sum up. Our major object has been to challenge the usual conclusion that when corporate managers are able to benefit themselves at the expense of the stockholders the decisions being made violate the profit-maximizing assumption basic to price theory. We have seen, in fact, that managers *are* the true entrepreneurs only to the extent that the entrepreneurial opportunities for personal benefit do in fact exist, and that where such opportunities are embraced this is fully in accord with the profit-maximizing rationale of the market system. (And, on the other hand, if the opportunities for personal managerial gain are not entrepreneurial in character, then we have seen that either short-run or long-run competitive forces, or both, can nevertheless be relied upon to ensure the universal tendency toward disposing productive resources in the most effective ways known to entrepreneurs.)

ENTREPRENEURSHIP AND KNOWLEDGE

Some remarks appear to be in order to clarify the relationship between the notion of entrepreneurial *alertness* developed in this chapter and the alternative idea that pure entrepreneurship represents superior *command over information*. There is a certain temptation to conceive of the entrepreneur as one who simply *knows* more accurately than others do where resources can be purchased most cheaply, where products can be sold at the highest prices, what technological or other innovations will prove most fruitful, which assets can be expected to increase most in value, and so on. By exploiting his superior knowledge the entrepreneur captures profits for himself. In this interpretation, entrepreneurial profit (and scope for entrepreneurial decision-making in general) disappears, in the general equilibrium market, because the perfect-knowledge assumption associated with the state of general equilibrium removes any possibilities for superior knowledge.

The difficulty with conceiving of entrepreneurship in terms of superior knowledge arises from the need to distinguish sharply between entrepreneurship and factors of production. The search for the elusive analytical category of entrepreneurship stems from the insight that an explanation of the market phenomenon of pure profits implies a role in the market which cannot be reduced to just a special kind of productive factor. Knowledge, or at least the services of men who possess knowledge, can, after all, be hired in the factor market. The more highly skilled worker tends to command higher wages in the labor market, and the better-informed individual tends to command higher wages in the market for the services of business decision-makers. If we are to maintain the position that entrepreneurship represents something not to be treated as a factor of production, it will not do to define it simply in terms of knowledge.[21]

And yet we can hardly deny that opportunities for pure

21. Cf. F. Machlup, *The Economics of Sellers' Competition* (Baltimore, Md.: Johns Hopkins University Press, 1952), pp. 225–31, for a discussion of the distinction between entrepreneurship and the exercise of managerial responsibility. See also G. J. Stigler, "The Economics of Information," *Journal of Political Economy* 69 (June 1961): 213–25, for a treatment of the *non*entrepreneurial aspects of knowledge in the market.

entrepreneurial profit are generated by the imperfection of knowledge on the part of market participants; that these opportunities can be seized by anyone discovering their existence before others have done so; and that the process of winning these profits is at the same time a process of correcting market ignorance. If all market participants were omniscient, prices for products and prices for factors must at all times be in complete mutual adjustment, leaving no profit differential; no opportunity for the worthwhile deployment of resources, through any technology knowable or for the satisfaction of any consumer desire conceivable, can be imagined to have been left unexploited. Only the introduction of ignorance opens up the possibility of such unexploited opportunities (and their associated opportunities for pure profits), and the possibility that the first one to discover the true state of affairs can capture the associated profits by innovating, changing, and creating.

But closely as the element of knowledge is tied to the possibility of winning pure profits, the elusive notion of entrepreneurship is, as we have seen, not encapsulated in the mere possession of greater knowledge of market opportunities. The aspect of knowledge which *is* crucially relevant to entrepreneurship is not so much the substantive knowledge of market data as *alertness, the "knowledge" of where to find market data.* Once one imagines knowledge of market data to be *already possessed* with absolute certainty, one has, as we noticed earlier,[22] imagined away the opportunity for further entrepreneurial (as distinct from "Robbinsian") decision-making. Conversely, we have also already seen that knowledge of opportunities that is possessed *without* the certainty required to capture them requires a separate, additional level of entrepreneurship capable of exploiting this possessed knowledge — such unsure knowledge being then a hired factor of production, with the entrepreneurial role filled by

22. See chap. 2, n. 4.

someone with the confidence that this hired knowledge is indeed capable of securing profits.[23]

That is why, in this book, I speak of the essentially entrepreneurial element in human action in terms of *alertness* to information, rather than of its possession. The entrepreneur is the person who hires the services of factors of production. Among these factors may be persons with superior knowledge of market information, but the very fact that these hired possessors of information have not *themselves* exploited it shows that, in perhaps the truest sense, their knowledge is possessed not by them but by the one who is hiring them. It is the latter who "knows" whom to hire, who "knows" where to find those with the market information needed to locate profit opportunities. Without himself possessing the facts known to those he hires, the hiring entrepreneur does nonetheless "know" these facts, in the sense that his alertness — his propensity to know where to look for information — dominates the course of events.

Ultimately, then, the kind of "knowledge" required for entrepreneurship is "knowing where to look for knowledge" rather than knowledge of substantive market information. The word which captures most closely this kind of "knowledge" seems to be *alertness*. It is true that "alertness," too, may be hired; but one who hires an employee alert to possibilities of discovering knowledge has himself displayed alertness of a still higher order. Entrepreneurial knowledge may be described as the "highest order of knowledge," the *ultimate* knowledge needed to harness available information already possessed (or capable of being discovered). A comparable relationship can be noticed in connection with the operation of *hiring* itself. A decision to hire a factor of production is not necessarily an *entrepreneurial* decision; after all, a personnel manager may be hired specifically for his talent in making wise hiring decisions. But where a factor of pro-

23. Cf. above, p. 60.

duction is making the hiring decisions, it is implied that this factor of production was itself hired by someone making a hired decision, and so on. The *entrepreneurial* decision to hire is thus the *ultimate* hiring decision, responsible in the last resort for all factors that are directly or indirectly hired for his project.[24] In exactly the same way the alertness of the entrepreneur is the abstract, very general and rarefied kind of knowledge which we must ultimately credit with discovering and exploiting the opportunities specifically unearthed by those whom he has been wise enough to hire, directly and indirectly.

It was stated in the first chapter that our emphasis on the market *process*, rather than on the more usually emphasized market equilibrium, stems from an awareness of the role of entrepreneurship, which is largely ignored by contemporary expositions of the theory of price. It is for this reason that I have given priority to the notion of entrepreneurship. I am now in a position to anticipate the discussions of later chapters and indicate briefly how the entrepreneurial role as I have developed it is in fact the crucial element in the market process.

A state of market disequilibrium is characterized by widespread ignorance. Market participants are unaware of the real opportunities for beneficial exchange which are available to them in the market. The result of this state of ignorance is that countless opportunities are passed up. For each product, as well as for each resource, opportunities for mutually beneficial exchange among potential buyers and sellers are missed. The potential sellers are unaware that sufficiently

24. Cf. the following statements by F. H. Knight in *Risk, Uncertainty and Profit* (Boston: Houghton and Mifflin, 1921): "What we call 'control' consists mainly of selecting some one else to do the 'controlling'" (p. 291); "The responsible decision is not the concrete ordering of policy, but ordering an orderer as a 'laborer' to order it" (p. 297). Cf. also Triffin, *Monopolistic Competition*, p. 184 and n. 39.

eager buyers are waiting, who might make it worth their while to sell. Potential buyers are unaware that sufficiently eager sellers are waiting, who might make it attractive for them to buy. Resources are being used to produce products which consumers value less urgently, because producers (and potential producers) are not aware that these resources can produce more urgently needed products. Products are being produced with resources badly needed for other products because producers arc not aware that alternative, less critically needed resources can be used to achieve the same results.

The task of a theory of the market is to provide insight into the course of events set in motion by the state of market disequilibrium. The crucial question concerns the nature of the forces that bring about changes in the buying, selling, producing, and consuming decisions that make up the market. And it is here that the entrepreneurial notion is indispensable. So long as we perceive all decision-makers as exclusively Robbinsian, each "mechanically" selecting the best course out of the alternatives believed to be available, our theory completely lacks a way of explaining how yesterday's plans are replaced today by new plans. So long as our decision-makers continue to believe that the alternative courses of action made available to them by the market are what they believed them to be yesterday, we are powerless (without resorting to exogenous changes in tastes or in resource availability) to account for any plan made today being different from that made yesterday. With the ends and means believed to be given today exactly as they were believed to be given yesterday, decision-makers will "automatically" arrive at the same optimum positions yielded by the data yesterday. For any price to change, or for any change in method of production or in the choice of product to occur, we must presume that some decision-makers are no longer attempting to carry out the plans they sought to carry out yesterday. There is nothing in the picture of a market of purely Robbinsian decision-makers, even with the injection of liberal doses of ignorance concerning the ends and means believed to be relevant, which can explain how yesterday's market experiences can account for changes in plans that might generate alterations in prices, in outputs, or in the use of inputs.

For this is it necessary to introduce the insight that men *learn* from their experiences in the market. It is necessary to postulate that out of the mistakes which led market participants to choose less-than-optimal courses of action yesterday, there can be expected to develop systematic *changes in expectations* concerning ends and means that can generate corresponding *alterations in plans*. Men entered the market yesterday attempting to carry out plans based on their beliefs concerning the ends worth pursuing and the means available. These beliefs reflected expectations, concerning the decisions other men would be making. The prices a market participant expected to receive for the resources or the products he would sell and the prices he expected to have to pay for the resources or products he would buy all went to determine the optimum course of market action for him. The discovery, during the course of yesterday's market experiences, that the other market participants were *not* making these expected decisions can be seen as generating changes in the corresponding price expectations with which market participants enter the market today.

For such a process of discovery of changing ends-means frameworks it is necessary to introduce something from outside the Robbinsian economizing terms of reference. For the purposes of the economist it is not necessary to explore the *psychology* of the learning process, which is the result of market experiences in which plans were found to be unworkable (or in which it has been found that alternative, preferable courses of action were in fact available).[25] But it is neces-

25. See F. A. Hayek, "Economics and Knowledge," in his *Individualism*

sary to build formally into our theory the insight that such a learning process can be relied upon. For this, the recognition of the entrepreneurial element in individual action is completely adequate. As soon as we broaden our theoretical vision of the individual decision-maker from a "mechanical" Robbinsian economizer to Mises's *homo agens*, with the universally human entrepreneurial elements of alertness in his makeup, we can cope with the task of explaining the changes which market forces systematically generate.

And the analytical device of concentrating *all* entrepreneurship into the role of the hypothetical pure entrepreneurs enables us to achieve the same kind of explanation. We may in this way continue to envisage a market in which consumers and resource owners are strictly Robbinsian economizers, exclusively price-takers, and shift the entire burden of price changes and changes in methods of production and of output quality and quantity upon the pure entrepreneurs. As we have seen earlier, this becomes all the easier once we perceive the near-inevitability of an entrepreneurial role's being filled by the producer.

All this leads me to express a certain dissatisfaction with the role assigned to the entrepreneur in the Schumpeterian system. We will return a little later in this chapter to Schumpeter's vision of the entrepreneur, as well as the views of the other leading writers on this topic. Here it is enough to observe that Schumpeter's entrepreneur and the one developed here can in many ways be recognized — and, let me add, reassuringly recognized — as the same individual. But there is one important respect — if only in emphasis — in which Schumpeter's treatment differs from my own. Schumpeter's entrepreneur acts to *disturb* an existing equilibrium situation. Entrepreneurial activity *disrupts* the continuing circular flow. The entrepreneur is pictured as *initiating* change and as gen-

and Economic Order (London: Routledge and Kegan Paul), 1949), p. 46; I. M. Kirzner, "Methodological Individualism," p. 795.

erating *new* opportunities. Although each burst of entrepreneurial innovation leads eventually to a new equilibrium situation, the entrepreneur is presented as a *disequilibrating*, rather than an equilibrating, force. Economic development, which Schumpeter of course makes utterly dependent upon entrepreneurship, is "entirely foreign to what may be observed in . . . the tendency towards equilibrium." [26]

By contrast my own treatment of the entrepreneur emphasizes the equilibrating aspects of his role. I see the situation upon which the entrepreneurial role impinges as one of inherent disequilibrium rather than of equilibrium — as one churning with opportunities for desirable changes rather than as one of placid evenness. Although for me, too, it is only through the entrepreneur that changes can arise, I see these changes as *equilibrating changes*. For me the changes the entrepreneur initiates are always toward the hypothetical state of equilibrium; they are changes brought about *in response to* the existing pattern of mistaken decisions, a pattern characterized by missed opportunities. The entrepreneur, in my view, *brings into mutual adjustment* those discordant elements which resulted from prior market ignorance.

My emphasis on this difference between Schumpeter's discussion and my own underscores the crucial importance of entrepreneurship for the *market process*. A treatment such as Schumpeter's, which invokes entrepreneurship as an exogenous force lifting the economy from one state of equilibrium (to eventually attain another such state as a result of "imitators"), is likely to convey the impression that for the *attainment* of equilibrium no entrepreneurial role is, in principle, required at all. Such a treatment is, in other words, likely to generate the utterly mistaken view that the state of equilibrium can establish itself without any social device to deploy and

26. J. A. Schumpeter, *The Theory of Economic Development* (Cambridge: Harvard University Press, 1934), p. 64.

marshal the scattered pieces of information which are the only source of such a state.[27]

It is to stress my contrary view, that it is only entrepreneurship which might (at least in theory, if exogenous changes are barred) eventually lead to equilibrium, that I feel it necessary to draw attention to entrepreneurship as a *responding* agency. I view the entrepreneur not as a source of innovative ideas ex nihilo, but as being *alert* to the opportunities that exist *already* and are waiting to be noticed. In economic development, too, the entrepreneur is to be seen as responding to opportunities rather than creating them; as capturing profit opportunities rather than generating them. When profitable capital-using methods of production are technologically available, where the flow of savings is sufficient to provide the necessary capital, entrepreneurship is required to ensure that this innovation will in fact be introduced.[28] Without entrepreneurship, without alertness to the new possibility, the long-term benefits may remain untapped. It is highly desirable to maintain a framework of analysis which shows the market process at work in essentially the same way both for a simple economy in which multiperiod plans are not made and for the complex economy in which such plans, involving the use of capital, are made. For this process it is utterly essential to invoke entrepreneurship. That most contemporary treatments of price theory fail to perceive this is perhaps the principal cause for my dissatisfaction with them. Schumpeter's unfortunate emphasis upon the entrepreneur as pushing the economy *away* from equilibrium helps promote the quite erroneous belief that entrepreneurship is somehow unnecessary to un-

27. See F. A. Hayek, "The Use of Knowledge in Society," *American Economic Review* 35 (September 1945): 529–30 (reprinted in *Individualism and Economic Order*, pp. 90–91), for the charge that Schumpeter himself in fact fell prey to this mistaken view.

28. See M. N. Rothbard, *Man, Economy and State* (Princeton, N.J., Van Nostrand, 1962), 2:493–94.

derstanding the way the market tends toward the equilibrium position.[29]

As was remarked earlier, one of our complaints concerning contemporary theories of price arises from their virtual elimination of entrepreneurship. What is required, I have argued, is a reformulation of price theory to readmit the entrepreneurial role to its rightful position as crucial to the very operation of the market. Despite my criticisms in this respect, however, it is by no means my contention that the entrepreneurial role has not received careful attention in the literature. There exists, of course, a well-developed line of contributions to the theory of entrepreneurship and entrepreneurial profit. Moreover, these discussions have involved several of the best-known names in modern economic thought. And from time to time articles still appear in the journals, dealing with one or another aspect of the problem. My complaint is not directed primarily at the shortcomings in this literature; rather I regret that the entrepreneurial role is not recognized as crucial to the market determination of the course of price movements. It seems desirable at this point to refer very briefly to the literature on entrepreneurial profit and to indicate the matters on which my approach diverges from the various strands of thought that are to be distinguished within that literature.[30]

As a general preliminary remark, it is worth noting that the primary concern of many of the contributors to this literature

29. For further discussion of the points raised in this section see I. M. Kirzner, "Entrepreneurship and the Market Approach to Development," in *Toward Liberty* (Menlo Park, Calif.: Institute for Humane Studies, 1971).

30. For general surveys of the literature see F. H. Knight, "Profit," in *Encyclopedia of the Social Sciences* (New York: Macmillan, 1934), reprinted in W. Fellner and B. Haley, eds., *Readings in the Theory of Income Distribution* (New York: Blakiston, 1949); J. F. Weston, "The Profit Concept and Theory: A Restatement," *Journal of Political Economy* 62 (April 1954): 152–70.

appears to be explaining *profit* rather than delineating the entrepreneurial role. The latter seems to have been undertaken merely as a step in completing the main task. In my own exposition we have seen that the phenomenon of profits is inseparable from the very possibility of entrepreneurship in general. But my concern has been with entrepreneurship as the prime moving force in the market process. I am concerned with profit because the notion of entrepreneurship is inseparable from the opportunity for profit. But it was the importance of entrepreneurship which inspired my inquiry, in contrast to much of the literature to which we now turn. I will comment briefly on the entrepreneurial role as it finds expression (1) in what Professor Bronfenbrenner has called the "naive profit theory"; [31] (2) in the system of Schumpeter; and (3) in the work of Professor Knight and his followers. Finally I will attempt to identify my own approach with that of Professor Mises.

1. The "naive" profit theory considers profits as a return to the entrepreneurial contribution to production. This contribution is, at least in earlier expositions, seen as ultimate decision-making or as ultimate uncertainty-bearing. Since this contribution is essential for all production processes, profit emerges as a "normal" distributive share — the "rewards for bearing uncertainty and risk." [32] As reformulated by Bronfenbrenner, the theory views profit "as compensation for merely the subset of uncertainties which arises from having no contractual claim to one's income." This "identifies entrepreneurship not with managerial, organizational, or innovational responsibili-

31. M. Bronfenbrenner, "A Reformulation of Naive Profit Theory," *Southern Economic Journal* 26 (April 1960): 300–309. Page references to this article will be to its reprint in W. Breit and H. Hochman, eds., *Readings in Microeconomics*, 1st ed. (New York: Holt, Rinehart and Winston, 1968).

32. Bronfenbrenner, "Reformulation of Naive Profit Theory." See also J. F. Weston, "The Profit Concept and Theory," p. 152, and J. F. Weston, "Profit as the Payment for the Function of Uncertainty-Bearing," *Journal of Business* 22 (April 1949): 106–18.

ties, but exclusively with the precarious nature of its legal claims."[33] Whether, in fact, the market will normally have to provide compensation for the function of providing productive services entrepreneurially (i.e., on a noncontractual basis) depends on such matters as possible aversion to uncertainty-bearing, tax considerations, the advantage of being one's own boss, the pleasures of a quiet life, and the like.

It is clear that the "naive" profit theory, as well as Professor Bronfenbrenner's reformulation of it, is concerned with a quite different aspect of the market process than I have considered in this chapter. There may well be a case for reserving the term "entrepreneurship" for the function of uncertainty-bearing (or of Bronfenbrenner's variant of it) and for identifying a separate distributive share as the normal compensation required to elicit its fulfillment. There is certainly no point in disagreeing over definitions; and the economic relationships which the "naive" theory of profit singles out for attention may well be important. But my own discussion has surely shown that there is present in the market process an element — which I have chosen to label entrepreneurship — to which the naive profit theory has simply not addressed itself; that the operation of the market depends almost entirely on the presence of this element; and that there is associated with this element the capture of opportunities for gain which remain unexplained by the "naive" theory. I offer no apologies for attaching the term "entrepreneurship" to this element; but I do need to distinguish the theoretical functions of my own discussions from those others have sought to fulfill. If bearing uncertainty or providing services on a noncontractual basis regularly involves a net disutility, it is indeed useful to point this out and to identify the compensation with which the market overcomes the general disinclination to provide such services. But this leaves us no less in need of a theory which recognizes the role of alertness to unrecognized oppor-

33. Bronfenbrenner, "Reformulation of Naive Profit Theory," p. 364.

tunities for gain. It will perhaps be helpful at this point to comment briefly upon the role of *uncertainty* in my own discussion of entrepreneurial alertness.

In one sense, of course, this discussion of entrepreneurship has been very much dependent upon the absence of perfect knowledge. Only in a world in which men make mistakes (in the sense of not perceiving the best opportunities) can there arise those opportunities for pure gain which offer scope for entrepreneurial activity. Only if opportunities are not immediately known can there arise a special role for alertness to new opportunities. And it is of course true that in such a world even the alert entrepreneur, discovering what *seems* to be an attractive opportunity, may have considerable misgivings concerning the venture. And the longer the time before the venture's required outlay can be expected to bring the hoped-for revenues, the less sure of himself the entrepreneur is likely to be. Thus entrepreneurial activity (as described here) undoubtedly involves uncertainty and the bearing of risk.[34]

But it should be clear that entrepreneurship as we have discussed it in no way depends on any specific attitude toward uncertainty-bearing on the part of decision-makers. Even if decision-makers displayed neither aversion nor preference toward uncertainty as such, even if they failed altogether to recognize the relatively precarious character of all perceived profit opportunities, we would yet have to find a place within our theory of the market process for entrepreneurial alertness

34. Schumpeter, of course, repeatedly denied that anyone except the capitalist bears risk. (See *Theory of Economic Development*, p. 137; *History of Economic Analysis* [London: Allen and Unwin, 1954], p. 556 n.) The sense in which this is undoubtedly true should not, however, prevent us from realizing that in another sense *only* the entrepreneurial element in decision-making (including that of the capitalist) faces risk. Robbinsian decision-making, as we have seen, sees ends and means as *data*; no matter how much uncertainty is given to us *in* these data, the fact that they *are* data shields the Robbinsian economizer from the ex ante possibility of changes in the ends-means framework.

and for its effect upon the continued availability of perceived opportunities for pure profit.

2. In the Schumpeterian system entrepreneurship consists of introducing new processes of production — of producing new products or producing old products in new ways. The innovator-entrepreneur disturbs the even flow of production and of the market by creating new ways of doing things and new things to do. In fulfilling this role he is at the same time *creating* profits for himself. By breaking away from routine activity the Schumpeterian entrepreneur is able to generate temporary gaps between the price of inputs and the price of output. The universal tendency for the "value of the original means of production to attach itself with the faithfulness of a shadow to the value of the product" [35] is for a brief period successfully defied by the daring pioneer who blazes new trails. Until imitators once again force prices and costs into conformity, the innovator is able to reap pure profits. Perhaps one of the most important aspects of Schumpeter's exposition is his very clear discussion of how pure profit is to be understood as containing no element whatsoever of compensation for the services of any factor of production. Profit, unlike payments for factor services, is not a "brake to production"; [36] nor can it be said of profit, as it can be said of factor costs, "that it just suffices to call forth precisely the quantity of entrepreneurial service required." [37]

In many respects the picture of the entrepreneur which I have sought to delineate shows much resemblance to that elaborated by Schumpeter. The Schumpeterian innovator is, after all, the decision-maker whose alertness to unnoticed opportunities has enabled him to depart from the routine repetitive working of widely known opportunities. The distinction which Schumpeter draws at length [38] between the way men

35. Schumpeter, *Theory of Economic Development*, p. 160.
36. Ibid., p. 153.
37. Ibid., p. 154.
38. Ibid., pp. 79 ff.

would act in "the accustomed circular flow" on the one hand and when "confronted by a new task" on the other is closely parallel to my own distinction between "Robbinsian" decision-making and entrepreneurial activity. "The assumption that conduct is prompt and rational," remarks Schumpeter, is, although never wholly realistic, sufficiently valid "if things have time to hammer logic into men." [39] In the routine of the circular flow, that is to say, we may excusably view decision-makers as wholly "economic"; but in contexts of potential change, the assumption of rationality becomes largely irrelevant. This is very similar indeed to my own contention that, although in an equilibrium world of perfect knowledge Robbinsian allocation presents an adequate framework within which to comprehend all decisions being made, the presence of imperfect information creates scope for an additional dimension in decision-making — the degree to which the decision reflects alertness to unexploited opportunities. This dimension cannot, as we have seen, be fitted into the Robbinsian ends-means framework. As Schumpeter remarks in contrasting the environment in which routine patterns of activity are subject to change with that of the circular flow; "[what] was a familiar datum becomes an unknown." [40]

Similarly, my entrepreneur and Schumpeter's innovator-entrepreneur have in common that, at least for their essentially entrepreneurial role, they contribute no factor services to production; the profit they win is not compensation needed to attract a necessary input into the production process. Production is entirely able to be carried on with the inputs whose remunerations have already been counted as costs in calculating pure profits. What the entrepreneur contributes is merely the pure decision to direct these inputs into the process selected rather than into other processes.

And yet my description of the entrepreneur does differ from

39. Ibid., p. 80.
40. Ibid.

Schumpeter's, and the entrepreneurial role in the Schumpeterian system is not identical with that which I have set forth. For me the important feature of entrepreneurship is not so much the ability to break away from routine as the ability to perceive new opportunities which others have not yet noticed. Entrepreneurship for me is not so much the introduction of new products or of new techniques of production as the ability to *see* where new products have become unsuspectedly valuable to consumers and where new methods of production have, unknown to others, become feasible. For me the function of the entrepreneur consists not of *shifting* the curves of cost or of revenues which face him,[41] but *of noticing that they have in fact shifted.*

What entrepreneurship achieves within the Schumpeterian system is the disruption of the circular flow, the creation of disequilibrium out of equilibrium.[42] For me, on the contrary, the entrepreneurial role, although of course the source of movement within the system, has an equilibrating influence; it is entrepreneurial alertness to unnoticed opportunities which creates the tendency toward the even circular flow of equilibrium. For Schumpeter, entrepreneurship is important primarily in sparking economic development; for me it is important primarily in enabling the market process to work itself out in all contexts — with the possibility of economic development seen merely as a special case.[43]

3. Professor Knight's theory of profit is well known. Profit

41. See Triffin, *Monopolistic Competition*, p. 168.
42. New products and methods introduced by the entrepreneur are described by Schumpeter as "disequilibrating" (J. A. Schumpeter, *Capitalism, Socialism and Democracy* [New York: Harper and Row, 1962], p. 132).
43. See further above, pp. 72–74, for additional comments on the difference between Schumpeter's discussion and my own. It may be observed that Schumpeter's well-known contention that perfect competition is incompatible with entrepreneurial innovation (*Capitalism, Socialism and Democracy*, pp. 104–5) displays unawareness that it is the *equilibrium* character of perfect competition which by definition rules out scope for entrepreneurship. See more on this below, pp. 129–31.

arises as a result of the constantly changing environment within which economic activity is carried on and the associated uncertainty concerning the outcomes of alternative courses of action. Profit is the residual, if any, left for the entrepreneur after he pays out the contractual incomes agreed upon for the factor he hires. The entrepreneur is identified as being ultimately in control of the venture, ultimately responsible for all receipts and all outlays, and thus subject to the uncertainty which surrounds the amount and sign of the difference between them.[44] Profits are not seen as compensation for shouldering this uncertainty; they are seen as uncertainty-bred differences between the anticipated value of resource services and their actual value.[45] The profits won by any particular entrepreneur depend on his *own* ability and good luck as well as upon the general level of initiative and ability in the market.[46] Followers of Professor Knight's theory of profit emphasize that the so-called profit-maximizing assumption in the static theory of the firm has (the possibly vital role it occupies in that context notwithstanding) nothing to do with the pure profits which are generated, within the dynamic context, by uncertainty and change.[47] The latter "cannot be deliberately maximized in advance."[48]

The Knightian entrepreneur does not display those distinctive features with which I have endowed the entrepreneur. The very emphasis on uncertainty in the Knightian system has tended to mask the fact that when an entrepreneur does enter into an admittedly risky venture he does so because he believes

44. Knight's theory of profit is presented in his *Risk, Uncertainty and Profit*. See also his essay "Profits" (cited above, chap. 2, n. 30).

45. J. F. Weston, "Profit as the Payment for Uncertainty Bearing"; also J. F. Weston, "Enterprise and Profit," *Journal of Business* 22 (July 1949): 141–59, and "A Generalized Uncertainty Theory of Profit," *American Economic Review* 40 (March 1950): 40–60.

46. Knight, *Risk, Uncertainty and Profit*, p. 284.

47. Weston, "Generalized Uncertainty Theory of Profit," p. 54; see also Bronfenbrenner, "Reformulation of Naive Profit Theory," 40:361–62, 369.

48. M. Friedman, "The Methodology of Positive Economics," in his *Essays in Positive Economics* (Chicago: University of Chicago Press, 1953), p. 21, n. 16.

that, on balance, it offers *an attractive opportunity*. The great interest with which Professor Knight considers the question of whether, ex post, profits outweigh losses deflects attention from the tremendously important insight that, viewed ex ante, every entrepreneurial decision taken envisages *only* profits. By averting our eyes from the nature of entrepreneurial activity viewed ex ante we are rejecting a useful instrument for understanding how decisions are made in the market and how these decisions determine the course of prices. What does not come through in the Knightian exposition is the active, alert, searching role of entrepreneurial activity. Treating profit as a residual fails to disclose that from the point of view of the prospective entrepreneur the profit opportunity is, with all its uncertainty, *there*; it is not seen as something that may or may not be left over after all contractual obligations have been met. The conclusion that entrepreneurial profits cannot be maximized in advance conceals the deliberate search for profit opportunities which we have seen is the essence of the entrepreneurial role.

On the other hand, although Knight's treatment of the entrepreneurial role is not quite satisfactory, his identification of where entrepreneurship is located is superb. Knight identifies entrepreneurship with *control* and *responsibility* [49] (with the latter to be understood as "uncertainty-bearing"). Moreover, Knight's concept of control is highly sophisticated — ultimate control is shown never to be separated from the bearing of ultimate responsibility.[50] Thus Knight's discussion of entrepreneurship in the modern corporate firm is not at all marred by that uncritical identification of entrepreneurial control with the activities of the corporate managers which I have objected to in Gordon's analysis of the same problem.[51] In my view, in fact, it is a sign of the excellence of Knight's concept of entrepreneurial control that it earned Gordon's disapproval

49. Knight, *Risk, Uncertainty and Profit*, p. 271 and passim.
50. Ibid., pp. 291–98.
51. See above, pp. 56–57.

as having become "so attenuated as to be of little significance in any analysis of active business leadership." It is, I maintain, precisely this "attenuated" quality of Knight's concept of entrepreneurship that enables him to analyze the economics of the corporate firm without confusion. It is easy to see that Knight's notion of ultimate control is immediately identifiable with my own notion of "ultimate knowledge"[52] — that is, with entrepreneurial alertness.

Another similarity between Knight's position and my own is the role of "profit maximization" in the theory of the firm. We have noticed that writers following Knight have pointed out the confusion that results from identifying the "static profits" relevant to the theory of the firm with the Knightian profits generated dynamically as a result of uncertainty. This keen observation parallels my own earlier remark[53] that the orthodox theory of the firm completely ignores the very possibility of and need for entrepreneurial decision-making. With revenue and cost curves viewed as data, the decision of the firm, within the framework of these curves, permits no entrepreneurial alertness to possible changes in these data. The difference between Knight's position in this respect and my own has already been stated. In the former the accent is not placed upon the entrepreneur's deliberate move to capture the profits he perceives to be forthcoming as a result of changes in the data which others have not perceived. In my own discussion it is precisely this deliberate exploitation of perceived opportunities which is essential to the entrepreneurial role.

MISESIAN ENTREPRENEURSHIP

It is in the writings of Professor Mises[54] that one finds, expressed concisely in a few pages, most of the ideas from which

52. See above, pp. 67–69.
53. See above, pp. 46–47.
54. See L. Mises, *Human Action*, pp. 253–57, 286–97; idem, "Profit and Loss," in *Planning for Freedom*, 2d ed. (South Holland, Ill.: Libertarian Press, 1962), 108–50. Mises bears, of course, no responsibility for shortcomings in the present chapter.

I have developed my own rather rambling and excursive discussion of the entrepreneurial role. And it is Mises's insights into the character of the market process that laid the groundwork for the construction of this theory of entrepreneurship. Mises's way of expressing what I have called entrepreneurial *alertness* is to define entrepreneurship as human action "seen from the aspect of the uncertainty inherent in every action." [55] "Entrepreneur means acting man in regard to the changes occurring in the data of the market." [56] To realize the essential similarity between my formulation and that of Mises, it is enough to consider his emphasis upon entrepreneurship as the driving force in the allocation of resources to correspond to consumers' wishes. The market, Mises emphasizes again and again, tends to eliminate from the entrepreneurial role all except those able "to anticipate better than other people the future demand of the consumers." [57]

My understanding of the Misesian view of the entrepreneur and of its similarity to my own can be expressed by characterizing the Misesian view of profit as well as my own as an *"arbitrage" theory* of profit. Profit opportunities arise when the prices of products on the product markets are not adjusted to the prices of resource services on the factor markets. In other words, "something" is being sold at different prices in two markets, as a result of imperfect communication between the markets. This "something," it is true, is sold in different physical forms in the two markets: in the factor market it appears as a bundle of inputs, and in the product market it appears as a consumption good. But economically we still have the "same" thing being sold at different prices, because the input bundle contains all that is technologically required (and no more than is required) to yield the product. The entrepreneur notices this price discrepancy before others do. What distinguishes this situation from the usual arbitrage case is that in-

55. Mises, *Human Action*, p. 254.
56. Ibid., p. 255.
57. Ibid., p. 288.

put purchases precede output sales; at the time of the production decision the product prices do not yet exist except as anticipations. The entrepreneur guesses that future product prices will not be fully adjusted to today's input prices. Although Mises's exposition emphasized more than mine the unavoidable uncertainty that surrounds entrepreneurial activity (in a world in which production takes time), it is clear that for Mises, as for me, profits arise from an absence of adjustment between the product market and the factor market; and that successful entrepreneurship consists in noticing such maladjustments before others do. "What makes profit emerge is the fact that the entrepreneur who judges the future prices of the products more correctly than other people do buys some or all of the factor of production at prices which, seen from the point of view of the future state of the market, are too low."

And, of course, it has been Mises's emphasis on *human action* which I have contrasted with Robbinsian economizing. My identification of an entrepreneurial element within human action which is by definition excluded from economizing simply repeats Mises's assertion that the entrepreneurial function — action seen from its *speculative* aspect — is inherent in *every* action.[58] (My discussion of entrepreneurial alertness has deliberately avoided emphasizing its speculative character. I have of course recognized [59] that in a world of uncertainty every entrepreneurial decision, no matter how much alertness it reflects, must to some extent constitute a gamble. But it has been my purpose to point out that the entrepreneur's decision — despite its unavoidably speculative character — represents his judgment that an opportunity for profit *does* exist. All human action is speculative; my emphasis on the element of alertness in action has been intended to point out that, far

58. Ibid., pp. 253–54.
59. See above, p. 78. On speculators as entrepreneurs see L. M. Fraser, *Economic Thought and Language* (London: A. and C. Black, 1937), 394–95.

from being numbed by the inescapable uncertainty of our world, men *act upon their judgments* of what opportunities have been left unexploited by others.)

Two others aspects of Mises's theory of entrepreneurship are of great importance to the main theme of this book. The first of these has to do with the essentially *competitive* character of entrepreneurship. The second has to do with the *welfare* implications of entrepreneurship. These important aspects of the theory will not be discussed at this time. Each of them will be taken up at the appropriate point in a subsequent chapter.

]3[
Competition and Monopoly

OUR EXTENSIVE DISCUSSION OF ENTREPRENEURSHIP HAS PLACED us in a position from which we can critically review the way contemporary price theory treats the issues of monopoly and of competition. Our own position will differ sharply from the dominant orthodoxy in regard to these crucially important aspects of a theory of price. And our disagreement with the dominant theory rests squarely upon the insights we have gained into the nature of entrepreneurship and the role it plays in the market process.

Contemporary orthodoxy examines the determination of prices and outputs within a number of alternative "market structures." Some of these are, with the addition of different qualifying adverbs, labeled "competitive"; others are (with similar qualifications) labeled "monopolistic." The vast literature dealing with this aspect of theory consists to a considerable extent of discussions of conflicting criteria for classifying market structures and for the appropriateness of the various labels. Dissatisfaction with this literature stems ultimately from dissatisfaction with theories of price that confine themselves to examining states of equilibrium. A theory which refrains from attempting to understand the market process, whatever its concern with competitiveness, is clearly going to be unable to provide insight into the differences between a competitive process and other processes. Contemporary ortho-doxy does, in fact, see competition (and of course monopoly) as a "situation" rather than as a process.[1] My own position will be to emphasize the need to examine the competitive character of the market *process*, and therefore the need to develop criteria for "competitiveness" as the term is to be used in this context. This will entail further disagreement with contemporary price theory in regard to meaningful use of the term *monopoly*, and in particular in regard to the theory of monopolistic competition. I will argue that the latter theory abandoned the earlier emphasis on perfect competition for the wrong reasons; and thus the new theory suffered from the very faults which rendered the old theory unhelpful.

COMPETITION: A SITUATION OR A PROCESS?

To the layman, the term competition undoubtedly conveys the notion of men vigorously *competing* with another, each striving to deliver a performance that outdistances his rivals. The essence of the idea is the awareness of what one's rivals are doing and the conscious effort to do something different and better. As has been explained again and again, the term competition in economic theory is used in just the *opposite* sense. "[Competition], in the broad sense in which business men understand it, largely consists in destroying competition in the narrow, economist's sense."[2] *Perfect* competition de-

1. On this see H. R. Edwards, *Competition and Monopoly in the British Soap Industry* (London: Oxford University Press, 1962), p. 5; P. J. McNulty, "A Note on the History of Perfect Competition," *Journal of Political Economy* 75 (August 1967): 398; H. Demsetz, "Perfect Competition, Regulation, and the Stock Market," in *Economic Policy and the Regulation of Corporate Securities*, ed. H. G. Manne (Washington, D.C.: American Enterprise Institute, 1969), p. 2.

2. J. Robinson, "The Impossibility of Competition," in *Monopoly and Competition and Their Regulation*, ed. E. H. Chamberlin (London: Oxford University Press, 1954), pp. 245–46; see also P. Hennipman, "Monopoly: Impediment or Stimulus to Economic Progress?" in *Monopoly and Competition and Their Regulation*, p. 426; A. Sherrard, "Advertising, Product Variation, and the Limits of Economics," *Journal of Political Economy* 59 (April 1951): 131–32.

notes for the price theorist the situation in which every market participant does exactly what everyone else is doing, in which it is utterly pointless to try to achieve something in any way better than what is already being done by others, and in which, in fact, it is not necessary to keep one's eyes open to what the others are doing at all. It is the state "of placid acceptance of the market's verdict concerning price."[3]

This difference between the terminology of the economist and that of the layman has frequently been deplored as generating confusion concerning the nature of competition in economics and as obstructing communication with the uninitiated. Only fairly recently has it come to be recognized that the terminology of the layman corresponds to an aspect of the market process which urgently demands theoretical attention in its own right, and that the terminology of the economist has in fact yielded a *dis*service to economic theory by deflecting attention from that aspect. By reserving the term competition for its special meaning in neoclassical theory, economists were for a long time led to ignore the need to analyze the role of the competitive *process*.

It was not always so. It has recently been pointed out that for Adam Smith competition was not a "situation" but an active process,[4] and that the notion of competition as a situation free of competitive activity in the layman's sense originated only later from Cournot's interest in the *effects* of competition (as distinct from the process itself). But it was the development of the Cournot notion of competition — perhaps because economists shared Stigler's judgment of it as "enormously more precise and elegant than Smith's"[5] —

3. See N. Georgescu-Roegen, "Chamberlin's New Economics and the Unit of Production," in *Monopolistic Competition Theory: Studies in Impact, Essays in Honor of Edward H. Chamberlin*, ed. R. Kuenne (New York: John Wiley, 1967), p. 32.

4. P. J. McNulty, "Note on the History of Perfect Competition," p. 398; see also P. J. McNulty, "The Meaning of Competition," *Quarterly Journal of Economics* 82 (November 1968): 639–56.

5. G. J. Stigler, "Perfect Competition, Historically Contemplated," *Journal of Political Economy* 65 (February 1957):5.

that came to dominate the profession. It was perhaps not (at least in Anglo-American economics) until Hayek's penetrating and pioneering paper "The Meaning of Competition"[6] that the distinction between the two concepts, competition as a process and competition as the state resulting from the process, was drawn with clarity. Whether or not it is fair to ascribe to the neoclassical economist a theory of price that depended entirely on perfect competition is not our present concern. Shorey Peterson's contention[7] that the leading neoclassicists, notably J. B. Clark and Marshall, were not at all unaware of the relevance and social usefulness of what later became J. M. Clark's concept of "workable competition" is well known. But the truth is that neither "workable competition" nor Schumpeter's process of "creative destruction"[8] (which Peterson seems to equate with "workable competition") — and least of all Chamberlin's development of "monopolistic competition" — involved any attempt to come to grips with competition as a market process. None of these departures recognizes that what renders the supposedly traditional perfectly competitive market notion unhelpful is neither the rarity or difficulty of its discovery in the real world nor the patent incorrectness of the claim that it is a necessary condition for a workable market economy, but rather its blandly *assuming* that "situation to exist which a true explanation ought to account for as the effect of the competitive process."[9]

That the "workable competition" theory failed to grapple with competition as a process was indeed recognized by J. M. Clark in his concern, during the fifties, with the dynamics of competition[10] (although we shall find cause for some dissatis-

6. Read as a lecture in 1946 and published in F. A. Hayek, *Individualism and Economic Order* (London: Routledge and Kegan Paul, 1949).

7. S. Peterson, "Antitrust and the Classic Model," *American Economic Review* 47 (March 1957): 60–78.

8. See J. A. Schumpeter, *Capitalism, Socialism and Democracy* (New York: Harper and Row, 1962), chap. 7.

9. Hayek, *Individualism and Economic Order*, p. 94.

10. J. M. Clark, "Competition and the Objectives of Government Policy," in *Monopoly and Competition and Their Regulation*, ed. E. H.

faction with his attempt even in this regard). Schumpeter's view of competition as a process of "creative destruction" seems on the surface to be closer to our own emphasis on the competitive market process. Upon more careful scrutiny, however, it seems more accurate to describe Schumpeter's dissatisfaction with the traditional notion of perfect competition as arising from its restriction to an unchanging pattern of productive activities. Schumpeter's emphasis on "the competition from the new commodity, the new technology, the new source of supply" [11] does not, it appears, reflect a recognition of the nature of the market process (as opposed to the situation resulting from it). Rather, this reflects his belief that the notion of perfect competition unnecessarily restricts the *kinds* of competitive pressure exercised by the market. But, as we will see, the real weakness of the perfect competition idea is not primarily, as Schumpeter believed, that it considers only price competition, within a framework of unchanging commodities and methods of production. Its real weakness is that, even with respect to price competition itself, it assumes that the course of competition has already been completely run, so that no active competition occurs within the perfectly competitive market even in terms of price.[12]

Nor did the emergence of the theory of monopolistic competition do anything at all to draw the attention of economists to the urgent need for a theory of the competitive process. On the contrary, its attack on the relevance of the theory of perfect competition tended to strengthen use of the perfectly competitive economy as a norm from which to judge the efficiency of the real world. And, again, the failure of the monopolistic-com-

Chamberlin (London: Oxford University Press, 1954), pp. 326–28; idem, "Competition: Static Models and Dynamic Aspects," *American Economic Review* 45 (May 1955): 450–62. Clark's ideas have been developed further in his book *Competition as a Dynamic Process* (Washington, D.C.: Brookings Institution, 1961).

11. Schumpeter, *Capitalism, Socialism and Democracy*, p. 84.

12. For a more extensive discussion comparing and contrasting Schumpeter's views and my own, see below, pp. 125–31.

petition theorists to detect the real flaw in the perfectly competitive model led them to replace it with a model suffering from the very same flaw. Both the perfectly competitive model and the monopolistically competitive model suffer from being equilibrium models — they represent situations in which the results of the relevant process are assumed to have already been attained. But the very vigor with which the proponents of the new theory of monopolistic competition attacked the old orthodoxy of perfect competition tended to direct attention away from the defect shared by both. We will discuss this theme in greater detail later in this chapter.

In the decades since Hayek's paper, however, some occasional attention has come to be paid in the literature to the need for a theory of the competitive process, and there is fairly widespread recognition, at least, that the perfectly competitive model does *not* provide a theory of any process at all. Although it would be too much to claim that Hayek's paper finally drove home to the profession the distinction between competition as a process and competition as the situation resulting from a process, it has come to be realized that the theory of competitive equilibrium must be supplemented by a process theory, and that the layman's notion of competition may provide at least a pointer toward the construction of such a theory.[13]

Competition in the sense of process is a principal theme of this book, and it is its close connection with entrepreneurship that we will be exploring in the next section. Thereafter, we will examine the possible role of monopoly within the kind of

13. Among the relevant references I may cite the following: F. Machlup, *The Economics of Sellers' Competition* (Baltimore: Johns Hopkins University Press), pp. 279 f., also p. 106; K. Arrow, "Toward a Theory of Price Adjustment," in *The Allocation of Economic Resources*, ed. Abramovitz et al. (Stanford, Calif.: Stanford University Press, 1959); G. B. Richardson, *Information and Investment* (London: Oxford University Press, 1960), pp. 23–24; D. McCord Wright, "Some Notes on Ideal Output," *Quarterly Journal of Economics* 76(May 1962): 173–85; Clark, *Competition as a Dynamic Process*; see also the references cited above, chap. 3, n. 4; D. Dewey, *The Theory of Imperfect Competition: A Radical Reconstruction* (New York: Columbia University Press, 1969).

price theory which emerges from our insight linking competitiveness with entrepreneurial activity.

The proposition I will attempt to explain here involves the notions of purely Robbinsian economizing activity and that of purely entrepreneurial activity (as developed at length in chapter 2), and of competitiveness (in the sense of "process") as discussed in the preceding section. The proposition runs something like this: *Purely Robbinsian economizing activity is never competitive; purely entrepreneurial activity* always *is*. In other words, I am asserting [14] that entrepreneurship and competitiveness are two sides of the same coin: that entrepreneurial activity is always competitive and that competitive activity is always entrepreneurial (rather than Robbinsian). Let us consider the proposition more closely.

For decision-making to be Robbinsian, we found in chapter 2, the decision-maker must be viewed within a *given* framework of ends and means. His task is to choose the best course of action out of all those feasible within the given framework. In the context of the market, the framework relevant to a Robbinsian economizer reflects the buying and selling opportunities he believes are available. These opportunities consist of alternative possibilities for buying or for selling, with each possibility identified in terms of both price and quantity. Although we have seen that the framework need not express ends and means known with certainty (so that the prices and quantities qualifying the exchange possibilities may be quite uncertain), the framework is a *given* framework, already containing *all* the information, fragmentary though it may be, to be used in selecting the best course of action. Thus the framework for Robbinsian economizing in the market expresses itself as a set of *given* demand situations facing the

14. The assertion is made for a market economy free of government limitations on individual economic activities.

economizer as seller and *given* supply situations facing him as buyer. In the preliminary treatments of price theory where uncertainty is assumed to be entirely absent, this means that the Robbinsian economizer faces given and known demand and supply schedules. With uncertainty introduced, the Robbinsian economizer is seen facing demand and supply situations which may not necessarily represent themselves as sharply defined demand and supply curves. But regardless of the fuzziness of these curves, the Robbinsian character of the situation requires us to see the decision-maker as choosing an optimal buying or selling program or both out of all the programs he believes, with varying degrees of conviction, to be feasible.

The proposition above is asserting that in selecting this optimal buying and selling program, the pure Robbinsian decision-maker is *not* seeking to outdistance his rivals — he is not intent on learning what opportunities *they* are about to make available to the market in order to attempt to make available still more attractive opportunities. It is of course true that, in order for the Robbinsian allocation situation *to be set up*, in order for the range of feasible programs (from among which the economizing selection is to be made) *to be perceived*, it may be necessary to notice very carefully what one's rivals are about to do and to judge what possible buying or selling programs are feasible in the light of what they are or are not doing. And this may mean that, after the Robbinsian economizing decision has been made, the decision-maker may seem to have indeed competed actively with his rivals. The final selling or buying program he adopts may well appear to aggressively go beyond what others are making available to the market. But, as was explained in chapter 2, pure Robbinsian decision-making presupposes that the framework has *already* been set up. It is precisely the "entrepreneurial" element responsible for *setting up* the Robbinsian framework, which is *not* itself a factor in the economizing decision. That which, ex post, may make it seem that the Robbinsian economizer has competed aggressively is precisely this entrepreneurial element which is by definition excluded from the analysis of the purely allocative decision. There is nothing in the calculative activity of which Robbinsian decision-making consists which calls for deliberately outdistancing one's fellow market participants. Thus, although in the sense in which competition is defined in the theory of perfect competition we view competitive buyers and sellers as Robbinsian economizers, this view cannot be maintained insofar as the term competition is reserved for the active process of offering the market opportunities which one believes are better than those others are able or willing to offer.

But my proposition asserts more than that all competitive activity (in the process sense) must involve an element of entrepreneurship. It also asserts that, insofar as the theorist is able to visualize *purely* entrepreneurial activity (and we have, I concede, seen that such visualization can never be more than an analytical device), such activity must *always* be competitive (in the process sense). This is probably the more important part of my proposition and it deserves careful consideration.

To perceive the correctness of this part of my argument it is necessary to clarify first of all what we are to understand by *an obstacle to the competitiveness* of the market process. In the theory of perfect competition it is easy to explain what one means by imperfection in competition — at least it is easy once one has specified the conditions for perfect competition. One merely sets forth a pattern of actions, or a pattern of possible actions, which is inconsistent with the set of actions admissible in the state of perfect competition. In fact, imperfection in competition, from the viewpoint of the theory of perfect competition, is usually taken to mean simply any absence of perfect elasticity in the demand (supply) curves facing sellers (buyers). This is because in that theory competition refers to a particular situation, a particular pattern of actions; thus absence of competition means simply that this particular situation (the absence of control over price by the individual market participant) does not prevail. Clearly, with competition in the process sense the notion of an obstacle to competition cannot be found in the description of situations or particular sets of actions. We must look for a way of identifying elements in the market which obstruct the *course* of the competitive process. There is no pattern of actions which, in and of itself, is necessarily inconsistent with a competitive market process. That in any given period a particular market participant (or for that matter *each* market participant) fails to engage in activities different from what others are doing, or that one participant is exploiting a lucrative opportunity without others' following suit, need not mean that market participants are not under competitive pressure to do their best. That in any one period aggressive competitive activities have not been engaged in does not necessarily mean that the competitive process has come to a halt. It may simply mean that with all their alertness market participants have not yet become aware of the opportunities which exist, but that they will nonetheless surely pounce upon them in a most competitive way as soon as they are perceived.

In order, then, for us to speak freely of a lack of competitiveness in a market process, we must be able to point to something which *prevents* market participants from competing. What is it that might succeed in rendering particular market participants secure from being competed with — that might make it possible for them to continue to offer inferior opportunities to the market, immune from the pressure of having at least to match the more attractive offers which other participants might be making available? What is it, in other words, which might halt the competitive process? Clearly this formulation of the question points to its answer. Competition, in the process sense, is at least potentially present so long as there exist no arbitrary *impediments to entry*. So long as others are free to offer the most attractive opportunities they are aware of, no one is free from both the urge and the need to compete. Only when one is aware that others, despite the possibility of their offering something more attractive to the market, will be barred from doing so can one feel secure from competition. The competitive process depends entirely on the freedom of those with better ideas or with greater willingness to serve the market to offer better opportunities. Every arbitrary impediment to entry is a restriction on the competitiveness of the market process.

The importance of freedom of entry for the competitiveness of the market has of course not gone unnoticed, especially in recent years. Especially in the context of what in the dominant terminology has been called *imperfect* competition, the role of entry has been explored extensively.[15] The importance of potential competition has frequently been acknowledged. And even within the context of competition in the neoclassical sense, competition came, not entirely understandably, to be associated with freedom of entry. As Triffin has remarked, the "traditional theory of competition was built upon two independent assumptions, needlessly jumbled together: the lack of influence of the seller upon his price, and free entry." It was, in Triffin's view, the great merit of "modern theory" that it "isolated the first assumption in its definition of pure competition."[16]

From the point of view of this book I appraise Triffin's judgment as follows. Triffin is perfectly consistent in objecting to the "traditional" jumbling together of the two assumptions, the lack of seller's influence upon price and free entry. To the extent that the traditional position in fact espoused the notion of competition as the situation *resulting* from the competitive market process, the emphasis on freedom of entry is almost

15. Classic references are J. S. Bain, *Barriers to New Competition* (Cambridge: Harvard University Press, 1956); P. Sylos-Labini, *Oligopoly and Technical Progress* (Cambridge: Harvard University Press, 1962); F. Modigliani, "New Developments on the Oligopoly Front," *Journal of Political Economy* 66 (June 1958): 215–32. See also Machlup, *Economics of Sellers' Competition*, pp. 102–11; P. W. S. Andrews, *On Competition in Economic Theory* (London: Macmillan, 1964), p. 16.

16. R. Triffin, *Monopolistic Competition and General Equilibrium Theory* (Cambridge: Harvard University Press, 1940), p. 136.

irrelevant (especially in the context of the usual postulation of large numbers of buyers and sellers). As Machlup has pointed out, the economist who states that an industry is characterized by "newcomer's competition" (Machlup's "pliopoly") is not thinking at all of a situation present at any moment of time; he is thinking, instead, "of a process which he expects to take place in the *course of time* and which would explain a future situation at the completion of the process."[17] On the other hand, Triffin's enthusiastic concurrence in the final excision of the element of freedom of entry from the formal definition of competition constitutes a step (and from my point of view an unfortunate step) yet further away from a recognition of the need for a theory of the competitive market process.

Be this as it may, for our own discussion of competition as process there can be no doubt that the necessary and sufficient condition for competition to exist without obstacle is complete freedom of entry into all kinds of market activity. When we assert that purely entrepreneurial activity is *always* competitive, we are then asserting that *with respect to purely entrepreneurial activity no possible obstacles to freedom of entry can exist.*

We can see this by recalling that purely entrepreneurial activity involves no element of resource ownership.[18] Now in the absence of government restrictions on given activities the only possible source of blockage to entry into a particular activity must arise from restricted access to the resources needed for that activity. Without oranges, one cannot produce orange juice. All imaginable obstacles to entry can be reduced, in basic terms, to restricted access to resources.[19] Therefore, for

17. Machlup, *Economics of Sellers' Competition*, p. 106.
18. See above, p. 40.
19. Statements describing barriers to entry are most frequently cast in terms that fail to emphasize this insight. But reflection will lead to the realization that with all resources equally accessible to all present and prospective producers, no barriers to entry can be imagined. A number of the usually cited barriers to entry can easily be seen to refer to short-run limitations on the accessibility of resources. See also S. R. Shenoy, "The Sources of Monopoly," *New Individualist Review* 4 (Spring 1966): 41–44.

activities which require no resources at all there can clearly not exist any obstacles to entry. Purely entrepreneurial activity, which by definition we have seen requires no initial resources, cannot, it follows, be subject to blocked entry. Although the actual carrying through of particular entrepreneurial decisions may very certainly call for the purchase of resources for subsequent sale (possibly in changed physical form), it is not the purely entrepreneurial aspect of this transaction which depends upon free access to the resources. To produce orange juice one needs oranges. With access to oranges blocked there exists no freedom of entry into orange-juice production. But it is not necessary to have access to oranges in order *to discover*, as an alert entrepreneur comes to discover, how unexploited opportunities for profit exist in orange-juice production. If entry into orange-juice production is blocked, this cannot be ascribed to any absence of freedom to enter the activity of entrepreneurship; the source of blockage must be sought in the availability of oranges or other necessary inputs. Conversely, if no limitations exist upon the availability of all the necessary inputs, it follows that orange-juice production must be carried on under fully competitive conditions (in the sense of process), since the entrepreneurial element necessary for undertaking orange-juice production is, almost by definition, not subject to obstacles to competition.

One may object that the distinction between the entrepreneurial element in a productive activity and its Robbinsian economizing element is a wholly artificial one introduced by the theorist. Thus if entry to that productive activity is blocked, there is little point in insisting that the obstacle relates only to the Robbinsian, and not at all to the entrepreneurial, element of the activity; the two elements are in reality always found together. But this objection cannot be sustained. Although it is entirely true that dissecting a given act into its Robbinsian and entrepreneurial components must remain an exercise in pure analysis,[20] it is by no means true that our demonstration of the necessarily competitive character of entrepreneurship is a mere game. As we will see, it will enable us to recast the entire concept of monopoly and throw a useful light on theoretical problems which have given rise to much discussion in the modern literature.

THE MEANING OF MONOPOLY

Both economists and laymen have always viewed monopoly as somehow antithetical to competition. Traditionally, the monopoly concept involved the notion of a seller with control over supply, protected from the possibility of others' entering his market. Under the impact of the theories of imperfect and of monopolistic competition, and the resulting attention paid to the polar case of perfect competition, some economists came to perceive the presence of some degree of monopoly in all situations where the demand curve facing a seller was less than perfectly elastic. (Chamberlin himself vigorously rejected this, and indeed all other attempts to depart from the traditional notion of monopoly.)[21] Other writers have tended, in formulating a precise concept of monopoly, to emphasize the *independence* of the monopoly seller from any effects of price changes on the part of other sellers.[22]

Despite this lack of unanimity on assigning a precise definition to the notion of monopoly, the formal *analysis* of the monopolized market has been pursued with relatively little disagreement. As with the perfectly competitive market, the analysis of the monopolized market has invariably revolved round the theory of the *firm*. The disagreements on definition have

20. See above chap. 2, n. 4 and n. 6.
21. E. H. Chamberlin, "Measuring the Degree of Monopoly and Competition," in *Monopoly and Competition and Their Regulation*, ed. E. H. Chamberlin (London: Oxford University Press, 1954), p. 255.
22. Triffin, *Monopolistic Competition*, p. 103; see also F. Machlup, *Economics of Sellers' Competition*, p. 544, and M. Olson and D. McFarland "The Restoration of Pure Monopoly and the Concept of the Industry," *Quarterly Journal of Economics* 76 (November 1962): 613–31.

mainly had implications for the problem of *classifying* different markets. Theoretical insight into how monopolistic and competitive elements may be present together, and discussions concerning the validity of the notion of *the industry*, have depended upon the particular monopoly notion espoused. The Chamberlinian revolution saw as its principal contribution the abandonment of an analytical framework in which monopoly and competition are mutually exclusive. In its place its adherents sought to introduce a picture of the market as made up of firms each exercising some degree of monopolistic control over its output but at the same time subject to competition from other firms producing "other" products.[23] The degree to which competition from other firms and other products weakens the effectiveness of a firm's monopolistic control over the supply of its own product depends on the degree to which the firm's "product" is in fact different from other products. The notions of both monopoly and competition are seen, for Chamberlinian as for pre-Chamberlinian theory, as referring to the *degree of control by the firm over the relevant "product."* The analysis of both monopolistic and competitive markets, and of "blended" markets, centers on the *theory of the firm.* The preceding discussions of entrepreneurship and of competition (in the process sense) require us to see the market, and the role of monopoly in the market, from a decidedly different point of view.

For a theory concerned with the market *process*, we need a concept of monopoly that lets us formulate the relevant questions concerning the impact of monopoly on the process. And here a difficulty seems to present itself. Our discussions of entrepreneurship and competition have taught us that the market process is always entrepreneurial, and that the entrepreneurial

23. "One can have a monopoly of Chateau d'Yquem, of all Sauternes, of all white wines from the Bordeaux region, or all Bordeaux wines, or of all white wines, of all wines, of all beverages. . . . And whatever the area monopolized, the monopolist will always face competition in some degree from the wider area beyond its limits" (Chamberlin, *Monopoly and Competition*, p. 255).

process is always competitive. How, then, is a monopoly concept to be made relevant to the market process, if the process is always competitive? The difficulty is only apparent. We have already seen that in considering the competitiveness of the market process the crucial question concerns freedom of *entry*. Now it is true that with respect to purely entrepreneurial activity no obstacles to entry exist. But it is no less true that obstacles to the *exercise* of entrepreneurial activity can very easily be imagined. Although no monopoly over entrepreneurship is imaginable (since no resources are required for pure entrepreneurship), we have already seen that restricted access to needed resources may effectively block potential entrepreneurs from discovering unexploited opportunities for profit — not because monopoly has restricted them from perceiving whatever opportunities can be perceived, but because monopoly over the resources may have erased the very possibilities themselves. Without access to oranges, entry into the production of orange juice *is* blocked.

Monopoly, then, in a market free of government obstacles to entry, means for us the position of a producer [24] whose exclusive control over necessary inputs blocks competitive entry into the production of his products. Monopoly thus does *not* refer to the position of a producer who, without any control over resources, happens to be the only producer of a particular product.[25] This producer is fully subject to the competitive market process, since other entrepreneurs are entirely free to compete with him. It follows, also, that the shape of the demand curve facing the producer does not of itself have bearing on whether he is a monopolist as I have defined the term. That a producer without monopoly control over resources perceives the demand curve facing him as that of the entire market for the particular product merely means that he believes he has discovered the opportunity of selling to this entire market be-

24. Of course the monopoly owner of a consumer commodity found in nature is also a monopolist in the sense developed here.
25. See below, pp. 132–33.

fore any one else has. Since he possesses no monopoly over entrepreneurial alertness, the competitive process is unimpeded by the downward slope of the demand curve facing this producer at the moment.[26] Conversely, monopoly control over inputs, effectively blocking entry into a particular productive activity, is not necessarily inconsistent even with a horizontal demand curve perceived to face the monopolist. (Such a case could occur, for example, when many other producers are producing the product at a going, universally known price with inferior inputs, whereas the monopolist has not yet discovered that the output he produces with his own monopolized resource is in fact a better product.) Only in a theory unconcerned with the entrepreneurial process —concerned only with the state of affairs facing firms after the process has presumably run its course — can the shape of the demand curve facing the firm seem of overriding importance. For us, with the focus of attention upon the competitive character of the entrepreneurial process, the concept of monopoly must be introduced so that it is relevant to discussions at the entrepreneurial level — a level at which the very idea of a given demand curve perceived as already facing the decision-maker begs the really important questions.

THE TWO NOTIONS OF MONOPOLY COMPARED

At this point it will be useful to examine somewhat more thoroughly the differences that separate the notion of monopoly

26. From this perspective it appears unfortunate that, in his discussion of the process of price adjustment in the disequilibrium competitive market, Arrow ("Toward a Theory of Price Adjustment") identifies the individual firms as acting "monopolistically," on the grounds that in disequilibrium each of the firms faces a downward-sloping demand curve. The truth is that the adjustment process is an entrepreneurial one whose competitive character, we have seen, is not affected by the downward slope which characterizes the demand curves faced by firms in the disequilibrium industry. See also the terse remark attributed to Professor Lewis (in W. J. Baumol, "Entrepreneurship in Economic Theory," *American Economic Review* 58 [May 1968]: 69 n) linking the pioneering aspect of the entrepreneur to the need to approach a theory of entrepreneurship by way of a relevant theory of monopoly.

just advanced from that which has dominated orthodox price theory.

1. The orthodox notion of monopoly has stressed the monopolist's control over the supply of his products. Shorn of some of the refinements introduced into its definition, monopoly in this sense has meant essentially the position of the single seller of a given commodity. Although some important attention eventually was paid to why new firms were blocked from entering the industry (and to the distinction between a merely short-run monopoly position and the monopoly position that is also protected in the long run), the analysis of monopoly situations meant analyzing single producers.

The notion of monopoly advanced here, on the other hand, does not depend on the uniqueness of the monopolist's product. Although it is of course true that the *profitability* of a monopolist's position will depend crucially on whether other producers are able to produce the same commodity, nonetheless the monopolist as defined here is a monopolist by virtue of his control over certain resources, which renders him immune from the competition of other entrepreneurs who might, in other circumstances, enter his field of activity. This immunity however, in no way protects him from the competition of other entrepreneurs who may decide to enter very similar fields of activity (including, possibly, the production of the *same* commodity with other, nonmonopolized resources).

2. The monopoly notion advanced here, then, does not depend on the validity of the concept of *an industry*.[27] Since for us the monopolist is not defined as the only producer in the industry, we (unlike the orthodox monopoly theorists) are not troubled by the insight that the monopolist may face the competition of close substitutes. Some further remarks in this

27. See Olson and McFarland, "Restoration of Pure Monopoly"; R. E. Kuenne, "Quality Space, Interproduct Competition, and General Equilibrium Theory," in *Monopolistic Competition Theory: Studies in Impact*, ed. R. E. Kuenne (New York: John Wiley, 1967), pp. 225 f. See further below, pp. 119–25.

regard follow, in connection with a related difference separating the two monopoly concepts.

3. For the orthodox notion of monopoly, the realization that competition may come from producers of *other* commodities came as a profound shock. This realization inspired Chamberlin to completely recast the theory of market value and to proclaim the virtual universality of market situations in which both monopolistic and competitive aspects exist simultaneously. It was this line of reasoning that led him, in other words, to abandon the notion of a *pure* monopoly as a realistic market case.[28]

For the notion of monopoly developed here, the insight that competition exists between producers of close substitutes and between different industries is not only not at all a threat to the monopoly concept, but is, on the contrary, essential to understanding how monopoly affects the market.

For us monopoly means the position of a producer who is immune from the threat of other entrepreneurs' doing what he does. The profitability of his position is certainly enhanced as his immunity extends to block other activities which although not *exactly* "what he does" are yet sufficiently similar to constitute a felt danger. But the monopoly notion itself is entirely independent of such extension. It is enough that the monopolist controls the entire available quantity of one of the inputs which he himself uses in his productive activities. The blockage to entry which protects the monopolist diverts the competitive, entrepreneurial process into other activities. The monopolist's position, which I have defined so as to perceive its impact upon the competitive process, creates a pocket of economic activity (*around* which competitive-entrepreneurial activity swirls) *within* which the monopolist hopes to enjoy his quiet life. But the quietness of his life is, by the very nature of his position, subject to the impact of the competitive turbu-

28. Olson and McFarland, "Restoration of Pure Monopoly," p. 615.

lence which *surrounds* and impinges upon his activity. In fact, our analysis of monopoly decision-making must *depend* upon this surrounding competitive-entrepreneurial process in order to define the framework within which the monopolist is viewed as operating. It is the competitive-entrepreneurial market process upon which we (and the monopolist) rely for the information on input and output availability and price prospects which sets up for the monopolist the cost and revenue curves from which we imagine him to select the profit-maximizing course of action. If I produce orange juice and have sole access to oranges, my monopoly over my activity is complete. Competing entrepreneurs cannot duplicate my activity. Of course they may produce other beverages; the whole point of the monopoly over oranges is that this *diverts* the entrepreneurial-competitive process into these other beverages. Moreover, the monopolist's perceived market for orange juice, as well as his opportunity, as buyer, in the factor markets, is a result of the entrepreneurial competition in the market. (We can *imagine* a series of monopolists with control over successively larger and larger volumes of resources until, in the extreme, we can imagine a monopolist controling *all* resources in the economy. In this series, the range of the entrepreneurial-competitive process is steadily being narrowed until, in the extreme, all market activity has ceased. As is well known, this latter extreme corresponds to the case of the fully socialized economy with all resources controlled by the state, in which the market process and all entrepreneurial and competitive activity are by definition absent.[29] Barring this case of total monopoly, the importance of monopoly is precisely its impact upon the course of the competitive market process.)

4. In the orthodox theory of monopoly, the analysis of monopoly involved, very importantly, the theory of the firm. The decision-making of the monopoly firm, in fact, came to mark

29. See L. Mises, *Human Action* (New Haven: Yale University Press, 1949), p. 277.

one of the significant differences between the monopoly market and the perfectly competitive market. In particular, as we have seen, the shape of the demand curve facing the firm was considered of supreme importance. We have already seen that for our notion of monoply the shape of the demand curve facing the firm is of little significance. More fundamentally, we can now see why for us the significance of monopoly does *not relate to the theory of the firm at all.* (It is because of this that the shape of the demand curve is irrelevant.)

In the discussion of entrepreneurship in chapter 2, I pointed out [30] that the framework within which the theory of the firm operates is narrowly Robbinsian and permits no consideration of entrepreneurship at all. The cost and revenue curves which enable the firm to select its profit-maximizing price-quantity combination are, for the theory of the firm, assumed to be already given and known. But we have seen earlier [31] that in such Robbinsian contexts the concept of competitiveness (in the sense of process) is entirely irrelevant. The competitive aspects of a firm's decision are those which determine which cost and revenue curves it considers relevant. Conversely, the notion of monopoly as obstructing the competitive process is equally irrelevant to all strictly Robbinsian situations. One cannot label one Robbinsian situation monopolistic (in our sense) and another competitive. The possibility of competitiveness has already been excluded by the Robbinsian specifications of the case. The theory of the firm, it follows, is by its very construction incapable of providing any help in discriminating between monopolistic and competitive cases. As soon as we draw the cost and revenue curves facing the firm, no matter what their shape, we have created a theoretical case in which all competitive behavior has by definition been ruled out. What is left is neither competitive nor monopolistic (in the process sense), but a problem in allocation. The level at which ques-

30. See above, pp. 46–47.
31. See above, pp. 95–96.

tions concerning the competitiveness of a market can be raised is different from that at which purely Robbinsian allocation problems are considered. Thus the theory of the firm has been so constructed as to render questions of competition and monopoly, in the process sense, completely idle. If we wish to investigate the competitiveness of market processes, and the impact upon them of monopolistic obstacles to entry, we must transcend the theory of the firm. The unfortunate preoccupation of orthodox price theory with *situations* of competition and monopoly, rather than with the implications of competition and monopoly for market processes, has naturally gone hand in hand with an analysis of competition and of monopoly which depends heavily upon the theory of the firm.

5. In the orthodox theory of monopoly there appear *monopoly profits* which are not lost by competition. Although these monopoly profits are, at least for most economists, a category quite separate from that of pure entrepreneurial profit, they appear in the theory, just as do entrepreneurial profits, as an unimputed surplus (or, if imputed, are ascribed to the "monopoly position" itself). For the notion of monopoly developed here, on the other hand, there is no room for possible confusion between monopoly profits and entrepreneurial profits. In fact it should be apparent that in our view of monopoly the term profits is hardly in place in this context in general. What the monopolist is able to secure for himself (beyond any possible purely entrepreneurial profits which his alertness may discover) is a *monopoly rent* on the uniquely owned resource from which he derives his monopoly position.

This way of looking at things emphasizes another aspect of the difference between the two notions of monopoly. Monopoly rents can, after all, be captured not only by monopolist producers but also by monopolist owners of resources selling their resources to entrepreneur-producers. The rents thus received may reflect the ability of the monopolist resource owners to obtain greater revenues *by withholding some of their resources from the market,* a course of action not generally open to resource owners who are not monopolists. By pointing out that monopoly profits are to be viewed as rents on the monopolized resources, we make clear the essential similarity between the role of the monopolist producer and that of the monopolist resource owner. Where a resource owner holds a monopoly over his resource he is immune from entrepreneurial competition in the resource market and may command a higher than competitive-equilibrium price for his resource. By engaging himself in productive activity with his monopolized resource, the resource owner again commands a higher than competitive-equilibrium (implicit) price for his resource. Even though it can be shown that the monopoly resource rent captured through producing is generally greater than that which the monopolist resource owner could have obtained by selling in the factor market,[32] it remains true that the monopolist's "surplus" of revenue over "costs" (i.e., the costs of the *non*monopolized resources) represents a receipt which other entrepreneurs are unable to capture only because capturing this surplus requires access to the monopolized resource. Were this resource available to all, the "surplus" would tend to be whittled away by entrepreneurial competition until it shrank to the competitive-equilibrium price of this resource. Because this resource is monopolized, the monopolist producer may be able to enjoy a larger surplus, just as he could have enjoyed more than a competitive-equilibrium price for the factor by selling it in the resource market. Where such a higher surplus is forthcoming, this too is because the owner of the monopolized resource has withheld the use of some of his stock from the market, forcing up the price the market must pay for the smaller remaining quantity. (Even if the monopolist-producer employs his entire stock of the monopolized resource, it may be advantageous to him to use it less intensively than it would have been used had

32. I am indebted to Professor R. L. Bishop for pointing this out to me in correspondence.

it not been monopolized. This means that consumers have been denied the additional output which the monopolized resource might easily have furnished, even though the urgency of their demand for output makes them willing to pay for the additional quantities of the *other* factors needed to elicit additional output at the intensive margin of use of the monopolized resource.)

This perspective upon the harmful effects of monopoly (from the point of view of the rest of the market) differs from that associated with the orthodox concept of monopoly. In the latter view, monopoly production involves resource misallocation not because the monopolist underutilizes an available and potentially valuable scarce resource, but because he is led by his search for maximum profits to produce "too small" an output of the monopolized product (as judged by a comparison of price and marginal cost). Not enough of the nation's resources in general are being channeled into producing the monopolized product, although consumers value this product more highly at the margin than they value other products. The approach to the analysis of monopoly which we have suggested, on the other hand, sees its harmful effects, where they apply, in the incentive which monopoly ownership provides for not using a scarce resource to the fullest extent compatible with the pattern of consumer's tastes in the market. (Of course an additional implication of this approach is that the other, nonmonopolized resources come to be allocated at the margin to productive purposes in which their fullest potential productivity is not being tapped.)

6. Let us note a final difference between the implications of the approach to monopoly advanced here and that of orthodox price theory. In the orthodox approach the welfare consequences of monopoly are appraised strictly in terms of the immediate allocation of resources. With the perfectly competitive equality of marginal cost and price as the norm, all traces

of monopoly, represented (as in orthodox theory) by a less than perfectly horizontal demand curve facing the firm (with consequent divergence between price and marginal cost), are branded as socially harmful.

For us, on the other hand, having sought for a concept of monopoly that is (like our concept of competition) relevant to the market process, a welfare appraisal in terms of the immediate allocation of resources cannot provide the only, or even the most significant, measure of economic effect. We are, after all, concerned with disequilibrium situations as well as equilibrium ones. And clearly the pattern of resource allocation during a given period may, for certain purposes, be considered profoundly unimportant as compared with the speed and smoothness with which misallocations can be discovered and corrected. Thus, apart from the possible harmful effects of monopoly resource ownership previously discussed, we must be concerned with the effect upon the competitive entrepreneurial process of the associated obstacle to entry. No more need to be said on this at this point. We will return to these considerations in chapter 6.

THE THEORY OF MONOPOLISTIC COMPETITION

We have reached a point from which we can appraise certain aspects of the large literature of the past thirty-five years that is based upon the work of Chamberlin and of Robinson. At the time of the first appearance of *The Theory of Monopolistic Competition* and *The Economics of Imperfect Competition*, these theories were represented as revolutionary. More recent appraisals and reappraisals have differed on the degree of innovation embodied in these approaches,[33] and some writers

33. See, for example, the literature reviewed in R. L. Bishop, "The Theory of Imperfect Competition after Thirty Years: The Impact on General Theory," *American Economic Review* 54 (May 1964): 33–43; the papers in R. E. Kuenne, ed., *Monopolistic Competition Theory: Studies in Impact* (New York: John Wiley, 1967); Dewey, *Theory of Imperfect Competition*, chap. 1; S. Peterson, "Antitrust and the Classical Model," *American Economic Review* 47 (March 1957): 60–78.

have vigorously criticized their usefulness.[34] But, divergent as these judgments have been, all of them concede one very important advance to the credit of imperfect or monopolistic competition theories — that they provide a more realistic framework within which to understand the real world. Critics may debate the advantages a complicated monopolistically competitive framework of analysis provides over a simple perfectly competitive one in explaining and predicting real-world phenomena, but there seems to be little disagreement that a model of monopolistic competition [35] does provide a more faithful representation of that real world. Oligopolistic situations aside, the real world, it is pointed out, simply does not correspond to perfectly competitive conditions in which the firm can sell as much as it wishes without having to lower its price. Nor, on the other hand, does the real world provide us with instances of pure monopoly, in which the producer of any given commodity is not affected by the activities of producers of other products. Phenomena such as advertising and other selling costs, brand names, and product differentiation are cited as evidence of the inadequacy of the pre-Chamberlinian picture of the world as "a smooth sea of perfectly competitive firms in equilibrium, interrupted here and there by a few monopolist whirlpools obeying a different law." [36] To incorporate these phenomena into our theory, we are told, it is necessary to replace the theory of perfect competition with the theory of monopolistic competition. The position developed thus far in this book makes it impossible for me to accept this approving judgment on the theory of monopolistic competition.

34. See, for example, G. J. Stigler, "Monopolistic Competition in Retrospect," in *Five Lectures in Economic Problems* (London: Macmillan, 1949); see also the literature criticized by E. H. Chamberlin in "The Chicago School," in his *Towards a More General Theory of Value* (London: Oxford University Press, 1957).

35. I follow Chamberlin in recognizing the significant differences between his theory and that of Mrs. Robinson. My subsequent discussion will refer to the former theory.

36. G. L. S. Shackle, *The Years of High Theory* (New York: Cambridge University Press, 1967), p. 43.

I judge the development of this theory most unfortunate. Although it is not to be denied that it brought a number of valuable insights which might otherwise have escaped attention, it appears that the very plausibility with which the new theory accounted for phenomena unexplained by the theory of perfect competition diverted attention from the real inadequacies of the older theory. The truth is that these inadequacies are fully shared by the theory of monopolistic competition. Moreover, a theory of the market which is able to avoid these common inadequacies will by that very token successfully come to grips with those real-world phenomena not accounted for by the perfectly competitive model. That we have already outlined such a theory of the market underscores my judgment that the theory of monopolistic competition was on balance a decidedly unfortunate episode in the history of modern economic thought.

The theory of monopolistic competition attempted to replace one equilibrium theory, in which the assumed conditions clearly violate the conditions of the real world, with another equilibrium theory in which the assumed conditions appear to be in closer conformity with those encountered in the marketplace. What it overlooked was that the old perfectly competitive equilibrium theory was rendered both theoretically unsatisfying and at odds with the facts not so much by its specific assumptions themselves, as because these assumptions made it an equilibrium theory. Thus, replacing the old equilibrium theory by a new equilibrium theory preserved the theoretical unsatisfactoriness of the old theory while failing to offer the simplest explanation of those real-world phenomena it left unaccounted for. Whatever attractiveness the new equilibrium theory of monopolistic competition possessed must be judged to have effectively impeded the attainment of the theory of market process which modern price theory has so sorely lacked.

The decisions producers make in the marketplace concern,

among others, the choice of output quality, of output quantity, and of the price to be asked. Each of these aspects of decision-making reflects many different alternatives. In particular the choice of output quality involves not only the choice of what commodity to produce (shoes, automobiles, or ice cream), but also such matters as the style of the commodity, the quality of materials, the sizes, the colors, the packaging, and the kind of selling effort. In each of these respects, as well as in respect to output quantity and asking price, the prospective producer chooses in light of the information available to him. In any given period of time the decisions being made by market participants, including these decisions of producers, are likely to constitute a disequilibrium set; that is, either some of these decisions will turn out not to be feasible (in light of the other decisions being made) or some of these decisions will turn out to be less than optimal from the points of view of the respective decision-makers (again, in light of the other decisions actually being made). In other words, we can expect this disequilibrium constellation of product qualities, styles, sizes, color, packagings, and so on to change systematically under the influence of the market forces set in motion by the state of disequilibrium. Not only the prices asked and offered change; product quality, too, is an economic variable. But recognizing this involves more than merely realizing that the state of equilibrium also determines the equilibrium constellation of product qualities that will be produced. To recognize that product quality is a variable is to realize that in the disequilibrium market, before market forces have shaken down decisions into smoothly dovetailing patterns, *a variety of product qualities may be produced for no other reason than that equilibrium has not yet been reached.* In other words, even where conditions are such that equilibrium will generate a uniform product quality, product differentiation can be expected during the equilibrating process. Just as the market for a product can, until equilibrium has been reached, display more than one price for the same product, so can the disequilibrium market display product differentiation which may, once equilibrium has been reached, come to be shaken down into product uniformity. And again, just as price differences in the disequilibrium market may themselves play an important role in generating the equilibrating market process, so may differences in each of the multitude of aspects of product quality play the same role.

The position outlined above may be expressed in a somewhat different way. The perfectly competitive market for a given product is characterized by a single price. Nonetheless, the process through which this single price is attained takes the form of competitive price bids and offers, in which entrepreneurs test the market, seeking at all times to offer a price which is attractive enough to forestall their competitors, but not more attractive than necessary. During this process of competing, numerous price offers and bids will be made for the same product, consistent with the imperfection of market information which characterizes disequilibrium. In quite the same way producers may compete actively by offering a better quality (or a slightly poorer quality at a significantly lower price), a different style, a different credit policy, and so on. Even where conditions for equilibrium eventually eliminate all differences in quality, we must recognize the interim arrays of different qualities of a product as essential aspects of the competitive process. One dimension along which competitive entrepreneurial activity may proceed is that of product quality. It is most unfortunate that what can be seen most simply and clearly as an earmark of the *competitive process* has come through Chamberlinian usage to be viewed as nothing else than a characteristic of *monopoly!* Product differentiation, which we have found to be a natural aspect of competitive activity, has come to be almost synonymous with the *absence* of competition.[37]

37. This unfortunate treatment of the competitive process of quality adjustment as monopolistic in character parallels the similarly unfortunate description of the competitive price adjustment process as monopolistic; see above chap. 3, n. 26.

The Theory of Monopolistic Competition

Thus far my criticism of the monopolistic competition view of the market has charged it (*a*) with overlooking the simplest available explanation of such phenomena as product differentiation [38] (namely, that these phenomena are the to-be-expected earmarks of the competitive process at work), and (*b*) with gratuitously advancing an alternative explanation ascribing these phenomena to the presence of monopolistic elements. But the insights we have developed into the roles of competition and monopoly in the competitive-entrepreneurial market process enable us to carry this criticism even further. The explanation provided by the theory of monopolistic competition not only fails to recognize the disequilibrium character of the phenomena it seeks to explain, it fails even as an equilibrium theory. This latter failure has come, in recent years, to be recognized in the literature; [39] the framework for discussion developed in this chapter enables us to perceive this failure immediately.

I have criticized the Chamberlinian approach for perceiving no other way to account for product differentiation than by constructing an equilibrium theory in which product differentiation is a built-in distorting element. The truth is, however, that the theory of monopolistic competition provides no explanation of how, in fact, product differentiation can persist, as a monopolistic element, in conditions of equilibrium. Of course the market process determines the array of products and product qualities being produced in any one period. And there is no reason to doubt that the equilibrium situation toward which

---

38. Product differentiation, and especially the theoretical problems raised by selling costs, will be examined more fully in chapter 4.
39. See D. Dewey, "Imperfect Competition No Bar to Efficient Production," *Journal of Political Economy* 66 (February 1958): 24–33, and idem, *Theory of Imperfect Competition*, chaps. 4, 5; H. Demsetz, "The Nature of Equilibrium in Monopolistic Competition," *Journal of Political Economy* 67 (February 1959): 21–30 and idem, "The Welfare and Empirical Implications of Monopolistic Competition," *Economic Journal* 74 (September 1964): 623–41; Edwards, *Competition and Monopoly in the British Soap Industry*, pp. 103–4.

the process tends will include a wide variety of products and product qualities. But to postulate that equilibrium is consistent with a unique product for each firm is to argue that, during the course of the competitive market process in which profits are being eliminated, entrepreneurs are somehow barred from duplicating profitable product qualities. Without introducing the assumption that certain resources, required to produce a firm's unique product, are in fact monopolized by that firm, we are surely out of bounds in maintaining the uniqueness of the firm's product in the face of the assumption, central to monopolistic competition theory, that entry is free. As Edwards has pointed out, the assumption "that the demand curve of the individual firm has a significant downslope — is indicative of the entrenched market position; but with this so for all firms, it is scarcely compatible with the second assumption, namely that new entry is easy." [40]

It may be useful to sum up my objections to the Chamberlinian approach. First, the theory of monopolistic competition suffers, like the theory of perfect competition, from being exclusively an equilibrium theory. This means that both theories begin by assuming that definite, known demand curves face each firm. By beginning in this way the theory of monopolistic competition has in effect ruled out any possibility of ascribing the phenomena it sets out to account for to the market process set in motion by the circumstance that real-world firms do not, in fact, face known and definite demand curves. The theory is set up so it cannot recognize the entrepreneurial-competitive forces generated by the efforts of firms to determine the actual demand situation facing them.

Second, apart from my dissatisfaction with the notion of given, known demand curves facing each firm, I have objected to the gratuitous assumption that, without any monopolized

40. Edwards, *Competition and Monopoly in the British Soap Industry*, pp. 103–4; see also H. R. Edwards, "Price Formation in Manufacturing Industry and Excess Capacity," *Oxford Economic Papers* 7 (February 1955): 94–118.

resources and without any impediments to entry, it can be assumed that such curves will be downward sloping even after the equilibrating process has run its course.

The first objection is central to the purposes of this book. This objection was stated very clearly by Hayek,[41] and separately by Mises,[42] more than two decades ago. The profession, it seems, either has altogether ignored or simply has not understood what Hayek and Mises were trying to say. Thus Professor Bishop found Hayek's refutation of the theory of monopolistic competition (because of its preoccupation with equilibrium) "pale and unconvincing," being not really a refutation of the theory at all but an "obscurantist effort to undermine all the standard techniques of economic analysis" and, if valid, applying to perfect competition even more directly than to monopolistic competition.[43] It would be difficult to provide a more eloquent commentary on the limitations of contemporary price theory than that so distinguished a theorist as Bishop has failed utterly to perceive that an attack on the equilibrium theory of perfect competition constitutes not an example of obscurantism but a devastating critique of monopolistic competition theory. I will pursue this critique further in the next chapter, with special reference to the role of selling costs.

SOME REMARKS ON THE NOTION OF THE INDUSTRY

My emphasis on the entrepreneurial character of the competition that characterizes the market process carries definite implications concerning the role of the *industry* in a theory of the market. In light of some recent controversy on this point it seems worthwhile to spell out these implications.

For particular-equilibrium theory the "industry" is a device that enables us to ignore the interdependence between different commodities, so that adjustments within the industry can

41. F. A. Hayek, "The Meaning of Competition," in his *Individualism and Economic Order* (London: Routledge and Kegan Paul, 1949).
42. See Mises, *Human Action*, pp. 356 f.
43. Bishop, "Theory of Imperfect Competition," pp. 37–39.

be assumed to be isolated from the changes occurring outside it. Triffin contended that the insights on product substitutability which Chamberlin had introduced with the theory of monopolistic competition called for abandoning any crucial role in theory for the group or the industry. Monopolistic competition "robs the old concept of industry (and also the Chamberlinian group) of any theoretical significance. . . . The theoretical problem is the problem of general competitiveness among goods."[44] The notion of an industry becomes useful only in empirical work, where it can "reduce to a manageable size the research work involved, without any serious loss in precision or exhaustiveness." In a general statement of value theory the industry concept can be of no help in reducing the complexity of the problems posed by the reality of competition between all *firms* in the entire system.

In Triffin's view the abandonment of the industry concept, entailed and made possible by the theory of monopolistic competition, emancipates the theory of value from its particular-equilibrium shackles and extends it along Walrasian lines. A "general theory of economic interdependence" does not require and cannot usefully employ the industry concept; such a theory must be built upon a recognition of the interrelations among all *firms*. In this way the theory of monopolistic competition can bridge the canyon separating the Marshallian school from the Walrasian.[45]

Kuenne[46] recently has sharply criticized Triffin's position. It is *not* true, Kuenne maintains, that the theory of general equilibrium emphasizes interrelationships between firms rather than between industries; abandoning the industry concept cannot, therefore, be claimed to bring Marshallian theory closer to Walrasian. Moreover, Kuenne argues, the core of Chamberlin's contribution lies not at all in any emphasis upon interfirm

44. Triffin, *Monopolistic Competition*, p. 88.
45. Ibid., p. 3.
46. Kuenne, "Quality Space, Interproduct Competition, and General Equilibrium Theory," pp. 225 f.

competition. Rather, Kuenne believes, Chamberlin's contribution altered the nature of inter*product* competition, replacing "the product" by the product group, and viewing markets as decomposed into clusters of closely competing submarkets. But the Chamberlinian theory, in this view, retains the "nonrivalrous," "anonymous" competition between firms which characterizes the theory of perfect competition. And for Kuenne there is no reason, in exploiting the possibilities opened up by the Chamberlinian innovations, to abandon the industry concept. In fact, Kuenne concludes, "retention of the essential outlines of the 'industry' or 'group' and the 'market' may afford the most promising methods of extending the newer techniques to general-equilibrium theory. The interrelation of nonrivalrous firms via product markets is the 'natural' extension of monopolistic competition into general equilibrium theory, and should be tried before ambitions are extended to introduce rivalrous types of interfirm competition as well." [47]

From a somewhat different point of view Triffin's abandonment of the industry concept has been criticized by Olson and McFarland.[48] Their criticism, too, challenges the view that the discovery of interproduct competition renders the industry concept unhelpful. But their criticism does not focus (as Kuenne's does) upon Triffin's view that, because of the uniqueness of each firm's product, consistency requires that a theory of interproduct competition be a theory of interfirm competition. Rather, Olson and McFarland challenge the view that once the ubiquity of interproduct competition has been recognized it is impossible to draw a line round an industry without arbitrarily ignoring the substitutability between the industry product and other products. It is entirely possible for a single ("monopoly") firm to be producing a product — or for a group of firms to be producing a product (or product group) — for which there are indeed many substitutes among other products,

47. Ibid., p. 231.
48. Olson and McFarland, "Restoration of Pure Monopoly."

but for which no one of the substitutes is close or competitive. In such a case, Olson and McFarland conclude, the monopoly firm (or the industry, or the group) is not subject to the direct reactions of other firms, and so analysis of the monopoly firm's price-output decision (or of the market adjustments within the industry or group) can proceed without being compelled to embrace the entire price system.

From the point of view developed here we need not, of course, take a position on the doctrinal implications of Chamberlinian monopolistic competition theory, or of Walrasian general equilibrium theory. We are not called upon to choose, that is, between Triffin on the one hand and Kuenne, Olson, and McFarland on the other in resolving whether the theory of monopolistic competition does or does not logically entail the excision of the industry concept. Nor is it necessary to take a position on whether, in Walrasian theory, the major focus for analysis is upon the individual *firm* (as Triffin maintained) or upon *industry* (as Kuenne has argued.) But our point of view does carry definite implications for the role of the industry within our own theory of the market process, and it turns out that our position on the role of the industry comes closest to that of Triffin.

Whatever pragmatic usefulness the industry concept undoubtedly possesses for applied research, it seems clear that for a theory of market process as I have outlined it in this book the industry concept can be of little help. We have seen that the market process proceeds through entrepreneurial competition. In this process market participants become aware of opportunities for profit: they perceive price discrepancies (either between the prices offered and asked by buyers and sellers of the same good or between the price offered by buyers for a product and that asked by sellers for the necessary resources) and move to capture the difference for themselves through their entrepreneurial buying and selling. Competition, in this process, consists of perceiving possibilities of offering opportunities to other market participants which are more attractive than those currently being made available. It is an essentially *rivalrous* process [49] (to adopt Kuenne's term); it consists not of market participants' reacting passively to given conditions, but of their actively grasping profit opportunities by positively changing the existing conditions. In explicating the nature of this process we cannot adopt the device of an industry, within which adjustments are assumed to be made in an anonymous and nonrivalrous fashion. Not only would adopting such a device force us to forgo our understanding of the competitive process within the "industry," it would also deprive us of our understanding of how market forces proceed by the interaction between the producers of *different* products (since this interaction proceeds, as always, through individual entrepreneurial activity). Only an equilibrium theory (whether particular equilibrium or general equilibrium, whether perfectly competitive or monopolistically competitive) can afford to ignore intra-industry processes. For a theory of market process, the emphasis placed upon the individual entrepreneurial activity which determines the course of market prices for any one product or product "group" immediately points to the extension of the *same* activity in explaining the course of market prices for many different products. Kuenne may be right in arguing that Chamberlinian theory did not significantly emphasize interfirm competition; he may be right in maintaining that for Walrasian theory the industry (rather than the firm) was the "production entity of sole concern."[50] But for a theory of market process we cannot afford to remove emphasis from rivalrous interfirm competition. Olson and McFarland may be right in denying

49. For our purposes the "rivalrous" character of competition consists not so much in the regard decision-makers have for the likely future reactions of their competitors as in their awareness that in making their present decisions they themselves are in a position to do better for the market than their rivals are prepared to do.

50. Kuenne, "Quality Space, Interproduct Competition, and General Equilibrium Theory," p. 226.

that substitutability between products necessarily means that adjustments within an industry cannot be understood without giving consideration to the consequences of these adjustments upon the markets for other products. But the essence of entrepreneurial activity, upon which our theory of market process depends, involves simultaneous participation in more than one "market" — in fact, this activity consists of *linking up* different markets. Thus the defense for partial analysis which Olson and McFarland have made, useful though it might be for equilibrium theory, is of little significance for an analysis of entrepreneurial process.

Moreover, for us (unlike Olson and McFarland) the rehabilitation of the industry concept is neither necessary nor sufficient for the reinstatement of the pure monopoly category. For equilibrium economics, in which the decision-making producing unit is the Robbinsian firm (and with monopoly understood primarily as an attribute of the *firm*), the pure monopolist requires the same insulation from the reaction of other firms as we must postulate to maintain the industry concept. Thus for Olson and McFarland the restoration of pure monopoly comes hand in hand with the restoration of the concept of the industry. The rehabilitation of the industry demand curve, insulated from the reactions (to intraindustry changes) of market participants outside the industry, is at the same time the rehabilitation of the demand curve facing the pure monopoly firm. We have sought a monopoly concept that should reflect the possibility of exemption from *entrepreneurial* competition — involving a level of discussion at which the very notion of a demand curve facing the firm begs the question. This monopoly concept was found in the uniqueness of resource ownership which may confer upon a producer a measure of immunity from the competition of other entrepreneurs, insofar as they are thereby blocked from some activities available to the monopolist producer. As we have seen, the profitability of a monopoly position so defined will indeed depend upon the degree to which substitutes can be found for the monopolized resource and for the product made from it. These considerations will affect both the extent and the significance of the shelter from entrepreneurial competition which the entry-blocking resource ownership can thus afford. Nothing in the monopoly notion so fashioned, we have seen, depends upon the integrity of the industry concept.

SCHUMPETER, CREATIVE DESTRUCTION, AND
THE COMPETITIVE PROCESS

The views on competition and the competitive process which we have developed will perhaps remind the reader of the well-known critique of perfect competition theory (and of associated policy positions) presented so vigorously by Schumpeter.[51] It will perhaps be thought that the entrepreneurial competitive process to which we have insisted upon drawing attention is simply that "perennial gale of creative destruction" which constitutes for Schumpeter both the manifestation of effective competition and the essence of the evolutionary capitalist process. Our concern with the layman's, rather than with the perfect competition theorists', understanding of what competition means — that is, acting *differently* from one's competition — may appear to overlap and even to coincide with Schumpeter's insistence that the important kind of competition in the market system is competition from the new commodity, technology, source of supply, and type of organization.[52]

Schumpeter's position has become most widely known through his associated critique of antitrust policies which take the model of perfect competition as their normative ideal. It is his thesis that perfect competition is inconsistent with technological innovation that has been most thoroughly discussed and tested.[53] For us it will be more important to examine

51. Schumpeter, *Capitalism, Socialism and Democracy*, chaps. 7, 8.
52. See above, p. 92.
53. See, for example, E. S. Mason, "Schumpeter on Monopoly and the Large Firm," *Review of Economics and Statistics* 33 (May 1951): 139–44;

Schumpeter's picture of the capitalist competitive process and to perceive how this picture *differs* from our own. This task assumes all the more significance because I hope it will clarify some aspects of our position which have not yet been sufficiently emphasized.

Briefly, the difference between Schumpeter's "perennial gale" and our own entrepreneurial-competitive process follows consistently from the distinction (developed in the preceding chapter)[54] between Schumpeter's concept of entrepreneurship and that developed here. This arises, paradoxically enough, from a circumstance that seems to clinch the apparent identity of our competitive process and Schumpeter's perennial gale: both processes are entrepreneurial. Schumpeter's dissatisfaction with the dominant price-theory view of capitalism consisted, as ours does, in recognizing the distortion that view represents in excluding the entrepreneurial role.

That our own competitive process is essentially entrepreneurial has been a principal theme of this chapter. That Schumpeter's perennial gale is nothing but the expression of (Schumpeterian) entrepreneurship becomes very clear from even a superficial study of his writings (even though he does not make this quite explicit in his own exposition of the process of creative destruction). Thus, for Schumpeter the kind of competition which shapes the course of capitalism is that "from the new commodity, the new technology, the new source of supply, the new type of organization."[55] This is closely parallel to the language Schumpeter uses in defining the role of the entrepreneur. The function of the entrepreneur, we read, "is to reform or revolutionize the pattern of production by exploiting an invention or, more generally, an untried technological possibility for producing a new commodity or producing an old one in a new way, by opening up a new source of supply of materials or

J. W. Markham, "Market Structure, Business Conduct, and Innovation," *American Economic Review* 55 (May 1965): 469–71.

54. See above, pp. 79–81.

55. Schumpeter, *Capitalism, Socialism and Democracy*, p. 84.

a new outlet for products, by reorganizing an industry." [56] It is this identification, both for Schumpeter's system and for our own, of the competitive process with entrepreneurial activity which can help us perceive that in fact the two systems are discussing two quite different processes.

In the preceding chapter both the similarities and the differences between the Schumpeterian concept of entrepreneurship and our own were pointed out. In both concepts it is the entrepreneur's alertness to hitherto unnoticed opportunities which enables him to depart from routine; it is only under disequilibrium conditions that his role emerges. But for Schumpeter the essence of entrepreneurship is the ability to break away from routine, to destroy existing structures, to move the system away from the even, circular flow of equilibrium. For us, on the other hand, the crucial element in entrepreneurship is the ability to see unexploited opportunities whose prior existence meant that the initial evenness of the circular flow was illusory — that, far from being a state of equilibrium, it represented a situation of disequilibrium inevitably destined to be disrupted. For Schumpeter the entrepreneur is the disruptive, disequilibrating force that dislodges the market from the somnolence of equilibrium; for us the entrepreneur is the equilibrating force whose activity responds to the existing tensions and provides those corrections for which the unexploited opportunities have been crying out.

Thus, for Schumpeter entrepreneurial activity, the dynamic competition to which he drew our attention, manifests itself in the long-run economic development of the capitalist system. It is the source of the evolutionary process of which capitalism consists — for Schumpeter as for Marx.[57] "The opening up of new markets, foreign or domestic, and the organizational development from the craft shop and factory to such concerns as U.S. Steel illustrate the same process of industrial muta-

56. Ibid., p. 132.
57. Ibid., p. 82.

tion . . . that incessantly revolutionizes the economic structure *from within*, incessantly destroying the old one, incessantly creating a new one. This process of Creative Destruction is the essential fact about capitalism." [58] In this process the entrepreneurial activity is that of the *leaders* — the innovators and trailblazers; it is sharply contrasted with the activity of the host of "imitators" who follow the entrepreneurs. Whereas it is the leaders who temporarily create profits by disrupting the state of equilibrium, propelling the economy toward a higher level of economic well-being, it is the mass of imitators which bring the economy to rest again at a new level of equilibrium. Their activity, that of restoring the even, circular flow, is not entrepreneurial; they are the pedestrians who, once they have learned to imitate the leaders, fall into yet another zero-profit routine. Capitalist development for Schumpeter consists of spurts of entrepreneurial, innovative energy, continually dogged by the imitators and routine-huggers.[59]

For us entrepreneurship is manifested in short-run movements fully as much as in long-run developmental changes, and is exercised by the imitators (who move in to exploit the opportunities exposed by the activities of the innovators) fully as much as by the innovators themselves. For us entrepreneurship ceases only when imitative activity has succeeded in squeezing out all profit opportunities. We see the process whereby an above-equilibrium price is beaten down toward equilibrium as an entrepreneurial process: it requires entrepreneurial alertness to the realities of the situation to adjust to the true eagerness (or rather, relative lack of eagerness) of prospective buyers. In fact it is precisely the short-run market processes, which are responsible for the ever-present agitation tending toward market equilibrium positions that we wish to illumine by our emphasis on entrepreneurship. These short-run

58. Ibid., p. 83 (italics in original).
59. See J. A. Schumpeter, *The Theory of Economic Development* (Cambridge: Harvard University Press, 1934), pp. 131 ff.

processes, being made up of the imitative activities of followers striking "at the margins of the profits and the outputs of existing firms," [60] do not, for Schumpeter, exemplify the exercise of entrepreneurship. Entrepreneurship is reserved for the brilliant, imaginative, daring, resourceful innovator. For us entrepreneurship is exercised whenever a market participant recognizes that doing something even a little different from what is currently being done may more accurately anticipate the actual opportunities available.

It is no accident, therefore, that for Schumpeter price competition exemplifies the *non*entrepreneurial, pedestrian kind of competition (which he wishes to relegate to the background), whereas the dynamic, entrepreneurial type of competition (which for Schumpeter is the essence of the capitalist process) is exemplified by the new commodity and new technology.[61] For us the *process* of price competition is as entrepreneurial and dynamic as that represented by the new commodity, new technique, or new type of organization. In fact, it is the essence of our position throughout this book that exactly the same competitive-entrepreneurial market process is at work whether it manifests itself through prices adjusting toward general (or partial) equilibrium patterns or through the adjustment of commodity opportunities made available, techniques of production, or the organization of industry. That Schumpeter clearly refuses to perceive such an identity sharply limits, from the perspective of this essay, the value of his otherwise masterly and pioneering insight into the entrepreneurial process.[62]

We may further clarify how our approach differs from Schumpeter's by referring to his often-cited views on the in-

60. Schumpeter, *Capitalism, Socialism and Democracy*, p. 84.
61. Ibid.
62. For a related criticism of Schumpeter's lack of interest in the market process (as it has been emphasized in this book), see F. A. Hayek, "The Use of Knowledge in Society," *American Economic Review* 35 (September 1945): 529–30. See also Mises, *Human Action*, p. 354.

compatibility of economic progress and the state of perfect competition.[63] It was Schumpeter's position that the perfect freedom of entry implied by perfect competition must remove all incentive for new methods of production and new commodities. Schumpeter (as well, indeed, as the writers who have evaluated this Schumpeterian thesis) seems to be forgetting that perfect competition theory is a theory of equilibrium, describing the conditions that will have to be fulfilled before a situation can be one in which *no* adjustments are needed. It follows that the question whether economic progress is or is not compatible with perfectly competitive conditions is really an idle one. Insofar as an economy possesses the potential for progress (e.g., new technologies are within reach and new commodities are capable of being commanded), then no equilibrium can be imagined *until this potential has already been exploited.* To criticize the perfectly competitive market as not conducive to technological progress is either to fail to recognize it as a state of equilibrium or to define as equilibrium any state of rest, even one in which maladjustments and tensions exist which demand (and will eventually surely win) market correction and adjustments. The theory of perfect competition is unsatisfying to us because it rules out (by definition) any consideration of the process through which equilibrium conditions may be achieved. For Schumpeter it is not possible for this objection to carry weight, since for him, as we have seen, the perfectly competitive market does *not* necessarily mean one in which all potential adjustments have already been exploited. The "dynamic" competition upon which Schumpeter relies for capitalist economic progress is therefore clearly not designed to meet this objection.

We agree wholeheartedly with Schumpeter's view that perfectly competitive conditions must be absent for technological progress to occur. But for us this truth is merely a special

63. Schumpeter, *Capitalism, Socialism and Democracy,* p. 105.

(even if highly important) case of the more general proposition, which asserts that the absence of perfectly competitive conditions (or, for that matter, *any* set of equilibrium conditions) is necessary for market adjustment of *any* kind to occur (even the simplest of price adjustments). It is because Schumpeter viewed the entrepreneurship that can give rise to technological progress as a spontaneous *disruption* of equilibrium (rather than the equilibrating *response* to preexisting tensions) that he could not perceive the essential homogeneity of the competitive-entrepreneurial process, whether it manifests itself through technological progress or through short-run market adjustments.

ENTREPRENEURSHIP AS A ROUTE TO A MONOPOLY POSITION

Among the inferences to be drawn from the monopoly concept developed in this chapter, one deserves to be carefully explained. Although this inference will concern us later, I will introduce it here in order to place our monopoly concept more clearly in perspective. The point I wish to emphasize is that *a monopoly position may be won by alert entrepreneurial (and hence competitive) action.*[64]

With monopoly understood as a position which confers immunity from the entry of competing entrepreneurs (this immunity arising out of unique ownership of resources), it becomes of interest to inquire into the *source* of such a monopoly position. Clearly the source may be simply the prevailing pattern of natural resource endowment as recognized by the relevant property rights system. In a society in which slavery has been ruled out, a man with unique natural skills possesses a built-in monopoly position; and so on. Here we must attribute whatever social disadvantages arise from the monopoly position to the initial endowment pattern made relevant by the institutionalized rights system. But it is clear that a monopoly position may also arise through deliberate action.

64. See above, pp. 22–23.

Thus where the initial resource endowment pattern has distributed a particular resource among *many* resource owners, but one farsighted entrepreneur buys up the entire supply for himself, he has acquired a monopoly position through alert entrepreneurial action. In his subsequent exploitation of his unique resource ownership he is a protected monopolist. If we appraise the benefits this entrepreneur extracts from the market because he owns the unique resource, we ascribe them to his strong position as a monopolist; at the same time we can ascribe them to the course of entrepreneurial actions which won him this position (over potentially competing entrepreneurs). Quite similarly, the social disadvantages that may arise from the monopoly position can be ascribed to the unique power of the monopolist; at the same time they can be ascribed to the competition in which the monopolist won his power (against these disadvantages we must then weigh the social *advantages* that may be traced back to the entrepreneurship involved in that competition). Clearly, one's evaluation of the final situation can be from a short-run point of view, in which the monopolist's position is a datum, or it can be from a long-run point of view, in which the existence of this position is itself explained in terms of the competitive-entrepreneurial market process. It has become apparent that a situation may not permit an unambiguous, positive label; and by the same token a situation may yield both a favorable and an unfavorable normative evaluation, depending on the perspective from which the judgment is made.

The case where an alert entrepreneur has (without any initial monopoly power) acquired a monopoly position through entrepreneurial action is not to be confused with the case in which an entrepreneur has by his alertness become the first (and for the moment the only) producer of a product *without* unique access to any necessary resources. The term "monopoly" is, in the contemporarily dominant theory of price, routinely applied to the latter case (although the relationship of the "monopolist's" activities to entrepreneurship is seldom recognized.) [65] In our own terminology, of course, the nimblest entrepreneur is not, as long as he possesses no unique resource control, termed a monopolist at all. His favorable position not only was won in open competition with other entrepreneurs, it *remains* a specially favorable position only for as long as it takes his competitors (to whom entry remains entirely free) to discover how to offer the market opportunities no less attractive than those *he* has already discovered. This is in sharp contrast to the case of the entrepreneur who acquires sole control of a unique resource and thereby gains a true monopoly position. In the latter case the favorable position was indeed won in open competition with other entrepreneurs, but once won this favorable position is safely and permanently excluded from the reach of would-be competitors.

Nonetheless, the case of the true monopoly position acquired through entrepreneurial activity *can* throw light on one important aspect of the situation in which the nimblest entrepreneur (*without* resource control) has temporarily placed himself in an unusually favorable position. It may be that the first discoverer of a market opportunity, even where he does not uniquely control any of the resources required to exploit it, is temporarily immune from the competitive activities of other entrepreneurs *even after they have discovered and have taken the steps necessary to duplicate this opportunity*. During the time that must necessarily elapse before the effects of these competitive measures impinge on the market, the first entrepreneur has what amounts to a temporary monopoly, a position he has won through superior entrepreneurship. This is a true monopoly position, in our own terminology, because the resources needed to produce the commodity under consideration without delay are in fact not available to other entrepreneurs. Others can marshal the resources capable of producing

65. See, however, the remark attributed to Professor Lewis, cited above, chap. 3, n. 26.

this commodity only sometime in the future; the "first" entrepreneur, simply by taking the first steps before any of his competitors, is the only producer capable of producing *now*. This monopoly position is of course temporary. One's evaluation of this situation will therefore involve a choice between a long-run and a short-run perspective, along yet another dimension beyond that discussed earlier in this section. We will return to a more detailed consideration of these matters in chapter 5.

]4[
Selling Costs, Quality, and Competition

THE PRECEDING DISCUSSIONS OF OUR VIEWS ON THE NATURE OF entrepreneurship and of the competitive market process make it convenient to take up at this point the closely related topics of selling costs and product variability. We shall discover that the insights we have gained concerning competitive-entrepreneurial activity immediately place these aspects of the market in an entirely new light.

Our position may be summarized in the following statements: (1) Entrepreneurs compete with one another, in the process sense, by seeking to offer better opportunities to the market. But an opportunity may be "better" in other ways than requiring (offering) lower (higher) prices from (to) prospective buyers (sellers). An opportunity may appear better to the market because for a given price it offers buyers something they seek more eagerly (or because it asks of sellers, in exchange for a given price, something they relinquish less reluctantly). Entrepreneurial competition expresses itself, therefore, in the kinds and qualities of goods and services being produced and offered for sale (and in the kinds and qualities of the factors sought for purchase). Market disequilibrium, it follows, means not only a pattern of prices and quantities subject to change under competitive pressures, but also a pattern of product types and qualities subject to change through these same pressures. (2) Positive economic theory cannot provide any means of distinguishing between so-called selling costs [1] and production costs. Both categories of costs are incurred by the entrepreneur as he attempts to offer opportunities which market participants will consider more attractive than those available elsewhere. In fact, once the character of the competitive process is correctly comprehended, "selling costs" present no new problems whatsoever for the theory of the market. That the opposite has been repeatedly asserted by orthodox price theorists — and it is this that makes the present chapter necessary — is a reflection of the incomplete understanding of the market process which orthodox price theory expresses. (3) As part of his *entrepreneurial* role, it is the function of the producer to go beyond the mere fabrication and delivery of a commodity to be available for the consumer. He must also *alert* the consumer to the availability of the product, and sometimes he must even alert the consumer to the *desirability* of an already known product. As we shall discover, this latter role cannot be understood merely as that of "producing knowledge" for the consumer concerning prospective or existing opportunities. Rather, it consists in *relieving the consumer of the necessity to be his own entrepreneur.* In order for him to perform this role, "costs of production" must often be higher than they would otherwise be. That the costs of production which most sensitively reflect this entrepreneurial role are usually those labeled selling costs places these costs in an entirely new light (and perhaps helps explain why it is so often mistakenly believed that these selling costs constitute a separate category).

Let us proceed, then, to elaborate this position. In the course of this elaboration, I will digress to explore some seldom-noticed difficulties raised by the attempt to formulate an economically valid definition of a given good.

1. On the treatment of buying costs see below, pp. 180–86.

ON THE PRODUCT AS AN ECONOMIC VARIABLE

Crucial to any discussion of these matters must be a clear understanding of how market forces determine the kinds and qualities of products being produced during a given period. Both Marshallian and Walrasian theory failed seriously in this regard. For Marshallian theory, it is quite clear, the concept of a given industry to which analysis is to be confined effectively begged the entire question: the scope of the Marshallian cross is defined by the given product to which it relates. Walrasian economics, despite its attention to interindustry relationships, did not provide any understanding of how the market determines — in fact, *originates* — the attributes of what is to be produced. Rather, the theory explained the determination of the output quantities of the various *given* product categories. Being an equilibrium theory, the Walrasian system failed even to explain the process whereby this equilibrium output pattern is hammered out; still less did it undertake to explain how the very specifications of the products to be produced are themselves generated by the market process.

This failure of the various neoclassical approaches is to be understood as consistent with their failure to incorporate the entrepreneurial role into their theory of price and thus to provide a theory of the market *process*. An equilibrium theory, being a nonentrepreneurial theory, must necessarily take as already determined the spectrum of products whose prices and outputs are being explained. At best, one can expect from an equilibrium theory only a statement of the equilibrium conditions to be fulfilled governing the relationships between the product, quantity, and price variables. And even this kind of statement was not forthcoming, within the neoclassical tradition, before the work of Chamberlin.

From the perspective of a theory of market process, the role of product quality is entirely analogous to, and in many cases almost inseparable from, that of price. At any given time market participants are engaged in a set of activities which is likely to be a disequilibrium set. In other words, the various decisions being made in the market are not in complete mutual adjustment. The most important case of maladjustment occurs where a bundle of resources is being used to produce units of commodity A at a time when the resources could be used to produce units of commodity B, for which consumers are paying (or would be prepared to pay) greater sums of money. The decisions of the resource owners, in this case, are not fully coordinated with the attitudes of consumers: owing to imperfect communication, resource owners are in effect selling their resources to a group of consumers at prices lower than those a second group is prepared to pay. This creates a classic opportunity for entrepreneurial discovery. Entrepreneurs, discovering the profit opportunity presented by this maladjustment, buy up the resources and put them to work in producing the more valuable product. The pressure of this kind of entrepreneurial activity brings about changes in resource and product prices, of course. It also brings about, at the same time, changes in the kinds of products being produced. Although this reasoning is most frequently used to explain the shifting outputs of existing industries, there is nothing in the above simple statement that does not cover the situation where "the more valuable" product is one that has not yet been produced at all. The products that do come to be produced as a result of entrepreneurial action are (like the various prices that emerge during the course of the entrepreneurial process) momentary features of the landscape, generated by the agitation of the competitive-entrepreneurial process and likely to be nudged and buffeted by the subsequent continuation of that process. Just as a spectrum of prices (for a single product) can be expected to give way, under the pressure of the market process, to a single price, so may a spectrum of various qualities of product give way, under competitive pressures, to a single set of product specifications. And just as a nonequilibrium price will be forced up or down toward equilibrium, so will a "nonequilibrium" quality of product be forced toward the specifications of the "equilibrium product."

The competitive-entrepreneurial character of this process determining product qualities is unmistakable. As soon as one describes an existing pattern of production as one of disequilibrium, it becomes clear that there exists a dimension for extra-Robbinsian decision-making. In the decision about which quality of product is to be produced the really significant aspect is not how to economize with given resources in attaining given ends, but the alertness with which the producer recognizes the kinds of goods consumers are eager to buy, the kinds of goods available technology and resources can create, and the kinds of resources that can be marshaled. It is the successful identification of relevant ends and means (rather than the efficient utilization of means to achieve ends) which marks the "right" decision on product quality. And with resource ownership not monopolized this decision is a strictly competitive one: each production decision is made in an attempt to provide opportunities to the market that will be judged more attractive than those otherwise available.

So difficult is it, in fact, to avoid recognizing the entrepreneurial element in the choice of product, that it is in discussions of the product as a variable that we find, in the contemporary orthodox theory of value, the closest approach to the position taken up here.[2] This seems particularly apparent in Chamberlin's essay "The Product as an Economic Variable."[3] Although Chamberlin himself seems to insist that this essay

2. For a fascinating account of the role of entrepreneurship in determining product quality in the British soap industry, see H. R. Edwards, *Competition and Monopoly in the British Soap Industry* (London: Oxford University Press, 1962), pp. 145–48.

3. E. H. Chamberlin, "The Product as an Economic Variable," *Quarterly Journal of Economics* 67 (February 1953): 1–29, reprinted in his *Towards a More General Theory of Value* (London: Oxford University Press, 1957); page citations will be from this reprint. It should be noted that Chamberlin observes that the substance of the article was "presented to successive generations of graduate students at Harvard since 1935" (p. 105 n).

is fully consistent with his *Theory of Monopolistic Competition*, a fairly strong case can be made for the claim that his later essay departs significantly from the earlier treatment. In the later work, for example, Chamberlin recognizes that it is not enough to analyze a market in which, although many different products are being produced, they are all *given*; it is necessary to treat the product itself as a *variable*.[4] The emphasis is less on the variety of products than on the fact that products are continuously being changed, "improved, deteriorated, or just made different — as an essential part of the market process."[5] He recognizes that admitting the product as a variable adds a new dimension for active competition.[6] The determination of the product-price-output equilibrium occurs, Chamberlin makes clear, through the interaction of entrepreneurs' decisions.[7] All this represents significant progress toward the analysis of product change. It is of course true that, from the point of view of our own treatment, we cannot be satisfied with a discussion which does not do sufficient justice to the *process* of product quality adjustment. Chamberlin has perceived that product quality is not to be taken as a datum, but is, like price, to be viewed as a variable determined by definite market forces. His treatment does not, however, proceed substantially beyond an enumeration of these forces. There is little recognition of the role of entrepreneurial alertness or of the competitive-entrepreneurial process it generates. But even the recognition that product quality is determined by entrepreneurial decision must be welcomed as a definite step in the direction of a theory of the entrepreneurial process of product quality adjustment.[8]

4. Ibid., p. 107, n. 4.
5. Ibid.
6. Ibid., pp. 111, 119.
7. Ibid., p. 115.
8. From the point of view of this book, by far the most perceptive and complete discussion of the competitive process through which product quality is determined is that of the work, unfortunately somewhat ne-

PRODUCTION COSTS AND SELLING COSTS

With a clear understanding of the entrepreneurial process as manifested in the ever-shifting arrays of product qualities available to the market, we are in a position to restate definitively the decisive theoretical objections to recognizing a category of "selling costs" separate from "production costs."

The position that selling costs can (and should) be clearly distinguished from production costs was made familiar to the profession through Chamberlin's emphatic endorsement in his *Theory of Monopolistic Competition*.[9] Citing earlier writers who had argued for such a distinction (as well as several who had explicitly denied it), Chamberlin considered failure to make the distinction a mistake so simple and obvious as to call for explanation. The distinction itself, Chamberlin maintained, is "as fundamental for value theory as the distinction between supply and demand, and indeed arises necessarily from it. Costs of selling increase the demand for the product on which they are expended; costs of production increase supply." Costs of production include "all expenses which must be met to provide the commodity or service, transport it to the buyer, and put it into his hands ready to satisfy his wants." In other words, costs of production are necessary for a particular product itself to be forthcoming, whereas selling costs are undertaken in order to alter the demand curve for that product.

The unacceptability of this distinction has been pointed out by a number of writers. As Stigler remarked, the distinction is either ambiguous in application or rests on arbitrary personal standards of value.[10] "Only he who assumes the right to make value judgements," Machlup observes, "would feel entitled to

glected, of L. Abbott, *Quality and Competition* (New York: Columbia University Press, 1955).

9. E. H. Chamberlin, *The Theory of Monopolistic Competition*, 7th ed. (Cambridge: Harvard University Press, 1956), pp. 123 ff.

10. G. J. Stigler, *The Theory of Price* (New York: Macmillan, 1946), p. 251.

draw the line." [11] The source of the difficulty has been most clearly identified by Kaldor, with the problem of judging what constitutes a "product." "If 'products' were merely thought of in the purely physical sense (as a certain quantity of 'stuff'), *all* costs could be looked upon as 'selling costs,' since they all have the effect of 'raising the demand curve' confronting them. . . . If, on the other hand, a 'product' were to be defined by market criteria (i.e., by the attitudes of buyers), then all costs would be 'production costs,' since they all involve a change of 'product,' as defined by the preferences of the consumers." [12]

Perhaps the least expected among the critics of the Chamberlinian distinction between production and selling costs has been Chamberlin himself. In a paper published in 1964 [13] Chamberlin acknowledged the inadequacy of his earlier formulation of the distinction. The problem with the earlier formulation, Chamberlin explains, is that it tacitly assumes a *given* product. If the product were actually a datum, the earlier definition of selling costs as those altering the demand curve would be entirely valid. But once the variability of the product is recognized, the earlier method of distinguishing between selling costs and production costs fails: "If an expenditure shifts the demand curve to the right, it remains an open question (so far) whether the expenditure has resulted in a new product

11. F. Machlup, *The Economics of Seller's Competition* (Baltimore, Md.: Johns Hopkins University Press, 1952), pp. 182–83.

12. N. Kaldor, "The Economic Aspects of Advertising," *Review of Economic Studies* 18 (1949–50): 1–27, reprinted in *Essays on Value and Distribution* (Glencoe, Ill.: Free Press, 1960), p. 131 (all page references are to this reprint). See also L. Mises, *Human Action* (New Haven: Yale University Press, 1949), p. 319; K. Gordon, "Discussion on Concepts of Competition and Monopoly," *American Economic Review* 45 (May 1955): 486–87; R. L. Bishop, "Monopolistic Competition and Welfare Economics," in *Monopolistic Competition Theory: Studies in Impact*, ed. R. E. Kuenne (New York: John Wiley, 1967), pp. 261–62.

13. E. H. Chamberlin, "The Definition of Selling Costs," in *Review of Economic Studies* 31 (January 1964): 59–64 (reprinted as an appendix in the 8th edition of *The Theory of Monopolistic Competition* [Cambridge: Harvard University Press, 1962]).

for which there is a stronger demand (and is therefore a production cost for the new product) or whether it has merely increased the demand for the old one (and is therefore a selling cost of the latter)." [14]

Chamberlin has thus clearly explained how his earlier faulty formulation arose: it came from regarding the product as a datum rather than as a variable. Awareness of the variability of product quality immediately erases the earlier Chamberlinian distinction between production and selling costs. The discussion earlier in this chapter of the entrepreneurial character of product-quality determination has made it possible to express this point in an even more illuminating way. The writers cited above as critics of the faulty Chamberlinian formulation seem not to have recognized that that formulation arose out of a profound misunderstanding of the role of the producer and of the character of production costs. It will be useful to show that this is so.

Although it is indeed true that the offending formulation arose out of a failure to recognize the variability of the product, it should be pointed out that this was based, in turn, upon a failure to perceive the entrepreneurial character of the decision to produce — even the decision to produce a *single* product. The truth is, as we have seen, that in all cases except that of equilibrium, each producer incurs costs in producing his product not as a Robbinsian decision-maker but as a Misesian entrepreneur. In incurring these costs he is in effect announcing that he has become alert to an opportunity of converting this expenditure into a hitherto unperceived revenue possibility. He believes this possibility to consist in the production of a good of a specific quality (accompanied perhaps by a range of auxiliary services) which will inspire consumers to purchase it at the anticipated price. No one else has quite perceived *this* revenue possibility until now, or, at any rate no one has hitherto discovered a way to realize it at quite so low

14. Ibid., p. 59.

an outlay. Clearly, the outlay undertaken in this way by the entrepreneur-producer cannot be divorced from the revenue possibility to which it is directed. The outlay is undertaken only to win the anticipated revenue; this revenue is anticipated only because *this* product, rather than any other, has been produced. Every penny of outlay is believed necessary to successfully market the product and thus capture the revenue that had been envisaged. The entrepreneurial character of the production decision means that no feature of the product was introduced by the producer without regard to its contribution to a salable finished product. Every aspect of the product (including such extras as friendly service, free parking, and the like) has been produced (and the associated outlays undertaken) strictly in the belief that it would enhance the salability of the whole product. No single penny of the outlay — even those usually considered as strictly production, rather than selling, costs — can be perceived as anything but costs incurred in order to "sell."

Only by assuming away the need for any entrepreneurial role in production (i.e., by assuming that each producer somehow knows *in advance* of his production decision the precise specifications of what he is to produce) is it possible to fall into the error of seeing the costs of fabricating a product as anything other than costs incurred in an effort to anticipate consumers' wishes. With entrepreneurship assumed away, with the product a datum, it is indeed easy not to perceive that the production of a product constitutes a *selection* by the producer of what he believes the consumer will be most eager to buy. With the decision on what to produce assumed to have been somehow made elsewhere, all the producer needs to do is undertake the outlays required to fabricate the product. In this faulty way of seeing things, the producer is viewed as producing a product for an *already guaranteed market* (or at least for a market that can be ensured through separate "selling" activity). Only with such a view could one believe that there can exist costs of production which do not partake of the nature of selling costs. But, as we have seen very clearly, such a view of the producer is appropriate only to a state of equilibrium. When we perceive the need for entrepreneurial decision-making by the producer, it is no longer possible to overlook the truth that all costs are selling costs. (It is of course entirely consistent with this reasoning to point out quite similarly that all costs are production costs.)

Our point of view, and the extent to which it goes beyond the standard criticisms of the earlier Chamberlinian formulation, can be succinctly presented as follows. The critics (including, as we have seen, Chamberlin himself) have pointed out quite correctly that if by selling costs we mean those which shift demand curves to the right, then fabrication costs too must be counted as selling costs (since consumer demand for the raw materials is less intense than that for the finished product). We have pointed out, in addition, that if selling costs are identified as such because they are undertaken to evoke buying eagerness on the part of consumers, then fabrication costs too must be counted as selling costs. This is so, I have argued, *not* primarily because consumers are prepared to pay more for a finished product than for its raw materials, but because the entrepreneur-producer's decision to produce a particular product reflects his alertness to the fact that *this* product can most effectively evoke consumer eagerness to buy. The assumption that the product is a datum makes it easy for our own perception of product costs as selling costs, as well as the corresponding perception of the critics cited earlier, to become suppressed.

If production costs were incurred by hired production managers under instructions to produce a specified product, it would be meaningful to separate the strictly fabricative outlays from those incurred by the sales department. But costs are incurred only by entrepreneurs. For entrepreneurs *all* outlays, no matter what department they originate in, are incurred only insofar as they contribute to a selling effort. (On the other hand, to attempt to isolate "pure" selling costs, that is, that supporting selling effort which does not in any way enhance "the product itself," is, as the cited critics have excellently made clear, to arrogate to oneself the position of being able to pronounce on what does and what does not constitute a "real" change in the product itself.)[15]

SELLING COSTS, CONSUMER KNOWLEDGE, AND
ENTREPRENEURIAL ALERTNESS

Our discussion of the essential homogeneity of costs, and of the invalidity of the selling cost–production cost classification, makes it of special interest to draw attention to a little-noticed function fulfilled in the market process by entrepreneur-producers. Awareness of this role will both confirm the invalidity of the distinction between selling and production costs and help explain the strength of the temptation, succumbed to by so many, to search for such a distinction.

The usual view of the matter is that the producer fabricates a product which the consumer (with or without the prodding of the producer's selling effort) thereupon purchases. The entrepreneurial aspect of the producer's role (if this aspect is recognized at all) is perceived to lie in his discernment of what the consumer stands ready to buy, or what the consumer can be persuaded to buy. Where the information content of advertising is recognized, the producer who sells his product with the help of advertising is perceived not only as producing his own product, but also as providing the consumer with the "knowledge" necessary for him to buy the product. (As we shall discuss later, the traditional "defense" of the role of advertising in the market system has been based chiefly on this informational element.) Here the entrepreneurial aspect of the

15. No attempt is made here to examine the efforts — unsuccessful, as they appear to me — of Kaldor and of Chamberlin (in their cited articles) to develop improved formulations for a distinction between selling costs and production costs.

producer's role is seen to consist in his discernment of that combination of product and information which the consumer stands ready to buy. This view of the matter, I wish to argue, does not do justice to the entrepreneurial role of the producer in the market economy.

It was pointed out in chapter 2 [16] that for analytical purposes it is often convenient to assume that the mass of market participants act as strictly Robbinsian decision-makers ("price-takers"), exercising no element of entrepreneurship whatever, but that a special group of market participants act as "pure" entrepreneurs, with the market *process* seen as being set in motion by their ("price-taking") activities. It will be useful to explain one implication of this model of the market.

If the Robbinsian market participants are to be *purely* Robbinsian, then we must of course view them as confronting *given and known* alternative courses of action. How shall we imagine the awareness of the existence of these alternatives to reach these Robbinsian economizers, during the agitations of market adjustments? It was all very well to examine how a Robbinsian economizer reacts to an *already perceived* problem. But surely the dynamics of the market process call for a series of *changes* in the way market participants perceive their available courses of action. With all elements of entrepreneurship assumed away from these Robbinsian market participants, changes in the price-quantity-quality opportunities available to them during the course of the market process cannot, without the use of some special device, be assumed to become known to these participants. (And even if the course of the market process makes *knowledge* itself available, the discussion in chapter 2 has pointed out that we have as yet no way of ensuring that Robbinsian market participants become aware of such newly available opportunities for acquiring knowledge.) And it is at this point that we realize that if we are to work with a market model based on the existence of purely Robbinsian roles and

16. See above, p. 39–43.

of purely entrepreneurial roles, these latter entrepreneurial roles must be tailored to fill yet an additional responsibility.

Our entrepreneurs, it now becomes apparent, must be charged with the responsibility not only of perceiving how an opportunity can be made available to a consumer (for which the consumer would be happy to pay more than it costs the entrepreneur to make the opportunity available), but also of making *the consumer perceive* that this is in fact available. This responsibility will not be discharged by the entrepreneur's merely making knowledge of the offer available to the consumer. After all, we have seen, a consumer may not even perceive that this offer of knowledge is available. The entrepreneur must somehow succeed *in making the consumer know* of the offer (or at the very least, of the availability of *knowledge* about the opportunities entrepreneurs are prepared to offer). In brief, the analytical division of labor envisaged in our models of pure entrepreneurs and pure Robbinsian maximizers makes it necessary to add a new feature to our picture of the entrepreneur. Until now we have seen the entrepreneur as being alert to opportunities that can be made available to the "Robbinsians" (which they are assumed not to be able to perceive themselves). Now we see the entrepreneur engaged, in addition, in *getting the Robbinsians to see* the availability of these opportunities.

Once this implication of the pure-entrepreneur-pure-Robbinsian model is understood, it is hardly possible to avoid understanding the role of so-called selling effort in the real world in an entirely new light. In the real world, too, producer-entrepreneurs are engaged in providing the consumers with the "entrepreneurship" which they (at least in part) lack. Producer-entrepreneurs are not only engaged in producing commodities for the consumers to purchase, they are concerned also *to make the consumer know* of the existence of these purchase opportunities. Thus we can see that the selling effort of producers goes beyond "persuasion" (attempting to change consumer's tastes), and beyond the mere provision of "knowledge" ("making available" information concerning the purchase opportunities). Selling effort fills the need for the producer-entrepreneur *to get potential consumers to know* about these purchase opportunities.

Later in this chapter we will return to examine some important implications of this new insight into the function of entrepreneurial selling effort. Here I will merely point out how this new view of the matter affects our earlier critique of the orthodox distinction between production costs and selling costs.

Superficially, the new insight into the function of selling effort offers a tempting criterion with which to *preserve* the orthodox Chamberlinian distinction and to defend it against the criticisms previously discussed. One is tempted to argue that "production costs" should be seen as those required to place an opportunity before the consumer, whereas the term "selling costs" should be reserved for the expenditures necessary to make the consumer aware of its availability. Surely, the argument would run, the very distinction between Robbinsian decision-makers and entrepreneurs depends upon the validity of a sharp distinction, in turn, between an opportunity that is "available" to a consumer and an opportunity that is *perceived* as available. Why, then, can we not validly distinguish between the expenditures necessary for the former and the additional expenditures that may be necessary to ensure the latter?

We must concede that such an argument possesses merit. (And, I may remark, its acceptance would not only rehabilitate the orthodox distinction between production costs and selling costs, but would entail, in addition, a drastic revision in the *normative* implications of the distinction. "Selling costs," identified under the new criterion, would be perceived as serving an entirely new social function, one whose utility can no longer be denied.) But although the merit of the argument may provide a measure of pragmatic justification for invoking the ortho-

149

dox distinction in specific cases, it should be apparent upon reflection that the general objections to the validity of the distinction are *not* removed by our new insight into the function of entrepreneurial selling effort.

Although it may be *conceptually* convenient to distinguish between the task of making an opportunity available to a consumer and the task of making the consumer aware of the opportunity, there is in fact no reason to expect that these tasks will be undertaken separately. The entrepreneur's selection of the particular opportunity he will make available is likely to take into account how easily consumers can be made aware of its desirability. The successful entrepreneur is likely to be the one who correctly anticipates those opportunities whose very existence impinges vividly on the consciousness of the consumer, *without* the need for a *separate* entrepreneurial selling effort. The "production costs" necessary to fabricate these commodity opportunities must surely in a sense be recognized as expenditures that ensure consumer awareness of their existence — that is, as "selling costs." Or, from a slightly different perspective, an entrepreneur may judge that the most effective way to convince consumers that his products are desirable is to take steps that in fact alter the nature of the "opportunity" being made available. These "selling costs" are clearly also "production costs." [17]

We thus once again reach the same conclusion. Our recognition of the entrepreneurial character of the production decision, and our insight into that aspect of the entrepreneur-producer's decision which undertakes to ensure consumer awareness of the desirability and availability of his products, converge to deny the validity of the distinction between pro-

17. Moreover, even at the conceptual level it can be argued that a valid distinction between the task of making an opportunity available to a consumer and that of making him aware of the opportunity cannot be consistently sustained. It must be pointed out that until he has been made aware of an opportunity that opportunity does not, in a real sense, exist for the consumer at all. Thus the task of making the consumer "notice" the opportunity turns out to be an integral part of making that opportunity available.

duction activity and selling activity and between production costs and selling costs.

The role filled by the entrepreneur in *making the consumer aware* of available opportunities needs to be further distinguished from the quite separate function of "providing information" to potential consumers as this is treated by many writers. In turning now to develop this distinction, we will have the opportunity to review briefly the widespread treatment of advertising as a major method of providing price and quality information to the market. Because so large a portion of selling effort does take the form of expenditure on advertising, and because many have "justified" the enormous volume of resources devoted to this solely by the information content of advertising, a careful consideration of the relevant issues is called for.

During the relatively few decades when economic theorists have paid explicit attention to advertising, they have almost invariably been quick to concede that advertising may fill a useful informational role.[18] "There can be no question," Kaldor remarks in his generally critical essay on the economic aspects of advertising,[19] "as to the genuine need for information . . . there is no doubt, also, that if advertising were *not* provided freely, the consumers would be quite willing to pay for the supply of market information. . . . There is no doubt, therefore, that advertising has a social function to fulfill." The critical views upon advertising have involved such issues as

18. For early examples see A. Marshall, *Industry and Trade* (London: Macmillan, 1919), p. 305; A. C. Pigou, *The Economics of Welfare*, 4th ed. (London: Macmillan, 1932), p. 196; D. Braithwaite, "The Economic Effects of Advertising," *Economic Journal* 38 (March 28): 16–37. See, however, E. A. Lever, *Advertising and Economic Theory* (London: Oxford University Press, 1947), chapter 6.

19. Kaldor, "Economic Aspects of Advertising," p. 103.

the "tainted" source of the information provided (since it is supplied by the producer, whose interest in providing objective information cannot be above suspicion); or the possibility that, as a result of profit-maximizing decisions of producers, consumers may be provided with more information than they are in fact willing to pay for.

Common to this line of ideas has been the general point of view that "information" is something which consumers are, in principle, willing to buy. If producers did not offer "free" information jointly with the product, consumers would be forced to use other techniques of purchasing information. In fact, the provision of free information through advertising has, in this line of ideas, come more recently to be integrated into the broader theory of the economics of information.[20] In this theory the provision of information is treated as a service clearly separated from the products to which market information is relevant. Moreover, it is a service whose usefulness is *valued* by the consumer *separately* from that of the relevant products. "Transportation costs are the prototype of all trading costs: costs of acquiring knowledge of products and other traders, inspecting quality. . . . Information costs are the costs of transportation from ignorance to omniscience, and seldom can a trader afford to take the entire trip."[21] The theory of information economics has in this way been deployed to explain why sellers rather than buyers have undertaken to provide the information contained in advertising.[22] It has similarly been deployed, in conjunction with the recognition of the role of transactions costs, to explain why, on efficiency grounds, information can generally be expected to be provided jointly with the product (thus blunting the impact

20. See G. J. Stigler, "The Economics of Information," *Journal of Political Economy* 69 (June 1961): 220f.

21. G. J. Stigler, "Imperfections in the Capital Market," *Journal of Political Economy* 75 (June 1967): 291.

22. See R. B. Heflebower, "The Theory and Effects of Nonprice Competition," in *Monopolistic Competition Theory: Studies in Impact*, ed. R. E. Kuenne (New York: John Wiley, 1967), pp. 179–81.

of criticism of advertising which points to the suspect source of advertised information).[23] Quite naturally, with this approach, the question of the optimum quantity of desired information — via advertising — has come to be discussed with the help of supply and demand curves relating only to the consumer-valued information component of advertising messages.[24]

In order to treat advertising in this way, whether at the positive or at the normative level, we must of course postulate a sharp distinction, in principle at least, between the informational aspects of advertising and such aspects as persuasion. The defense of advertising, as based on its informational aspects, assumes that information is useful to the consumer. But a consumer cannot be presumed to have an interest in subsidizing an attempt to persuade him to buy something for which he at present has no desire. Several writers have, for different reasons, expressed serious reservations on this score. Thus Chamberlin considered the emphasis on information greatly overdone. "Those who stress it evidently have in mind *technical* information about the product and its uses, and presented with zero emotional appeal, but it is not the only kind people want. They are perhaps more interested in knowing that a famous movie star smokes a certain brand of cigarette than in knowing what the cigarette is made of; and both are information." Chamberlin argues "that the line between information and emotional appeal is not easy to draw, and also that human beings actually enjoy appeals to their emotions as well as to their limited rational powers."[25] Here Chamberlin is taking issue with those who deny that advertising has social utility upon any basis other than the provision of strict information.

23. L. G. Telser, "Supply and Demand for Advertising Messages," *American Economic Review* 56 (May 1966): 458 f.

24. P. O. Steiner, "Discussion" (of the Economics of Broadcasting and Advertising), *American Economic Review* 56 (May 1966): 473; P. Doyle, "Economic Aspects of Advertising: A Survey," *Economic Journal* 78 (September 1968): 580.

25. E. H. Chamberlin, "Some Aspects of Nonprice Competition," in his *Towards a More General Theory of Value*, pp. 146–47.

Chamberlin's case is that just as we are prepared to ascribe social utility to strictly informational advertising because consumers desire information, so must we concede that "appeals to the emotions" fill an equally strong demand.

Hicks, too, has criticized those who have judged the social function of advertising to be confined to its strictly informational aspect. Advertising that is merely "bleakly informative" — in Hicks's phrase — is not fulfilling its social function of educating the public concerning available opportunities. "The attention of the consumer has to be attracted and his interest aroused. In order to perform its social function, advertising has to be attractive and (let us not be afraid to say) persuasive." [26] In other words, Hicks is pointing out that if consumers require information, they require it in a form that is indistinguishable from persuasion. Hicks, like Chamberlin, denies the existence of a clear line separating information from persuasion. But whereas for Hicks the persuasive aspects of advertising may be necessary to its purely informational function, Chamberlin has argued that some such persuasive aspects may be valuable to consumers because they enjoy appeals to their emotions.

We should notice, however, that both Hicks and Chamberlin, although they question the existence of a clear line of distinction between information and persuasion, do not quarrel at all with the approach — central to the defense or evaluation of advertising upon its informational content — that sharply separates the usefulness of the information contained in advertised messages from the usefulness of the products they advertise. In Hicks's own words, we are considering "two distinct services — that of providing the article and that of providing the information upon which the decision to buy it is based." [27] Chamberlin, indeed, insists similarly that advertising

26. J. R. Hicks, "Economic Theory and the Evaluation of Consumers' Wants," *Journal of Business* 35 (July 1962): 257.
27. Ibid.

be viewed as "itself a product which might be separated from the product advertised,"[28] and considers that his recognition of the possible value of the noninformational aspects of advertising is reinforced by such a view of the matter. Certainly those who have treated the information component of advertising as conceptually distinct from other components have quite simply proceeded to consider this information as clearly distinct from the advertised product itself.

In other words, the literature defending the social value of advertising because it provides information adopts the following position. Advertising is different from other forms of selling effort, which affect the demand curve *for the product being offered for sale*. Advertising provides a service *different from* the product being advertised. This way of putting the matter underscores the distinction between advertising perceived as the "provision of information" and as that facet of entrepreneurship (emphasized earlier in this chapter) in which the consumer is "made aware" of available opportunities.

Let it be immediately conceded that a substantial portion of advertising may indeed, as the cited literature argues, be viewed as providing a service quite distinct from the advertised product. And let it further be granted that it is entirely plausible to identify this service as the provision of knowledge and information. We have no quarrel, therefore, with the attempts to subsume this aspect of advertising under a broader theory of the economics of information. What I wish to point out is simply that to treat *all* informational aspects of advertising *exclusively* as providing a separate, distinct service ("information") fails utterly to perceive the crucially important role of the entrepreneur as one who *brings available opportunities to the awareness of the consumer*. In other words, there is an aspect of advertising which, although clearly aimed at making the consumer "better informed" about the advertised product, does *not* lend itself to an analytical treatment in which it is

28. Chamberlin, "Some Aspects of Nonprice Competition," p. 147.

handled as a separate service which for one reason or another happens to be provided by the producer of the advertised product. That there are informational aspects of advertising which *do* admit of such "separate" consideration renders it the more important and the more difficult to point out carefully the distinction between these quite different aspects of the matter.[29]

The distinction can be made clear in the following way. In attempting to explain why advertising information is jointly supplied with the advertised products, Telser compares advertising information to carburetors. Carburetors can be supplied separately, and yet there are powerful production economies which explain "why we buy complete cars instead of the parts which we could assemble ourselves in our back yards. . . . Similarly, there are economies that can explain why advertising services are seldom sold separately."[30] The point I wish to make here can be expressed by showing that the relationship between the knowledge provided by advertising and the advertised product differs sharply from that between the carburetor and the other components of an automobile. Even in the absence of the carburetor, we can conceive of a demand for the other parts of the automobile; *there are aspects of knowledge concerning a product without which it is absurd to conceive of demand for the product at all.* It is not nonsense to talk of the demand curve for one of several goods used in strict complementarity. It is nonsense to talk of the strength of a consumer's demand for an unknown opportunity. In other words, there are aspects of knowledge which render its provision more than merely a service whose utility strongly complements that of an advertised product; providing information turns out to be essential in order to attach meaning to the general notion that a demanded product exists.

In our earlier discussion of the invalidity of the distinction

29. For an excellent review of the relation between advertising and the advertised product, see L. G. Telser, "Advertising and Competition," *Journal of Political Economy* 72 (December 1964): 539–40.

30. Telser, "Supply and Demand for Advertising Messages," p. 458.

between selling costs and production costs, I mentioned that production costs, like selling costs, "shift the demand curve to the right." The demand curve for the finished product is quite different from that for the raw materials in it. We must insist now that it is invalid to treat *all* knowledge concerning a product as a service whose availability shifts the demand curve to the right. It is invalid to argue that with respect to *all* knowledge concerning products, the demand curve for product-plus-knowledge is to the right of that for the product-without-knowledge. There are some aspects of "knowledge" which are required in order for us to talk sensibly about any kind of demand curve at all.[31]

Suppose that a man knows the commodity he needs is available at a reasonable price in a number of stores but does not know where these stores are. Then an advertisement which contains the address of a store carrying this commodity can be said to provide information which can, in principle, be considered separately from the commodity itself. The would-be customer would have had to engage in a more or less costly search for the address of such a store; it is perfectly in order to consider that he has been provided with a service which makes the search unnecessary. This service is quite separate from the commodity itself. It is entirely proper to consider that this would-be customer, even before he discovered the address of the store, had a particular demand for the commodity. He knew, even without knowing the store's address, that this opportunity existed. Moreover, it is entirely in order to say that the intensity of his demand for the commodity, so long as a costly search is required before it can be purchased, is lower than it would be for a commodity available without search. It is in order, that is, to treat the information concerning the location of the store as a service complementary to

31. Cf. the following statement: "There cannot be demand unless buyers know who are the sellers, what they are selling, and the terms of sale" (Ibid., p. 462).

the commodity which must be searched for. It is reasonable therefore, to draw the consumer's demand curve for this information in exactly the same way that one may, if one chooses, draw the demand curve for a carburetor. As was cited earlier, such provision of information may indeed be compared to the provision of transportation. No doubt much of the "information" contained in advertising is of this kind.

But consider now the case of the man who has no inkling that a certain commodity exists. We may, of course, *imagine* his demand curve for this commodity once its existence has become known to him. But if we wish to discuss the commodity in its unknown state we are simply unable to talk of the consumer's demand for it. It is not that his demand curve coincides with the price axis; that he would buy none of it at any given price. It is rather that the very notion of demand has no place under these circumstances. It is nonsense to discuss the upper limit of the price this consumer is willing to pay for this unknown commodity; it is nonsense to discuss the quantity he would be prepared to purchase at a given price. These discussions refer to the eagerness with which a consumer wishes to pursue *perceived* opportunities. With no opportunities perceived the notion of consumer demand has no meaning. Under these circumstances an advertisement which informs the consumer that the commodity is available must be viewed as performing a function quite different from that in the preceding example (in which the store's address was provided). In no sense can the provision of this kind of information be treated as the provision of transportation which enhances the availability of an already-perceived product. In this instance the "information" provided by the advertisement renders the notion of the consumers' demand for the advertised product meaningful for the first time. It is therefore clearly improper to treat the product itself and the advertised "information" as two complementary ingredients that might in principle be purchased separately. It is improper to consider the value the consumer places upon this kind of information in the sense of asking how much the consumer himself might have spent to obtain it. The same considerations which made it absurd to talk of the demand for an unknown commodity make it absurd to talk of the demand for information whose existence is not even dreamed of. No doubt not all advertised information is of the kind described in this case. But no less surely must it be recognized that much advertising does assume the character described here — that is, it consists of messages making the consumer aware of unknown commodities or of unperceived desirable qualities of already known commodities.

ADVERTISING, INFORMATION, AND PERSUASION

The preceding sections help us understand more clearly why, as a number of writers have remarked, it is difficult as a practical matter to draw the line separating the purely informational aspects of advertising from the purely persuasive. It might seem that the *conceptual* distinction, at least, between informing and persuading is unambiguous. We talk of a man's "tastes" — of the way he would rank given, known alternatives — and we have something fairly definite in mind when we refer to a sequence of experiences which change these tastes. We also talk of a man's knowledge (whether true or false) of the alternatives which lie before him (regardless of the way in which they might be ranked). And here again we have something definite in mind when we refer to a learning experience which has altered a man's knowledge. To be sure, when we observe a man who yesterday chose alternative A over alternative B today making the opposite choice, it may be difficult to determine whether he has learned new information concerning one or both of the two alternatives or whether he has "learned" a new set of tastes.[32] (In denying earlier the validity of the orthodox Chamberlinian distinction between production costs and

32. Cf. K. Boulding, "The Economics of Knowledge and the Knowledge of Economics," *American Economic Review* 56 (May 1966): 7.

selling costs we were, quite similarly, pointing out the impossibility of an external observer's being able to determine whether such a switch signifies a genuine alteration in the ranking of the alternatives — that is, a change in "demand" — or whether it reflects a change, unnoticed by the external observer, in the nature of one or both of the two alternatives, at least as perceived by the chooser — that is, a change in "product." Clearly, the latter possibility includes the case where the chooser has acquired new knowledge concerning one or both of the alternatives.) But despite the difficulty of making this determination — and despite the possibility that the distinction may not always be respected in the psychological processes involved in choice — it does seem possible to identify polar cases of pure persuasion on the one hand and of the pure provision of information on the other.

In advertising it is the obviously persuasive elements which command the immediate attention of the observer, so much so that its possibly valuable role in providing information has often been totally ignored, or if recognized, has been considered of distinctly minor importance. For those who have considered the informative aspects of advertising to be at most a secondary function there is no need, of course, to account for its generally persuasive character. For those who have recognized the at least potentially important informative function of advertising, however, there is need to explain why the information comes packaged in so thick a coating of apparent persuasion.

It should be pointed out in this regard that it is by no means obvious, on a priori grounds, why persuasive advertising should play a large role in market activity at all (quite apart from the persuasive wrappings in which information is delivered). One might argue, surely, that entrepreneurs would do better for themselves by producing those commodities which consumers already want most urgently, rather than by producing less urgently desired goods which they are able to sell only through costly efforts of persuasion. There are, of course, several explanations for the profitability of efforts to change men's tastes. First, even if the most urgently desired commodity has in fact been produced, it may be judged possible and profitable, through a relatively cheap campaign of persuasion, to make consumers demand this commodity even more eagerly. As a special case of this it may be possible, through judicious expenditure on persuasion, to profitably change a mildly desired commodity into a wildly sought after favorite. In these cases, entrepreneurial alertness to these profitable opportunities may suggest that they are even *more* profitable than simply producing already popular commodities (which may of course, already be in abundant supply). Second, where past decisions of entrepreneurs have led them to mistakenly produce (or to take preliminary steps toward producing) commodities which are in fact *not* in strong demand, persuasion may clearly be a way to avoid the abandonment and waste of the efforts and resources already invested. Short-run considerations, in other words, may suggest persuasion as a way to turn an inventory or a plant with an initially low market appeal into something more valuable on the market.

These two kinds of situations in which profit-motivated entrepreneur-producers are led to advertise persuasively may be sufficient to account, at the same time, for the *persuasive character* of the *information* contained in advertising messages. In addition, we have already noticed [33] Hicks's contention that for advertising to fulfill its social function of providing information it must be not merely informative but also attractive and persuasive. In other words, even if no attempt is to be made to change people's tastes, the task of "informing" the public consists in "persuading" them to give up their faulty image of the world and to replace it with a more faithful one. The very same tactics of persuasion that are necessary to change men's minds are necessary, in this view, to change the knowledge men be-

33. See above, p. 154.

lieve they possess concerning the factual state of the world. This view, although it does not deny the conceptual distinction between changing men's tastes and changing men's knowledge, claims that substantial psychological parallelism exists between pure provision of information and pure persuasion. In the words of one writer on the topic, "all effective communication is persuasive . . . both information and recommendations must be presented persuasively if they are to have any effect on purchasing decisions." [34] Our discussion in the preceding sections will enable us to understand the almost inevitably persuasive character of advertising from a fresh perspective.

Our discussions have shown us that the function of the producer-entrepreneur is not merely to present the consumer with a particular buying opportunity, but to present it to him so that he cannot fail to "notice" its availability. The information such a producer-entrepreneur provides to prospective consumers in the course of his market activities was not, we found, to be understood exclusively as something, separate from but complementary with a product, that happens to be produced and supplied jointly with that product. Rather, we found, some of that information is to be considered as inseparable from the product itself: the product itself simply *does not exist* for the consumer until its existence and usefulness have been brought to his attention. It follows that the entrepreneur's task is not completed when he makes information available to the consumer. He must also get the consumer to notice and absorb that information. It is therefore not at all surprising to discover that the information that might be provided in a modest two-line newspaper announcement (that might be read by millions) is instead emblazoned in color on giant billboards, embellished by all kinds of vivid, but superficially irrelevant illustrations. It is not so much, perhaps, that effective communication needs to

34. W. Alderson, *Dynamic Marketing Behavior* (Homewood, Ill.: Richard D. Irwin, 1965), quoted in P. Doyle, "Economic Aspects of Advertising: A Survey," *Economic Journal* 78 (September 1968): 582.

be persuasive as that it needs to be eye-catching, mind-catching, and reinforced by constant repetition.

And as the opportunities being made available by producer-entrepreneurs increase both in number and in variety the task of ensuring that a particular opportunity is noticed by consumers becomes more and more difficult (although it *may*, by the very same circumstances, be rendered more and more important). With so many pieces of advertised information bombarding the consumer, successful entrepreneurship turns out to depend more and more upon the success with which the qualities of one's product can be brought to the notice of consumers. Greater and greater portions of entrepreneurial effort and alertness are dedicated to discovering ways to communicate effectively with consumers. It is not surprising, therefore, that the more affluent an economy becomes, the more provocative, intrusive, shrill, persuasive, and pervasive becomes the character of its advertising. It is entirely to be expected that the superficial observer of advertising in an affluent society will perceive a smaller relative information content in its advertising messages than is found in less affluent societies.

ADVERTISING, SELLING EFFORT, AND COMPETITION

From the point of view developed here, the debates in the literature over the influence exercised by the forces of selling effort and of competition acquire a special interest. The alleged incompatibility of selling effort (particularly advertising) and competition was expounded for many years almost without disagreement. Two circumstances were widely advanced as grounds for this position. On the one hand, with the dominance of the perfectly competitive model of the market, it inevitably was emphasized that the conditions for perfect competition render selling effort pointless; even without advertising or other selling effort the perfectly competitive market will take, at the market price, as much as any firm wishes to sell.[35] It follows that, since perfect competition precludes selling effort, where advertising or other selling effort *is* in fact engaged in, this must be attributed to the monopolistic elements in the market structure.

On the other hand, selling effort in general (and advertising in particular) has been considered not merely as *made possible by* departures from perfectly competitive conditions, but as *responsible for* the emergence of monopolistic features in the structure of markets. Selling effort, it is pointed out, enables individual producers to differentiate their products in the eyes of the public and thus permits producers to carve out for themselves segments of the market within which they are relatively immune to the winds of outside competition. Thus Henry Simons considered advertising "a major barrier to really competitive enterprise and efficient service to consumers."[36] In a widely cited critique of advertising, Kaldor presented the case for "a general presumption that advertising promotes industrial concentration."[37] This case rests on the possibility that in advertising there may exist economies of scale that will favor the expansion of the already larger firms. A considerable literature has emerged attempting to test empirically the extent to which increased industrial concentration can be attributed to advertising.[38]

At the same time it has been recognized that advertising is done "competitively" — that is, to win customers from other sellers. But this aspect of advertising has been considered *not* to merit the generally favorable view with which economists have treated competition. When Pigou discussed "competitive

35. Pigou, *Economics of Welfare*, p. 196 n; E. H. Chamberlin, *Theory of Monopolistic Competition*, 7th ed. (Cambridge: Harvard University Press, 1956), p. 128.

36. H. C. Simons, *Economic Policy for a Free Society* (Chicago: University of Chicago Press, 1948), p. 95.

37. Kaldor, "Economic Aspects of Advertising," p. 118.

38. This literature has been exhaustively presented and critically evaluated in J. Backman, *Advertising and Competition* (New York: New York University Press, 1967). See especially chap. 4.

advertisement," [39] he was referring to that category of advertising which Marshall had labeled "combative" and which was contrasted with the "constructive" kind of advertising which provides service to the consumers. Pigou's competitive advertising does nothing for the consumer. It does not improve the product, it does not provide information about the product — it has "the sole purpose of transferring the demand for a given commodity from one source of supply to another." From the consumer's point of view, Pigou believes, this kind of advertising is wholly wasteful. It gives him the identical product at a higher cost. Yet despite this decidedly unfavorable view of competitive advertising, it remains significant that, side by side with those numerous pronouncements in the literature declaring advertising a result of or a cause for monopolistic market control, or both, the insight that advertising and selling effort are weapons of rivalrous competition was never completely submerged. As long ago as 1933 Mrs. Robinson, in the course of discussing how "competition, in the plain sense of the word" is inconsistent with perfect markets, lists advertising as one of the weapons of rivalrous competition.[40] More recently, H. R. Edwards has remarked that "so long as one's view is not confined by the blinkers of Perfect Competition as a standard," advertising must be accepted as "a natural weapon of competition in a market." [41] P. W. S. Andrews has made this competitive aspect of advertising a major argument in his case against the dominant theories of monopoly, monopolistic competition, and oligopoly.[42]

39. Pigou, *Economics of Welfare*, p. 196.
40. J. Robinson, *The Economics of Imperfect Competition* (London: Macmillan, 1933), p. 90 and footnote. See also J. M. Clark, *Competition as a Dynamic Process* (Washington, D.C.: Brookings Institution, 1961), p. 16. Abbott has pointed out that informative advertising sharpens quality competition by facilitating quality comparison. (*Quality and Competition* [New York: Columbia University Press, 1955], p. 112).
41. Edwards, *Competition and Monopoly*, p. 13.
42. P. W. S. Andrews, *On Competition in Economic Theory* (New York: St. Martins, 1964), pp. 123–27. See also Telser's observation: "ad-

Selling Costs, Quality, and Competition

The perspective upon advertising, selling effort, and non-price competition in general that has been developed in this chapter enables us to see the competitive character of advertising in a rather different light. For us, that we find advertising treated in the literature both as an exploitation of imperfections in competition and as a weapon of rivalrous competition turns out to be a clue to its true role. Advertising and selling effort in general are steps entrepreneurs take in their attempts to place more eagerly desired opportunities before consumers. As such, these steps *must* be competitive, as this term has been defined for the purposes of this essay, since we have discovered that *all* entrepreneurial activity is competitive in this sense. At the same time, there is nothing in our recognition of this competitive character of advertising that renders it surprising that advertising has been considered in the literature to be inconsistent with perfectly competitive equilibrium and thus "monopolistic." We have discovered that this is entirely typical of the way rivalrous competition of all kinds has been treated in the literature.

In making these assertions we must bear in mind a number of propositions already discussed at length. We bear in mind, first of all, that without making arbitrary judgments of value it is impossible to distinguish between "production" costs and "selling" costs. For positive economic science both kinds of expenditure are incurred by the entrepreneur in the course of his attempts to offer the most attractive opportunities to the market. We bear in mind, second, that for an opportunity to have been "placed before a consumer" he must be alerted to its availability and to its desirability. We bear in mind, finally, that the competitive-entrepreneurial adjustments set in motion by the absence of market equilibrium include (beside competitive adjustments in prices asked or offered) competitive-entre-

vertising is widely believed to be the main avenue of competition among cigarette companies" (L. G. Telser, "Advertising and Cigarettes," *Journal of Political Economy* 70 [October 1962]: 472).

preneurial adjustments in the *kinds* of opportunities placed before the market participants.

When one accepts these insights, one is immediately aware that selling effort (including advertising) that alters the opportunities perceived by consumers constitutes an entirely normal avenue of competitive-entrepreneurial activity. It is activity which would indeed be precluded by a state of equilibrium, since such a state is by definition one in which maladjustments do not occur.[43] In equilibrium there is no way available resources can be more successfully deployed (by exchange or production or both) to coordinate individual goals through any reshuffling of the kinds of opportunities offered to the market. Since selling effort, including advertising, modifies the kinds of opportunities available in the market (through altering the character of the opportunities as perceived by consumers, or through altering consumer awareness of these opportunities, or through altering consumer tastes), the opportunities perceived by entrepreneurs for profitable selling effort represent hitherto unexploited "misuses" of resources, characteristic of disequilibrium. The exploitation by entrepreneurs of these opportunities for profit is entirely of the same kind as entrepreneurial profit-making activity in general. This activity necessarily proceeds competitively, in the sense in which the term is used in this essay; that is, it proceeds by each entrepreneur's attempting to offer opportunities to the market which, to his knowledge, are not less attractive to consumers than the opportunities made available by others (but are no *more* attractive

43. In his paper "Advertising and Competition," *Journal of Political Economy*, vol. 72 (December 1964), L. G. Telser has argued that even in the state of perfect competition there may yet be an informational role for advertising. It will be observed that this would confirm our contention that the "information" relevant to Telser's thesis is something other than the "awareness" we have recognized as relevant to the function of advertising. See also W. H. Hutt, "Economic Method and the Concept of Competition," *South African Journal of Economics* 2 (March 1934): 10 f; Abbott, *Quality and Competition*, pp. 112–13.

than is necessary to nose out his competition). That this activity may consist to a large extent of efforts to make consumers more fully alive to the desirable qualities of his own product than they are to the "similar" qualities of the products of other suppliers does not alter the situation one iota (so long as we recognize that the liveliness with which a consumer is aware of an opportunity is an integral part of the very "existence" of that opportunity). This kind of competition (i.e., competition with respect to the effectiveness with which entrepreneurs communicate with potential consumers) is simply a special case of the general category of quality competition, which it has been the principal purpose of this chapter to expound.[44]

Recognizing the entrepreneurial-competitive character of selling effort also provides us with the proper perspective from which to evaluate the possibility that advertising may be conducive to the *elimination* of competition. It will be recalled that the widespread acceptance of this possibility as fact depends first upon the claim that advertising differentiates the product in the eyes of consumers (thus protecting the product from the competition of substitute products) and second upon the claim that economies of scale in advertising favor the expansion of the already larger firms. Our previous discussions of the role of *entry* in the competitive process are of direct relevance here. For us, the crucial question (in evaluating the claim that advertising "monopolistically" differentiates the product in the eyes of the consumer) must always be whether the advertising activities engaged in by the differentiating "monopolist," are or are not open also to his competitors. So long as others enjoy "freedom of entry" — that is, so long as they can duplicate the messages to consumers which have been projected by the "monopolist" — it is difficult to look upon the "uniqueness" of his

44. The statement in the text deliberately refrains from emphasizing that we should in fact expect the most likely opportunities for profitable advertising to occur when there is indeed something "new" to communicate to the consumers.

product as resulting from anything but his entrepreneurial (and hence competitive) alertness and nimbleness.[45]

Somewhat similar considerations are also relevant, in part, to the argument that economies of scale in advertising may lead to industrial concentration. Let us suppose that such economies of scale do in fact exist. Then, so long as advertising possibilities are open to all, the firms who will exploit these scale economies (and will thus become the larger firms) will not necessarily be those firms which were *already* the larger firms; they will simply be the firms most entrepreneurially alert to these scale opportunities. Moreover, regardless of *which* firms turn out to be the surviving giants, if the industry concentration has increased as a result of economies of scale in advertising, with entry free in all respects, we are not entitled to view the situation any differently from *all* situations in which, with entry free, economies of scale in manufacturing tend to generate industries with few firms. It is only Kaldor's insistence on a difference between production costs and selling costs that permits him to conclude that if "the concentration is not justified by the existence of economies of large-scale production . . . concentration brought about by advertising is definitely harmful."[46] So, far from having justified their criticisms of advertising by demonstrating its monopolistic character, it turns out, not entirely to our surprise, that the "critics of advertising are really attacking the competitive process."[47]

WASTE, CONSUMER SOVEREIGNTY, AND ADVERTISING

Although the broader normative aspects of the competitive process will be taken up separately in a later chapter, it seems desirable to discuss here some of the questions raised in the literature concerning the net effect of advertising on economic

45. We recognize, of course, that entrepreneurial alertness may permit the achievement of a position of temporary monopoly. See further on this above, p. 133, and below, p. 208.
46. Kaldor, "Economic Aspects of Advertising," p. 119.
47. Backman, *Advertising and Competition*, p. 32.

welfare. These questions turn out to involve many of the issues we have examined in this chapter. Although I will reserve for later treatment, then, the general discussion of the possible usefulness of the competitive process, let me pause to point out how the insights gained in this chapter relate to several specific problems concerning advertising.

Many economists and social critics have argued that advertising is economically harmful on many grounds. My present concern is with that class of criticisms which indicts advertising as involving *waste*. Although these criticisms take various forms, for my purpose it will be convenient to point out that most of the objections rest upon a common premise — that in paying a price for a product sufficiently high to include the advertising expenditures committed to its marketing, the consumer is paying more than the lowest cost necessary to ensure its availability. It is the identification of this common basis for this class of criticisms, which demands that we relate these criticisms to the earlier discussions of this chapter.

In perhaps its simplest form, the criticism that advertising wastes resources rests directly on Marshall's classification of advertising as either "constructive" or "combative." [48] If an advertising message is branded as not being "constructive," as not providing the consumer with information or some other service increasing the usefulness of the product to the consumer, then it has been stamped wasteful by definition. Thus all "combative" advertising, engaged in purely to anticipate or counter the activities of competitors, is viewed as obviously wasteful. [49] This alleged waste in advertising is seen as most blatant in cases where, in oligopoly situations, firms advertise only because their rivals are advertising. In Kaldor's words (paraphrasing Pigou), "it would be a sheer waste if advertising by one firm led to the adoption of similar advertising by its

48. Marshall, *Industry and Trade*, pp. 304–7.
49. See Pigou, *Economics of Welfare*, pp. 196–200; K. Rothschild, "The Wastes of Competition," in *Monopoly and Competition and Their Regulation*, ed. E. H. Chamberlin (London: Macmillan, 1954), pp. 305–6.

rivals, since the advertising efforts of the various firms would largely cancel each other out, leaving the sales, etc., of particular firms pretty much as they were." [50] Professor Backman has pointed out that where criticisms of advertising are aimed at apparent duplication of effort what is being attacked is really typical of competition in general. "Competition," he remarks, "involves considerable duplication and 'waste.' The illustrations range from the several gasoline stations at an important intersection to the multiplication of research facilities, the excess industrial capacity which develops during periods of expansion, and the accumulations of excessive inventories." [51]

Perhaps the more serious form of indictment against advertising as wasteful revolves more explicitly around the role of advertising (as well as other kinds of selling effort) in changing consumers' tastes. It is this kind of attack upon advertising (and upon the market system which permits and encourages its emergence) which is most frequently offered in popular discussion. Critical emphasis on the persuasive role of advertising has assumed various forms. In the Marxist view of contemporary capitalism its "significance stems from its promoting a continual enlargement of the economy's unproductive sector, from its constituting one of the most powerful devices for the propagation of artificial obsolescence and irrational differentiation of consumer goods." [52] It has of course been J. K. Galbraith who has most insistently argued that advertising, among other aspects of affluence, makes a mockery of the notion that a price system efficiently serves the wants of consumers. It is not true, Galbraith asserts, that independently determined consumer

50. Kaldor, "Economic Aspects of Advertising," p. 116. See also J. K. Galbraith, *The New Industrial State* (Boston: Houghton Mifflin, 1967), pp. 214–5; R. M. Solow, "A Comment on Marris," *The Public Interest,* no. 11 (Spring 1968), pp. 48–49.

51. Backman, *Advertising and Competition*, p. 32.

52. P. A. Baran, "Reflections on Underconsumption," in *The Allocation of Economic Resources,* ed. Abramovitz et al. (Stanford, Calif.: Stanford University Press, 1959), p. 59. See also P. Baran and P. Sweezy, *Monopoly Capital* (New York: Monthly Review Press, 1966), chap. 5.

desires dictate the pattern of production. The "institutions of modern advertising and salesmanship . . . cannot be reconciled with the notion of independently determined desires, for their central function is to create desires — to bring into being wants that previously did not exist."[53] That the resulting market process is wasteful follows, in Galbraith's view, as soon as it is recognized that the scarce resources of society that are thus devoted to producing goods for which consumers have little independent desires (and which can be sold only after the allocation of massive amounts of additional resources to arouse consumer interest) are so devoted at the expense of the starved public sector of the economy.[54] More generally, the persuasive aspects of advertising have been cited as virtually destroying the notion of consumer sovereignty.[55] The volume of resources devoted to placing a product before the consumer so as to ensure that he will purchase it may bear no relation to the urgency with which the consumer would, in the absence of the allocation of these same resources, have desired that product. (Where a consumer is unable to afford the products for which his desire has been thus artificially aroused, the resulting dissatisfaction has been labeled by one writer "psychological waste.")[56]

These criticisms, it will be observed, appraise the consequences of advertising activity (*a*) against the background of the tastes of consumers, as these tastes were reflected in the demand curves of consumers before that advertising activity, and (*b*) on the assumption that these tastes were already, before that activity, known to relevant decision-makers. If one chooses to evaluate efficiency only against the yardstick of con-

53. J. K. Galbraith, *The Affluent Society* (Boston: Houghton Mifflin, 1958), p. 126.
54. Ibid., p. 205.
55. See the discussion in J. Rothenberg, "Consumers' Sovereignty Revisited and the Hospitability of Freedom of Choice," *American Economic Review* 52 (May 1962): 278–81.
56. Rothschild, "Wastes of Competition," p. 306.

sumer wants "independently determined," as expressed in the demand curves before advertising, and if one moreover assumes that these wants are fully and costlessly known to all relevant market participants without advertising, then indeed it follows that the resources devoted to advertising are wasted, since they cannot improve the allocation of resources from the point of view of the relevant consumer demand. Moreover, to the degree that advertising alters consumer choice, the resulting allocation of resources between products must be inefficient and wasteful, as judged by the demand pattern declared to be relevant. The earlier discussions should have made clear, however, how arbitrary these crucial assumptions are. And as soon as one is prepared to relax one or another of them, one is forced to conclude that the case which charges advertising with waste remains unproved.

To measure the efficiency of resource allocation by the yardstick of the consumer-demand patterns that prevailed before advertising, it is necessary to assume, first, that the "product" has not been improved by the advertising activity and, second, that the consumer tastes that prevailed before the activity are in some sense more important or a more accurate reflection of the truth than those evinced after that activity. Our discussion of the invalidity of the production cost–selling cost dichotomy has set forth the arbitrariness of the first assumption. The arbitrariness of the second assumption too has, as we shall see, been pointed out by several writers.

In order to argue that advertising is wasteful in the sense outlined here, it is not sufficient to arbitrarily adopt the preadvertising pattern of consumer demand as a yardstick (as under point *a* above); it is also necessary to assume (as under point *b* above) that advertising plays no role in the market process by which a given pattern of consumer demand determines resource allocation. This would be the case if, as in a world of perfect, costless knowledge, we were assured of instantaneous market equilibrium. As soon as one concedes the existence of imperfect knowledge and of the role, as outlined in this chapter, of advertising in the entrepreneurial-competitive process through which adjustments in the allocation of resources are achieved, the case against advertising collapses.

The view (represented above by passages from Baran and from Galbraith) that advertising is significant primarily in altering consumer tastes is based on the premise that no significant services to the consumer (as measured by his prior tastes) are provided by advertising. This premise underlies the judgment that the "rightward shift of 'the' demand curve" that is induced by advertising represents not any alteration in the "package" being offered to consumers, but only a change in the eagerness with which consumers desire given packages. Advertising, in this view, adds nothing of value to the information possessed by the consumer, or to the prestige and glamour he associates with the product. If an advertised perfume is in fact a "different" perfume from the "same" perfume unadvertised, than clearly it would be inappropriate to use the demand curve for the unadvertised perfume to measure the volume of social resources warranted for the production of the advertised perfume. To insist on the relevance of only the "unadvertised" demand curve must be to *assume* that advertising leaves the "product" unchanged. The discussions in this chapter have emphasized that in the absence of arbitrary judgments of value no such view can be maintained. (At least some of the writers arguing that advertising destroys the notion of consumer sovereignty have been frank in their willingness to make the value judgments necessary to support their argument. Baran and Sweezy excoriate modern economists for regarding "whatever is produced and 'freely' chosen by consumers" as the only relevant output, with all costs incurred in the process considered necessary. "From this starting point," they concede with evident disgust, "it is only logical to reject as unscientific any distinction between useful and useless output, between productive and unproductive labor, between socially necessary costs and surplus.") [57]

At the same time, the Galbraithian view of advertising as responsible for a "wasteful" disregard by producers of the "true" wishes of the public involves, besides the assumption that advertising does not alter the product, the additional assumption that the "really" important needs of the public are those which they would have expressed independently of advertising. This view, too, has been sharply criticized. As Professor Bergson has insisted, "the fact that changes in tastes are induced by advertising does not in itself mean that the changes are for the worse." [58] Demsetz has pointed out that Galbraith's attack on the practice of economists' taking consumer wants as given "creates confusion between the scientific sense in which wants are taken as given (it makes no difference whatsoever whether we know that these wants stem from hidden persuaders, hunger, or mother's breast) and the normative sense, in which wants are judged to be moral or immoral." [59] Hayek has criticized the illogic of concluding, as Galbraith suggests, that merely because a want might not be experienced spontaneously by the individual if left to himself, it must therefore be neither real nor important. [60]

From the point of view developed here, the objections to elevating the demand pattern, as it would have been without advertising or other selling effort, into the yardstick against which the efficiency of producer performance is to be appraised

57. Baran and Sweezy, *Monopoly Capital*, p. 134. See also T. Scitovsky, "On the Principle of Consumers' Sovereignty," *American Economic Review*, vol. 52 (May 1962), for the position that once one grants that consumers' tastes are *not* independent of the economic environment, explicit value judgments *must* be introduced into any evaluation of the operation of the market.

58. A. Bergson, "The Doctrine of Consumer Sovereignty: Discussion," *American Economic Review* 52 (May 1962): 284.

59. H. Demsetz, "The Technostructure, Forty-Six Years Later," *Yale Law Journal* 77 (1968): 802; at p. 810.

60. F. A. Hayek, "The Non-Sequitur of the 'Dependence Effect,'" *Southern Economic Journal* 27 (April 1961): 346–48.

can be stated even more forcefully. I have been at pains to distinguish a "Robbinsian" production decision (i.e., a decision to produce a preselected product for which the demand is assumed to be given and known, quite apart from the production decision) and the "entrepreneurial" production decision, in which the decision itself includes selecting the product to be produced, simultaneously with estimating the strength of the demand for it. In Robbinsian production decisions, it is perhaps possible to view fabrication costs apart from their effectiveness in evoking consumer demand. In the entrepreneurial production decision, we saw, fabrication costs (just as much as advertising costs) must be seen as undertaken to evoke an anticipated consumer demand. When we speak of consumer sovereignty, of production patterns dictated by the pattern of consumer demand, we can only mean that production decisions are determined by entrepreneurial anticipation of the patterns of demand that will be evoked by alternative production plans. These patterns of demand, we must remember, are those entrepreneurs *anticipate* will be caused by alternative opportunities they might place before consumers (in a manner capable of ensuring their awareness of the opportunities available.) The only consumer wants that can be considered relevant for a discussion of the efficiency of production decisions, then, are those that are manifested *after* production decisions have placed opportunities before consumers (in a manner securing their attention.) It is the failure to perceive this which vitiates all those Galbraithian discussions of the fallacy — to which economists are allegedly subject — of taking consumer wants as given, when in fact, these discussions insist, consumer wants are modified by the very process of production supposedly designed to cater to them. What vitiates these discussions is the quite incorrect belief (for which economists are certainly to blame) that the demand curves which help determine production decisions in the theory of the firm (and which thus presumably support the doctrine of consumer sovereignty) are given and known apart from the production decisions. As soon as we recognized that these are anticipated, entrepreneurially guessed curves, it becomes apparent that (except in equilibrium, where product qualities have already settled) the only sense in which we can consider production as responsive to demand is that which perceives entrepreneurs striving to anticipate the demand for what they will produce, as this demand will be manifested *after* production has taken place.

It was Chamberlin, in introducing curves of selling cost to the geometry of the theory of the firm, who perhaps helped most to perpetuate the error which has trapped Galbraith and those who have shared his views. Chamberlin assumed it was possible to superimpose the curve of selling costs upon the diagram (showing a firm's revenues and production costs) *without changing the quantity axis in that diagram.* This treatment reflected Chamberlin's postulation of a clear-cut distinction between production costs and selling costs, with the latter viewed as not altering the product. As soon as one recognizes the possibility that "selling costs" may change the quality of the product, one realizes, of course, that the demand curve facing the firm may have to be redrawn entirely, on a different set of axes, for each level of selling costs (depending on the entrepreneurially selected character of the selling effort for which these costs are incurred).[61] In other words, the revenue curves that

61. In his incisive refutation of Chamberlin's excess-capacity doctrine, Demsetz ("The Welfare and Empirical Implications of Monopolistic Competition," *Economic Journal* 74 [September 1964]: 623–41), bases his criticism of Chamberlin's welfare conclusions upon the insight that if consumers are willing to pay a higher price for more expenditure on location, quality, and promotional costs, then we must assume that they derive some utility from these cost expenditures. Demsetz fails to recognize that this denial of the Chamberlinian position (which maintains that selling costs leave the "product" unchanged) at the same time invalidates the Chamberlinian geometrical analysis which Demsetz is using to expound his refutation. For further discussion on the geometry of demand curves in the presence of selling effort, see E. H. Chamberlin, "Advertising Costs and Equilibrium," in his *Towards a More General Theory of Value* (London: Oxford University Press, 1957); F. A. Hahn, "The Theory of Selling Costs," *Economic Journal* 69 (June 1959): 293–

are considered by the entrepreneur-producer in conjunction with his cost curves are those he estimates will prove relevant after the proposed production plan is undertaken — with this plan understood to incorporate all the "selling" effort associated with it. Only in this sense can the doctrine of consumer sovereignty be maintained at all — except in the context of the equilibrium state.

It seems difficult to understand what criterion for the efficiency of production can be considered relevant *other* than one which measures the success with which accomplished production plans conform to postproduction tastes. After all, the demand that is expressed in the demand curve for a product *means* the quantities of it that consumers will be prepared to buy, at given prices, *when offered the opportunity of doing so.* It does not refer to the present desire of consumers for a hypothetical product not yet produced. *Of course* one cannot rule out the possibility that the selected production plans themselves modify tastes; surely, for this very reason, the efficiency of production plan selection can be appraised only against postproduction tastes. A market system in which entrepreneurial production plans are necessarily geared to the anticipated wants of consumers seems entirely capable of being judged in terms of the relevant norm. One may indeed adopt as one's own arbitrary standard of normative judgment for the market the pattern of needs that one believes relevant to a given set of consumers, or the pattern of wants that one believes these consumers themselves would have manifested under some other set of production plans. But one cannot, on the basis of logic, criticize others who do not happen to share these beliefs, or who wish to refrain entirely from introducing their own beliefs into their appraisals of the market.

312; R. Heiser and C. Soper, "Demand Creation: A Radical Approach to the Theory of Selling Costs," *Economic Record* 42 (September 1966): 384–96; R. J. Ball, "Classical Demand Curves and the Optimal Relationship between Selling Costs and Output," *Economic Record* 44 (September 1968): 342–48.

Closely related to these critical comments on using preadvertising demand curves to evaluate market efficiency is the criticism, referred to earlier, that must be directed against the assumption that, without advertising, all consumer tastes are already fully known to the relevant potential decision-makers. The truth is that until equilibrium has been attained producers are forced to make guesses concerning the precise product qualities that will evoke consumer interest. The entrepreneurial-competitive process consists, as we have seen, of selecting by trial and error opportunities to be placed before consumers. The precise mix of physical qualities and "sales effort" that are combined in the opportunity-package which any one producer offers to consumers at a given time is the expression of his entrepreneurial estimate of consumer demand patterns. To ask for a market system without advertising is to ask for a system in which entrepreneurs are barred from experimenting with one enormous range of possibilities, through which to probe, explore, and discover the pattern of consumer demand.

To condemn duplicated (and apparently unnecessary) advertising effort on the part of two rivals [62] is to condemn the duplication that occurs generally during the competitive process. In calling such duplication wasteful one is presumably passing judgment from the perspective of assumed omniscience. In the absence of such omniscience, to criticize competitive duplication as wasteful is to criticize the very process through which the market assembles the entrepreneurial knowledge required to perceive the occurrence of waste. (We will return to this theme later in broader context.) As Rothschild has pointed out, competition "even in its most ideal *practical* form, is therapeutic, not prophylactic." [63] This surely requires us (unlike Rothschild himself) to ascribe any resulting waste-

---

62. We should not fail to notice that if advertising (or any other apparently duplicative effort) were in fact "unnecessary" there would arise incentive for merger to eliminate the incentives to engage in such effort.

63. Rothschild, "Wastes of Competition," p. 307.

fulness not to the competitive therapeutic process but to the imperfection of knowledge which that therapeutic process is to heal.

It will be useful, before concluding this chapter, to pay attention briefly to the neglected role of "buying effort" and its relation to the competitive determination of quality. Nothing in the discussions thus far has explained why advertising, say, should be engaged in by sellers rather than by buyers; nor have we considered how the costs expended upon buyer's advertising or other "buying effort" are to be treated.

Superficially, it might seem that our refusal to accept the classic Chamberlinian distinction between production costs and selling costs has created a difficulty in regard to buying costs. Were one, like Chamberlin, to consider selling costs as shifting the demand curve for a given product without changing the product, then one would be free to treat buying costs, quite similarly, as simply shifting the supply curve facing a potential buyer of an unaltered, given commodity or service. But our insistence upon the homogeneity of production costs and selling costs raises the question of what might seem an asymmetry between buying costs and selling costs. Although an impartial observer might be willing to accept our position that selling effort may in some way change the character of the opportunity placed before buyers, it must surely be a difficult task to convince him that buyer's advertising does anything else but increase the seller's interest in selling an unaltered product or service. More careful consideration will provide useful insights into the relevant relationships.

It will be helpful to consider, as an example, a case in which buying effort clearly provides a direct utility to the seller. Suppose an employer, in order to attract workers at lower wage rates than they can command elsewhere, improves the working conditions for his employees. Here we have an example of buying effort that is symmetrical with the effort a seller might put forth, say, in the form of free gifts to customers. And clearly this "buying effort" (which, since it provides obvious utility to workers, cannot be understood symmetrically with Chamberlinian selling costs) can be treated in two possible ways. We can continue to view the labor service purchased by the employer as unchanged by the improvements in working conditions (always assuming, of course, that no change in labor productivity is generated by these improvements). In this view the buying effort must be seen as providing a higher "wage" payment to workers. The expenditure upon improvements in working conditions is a form of wage supplement enjoyed directly by workers. To view the selling effort that takes the form of free gifts to customers in symmetrical fashion, one would say that these gifts do not represent any "improvement" in the commodity being sold to consumers, but constitute a "rebate" on the price paid. That is, the utility provided to consumers in the form of free gifts lowers the "net" price these consumers pay for an unchanged commodity.[64] There is nothing inherently unacceptable in this way of viewing these cases. However, the fact that this has *not* been the way we have treated selling effort thus far suggests that we consider an alternative perspective for buying effort.

Thus far we have treated selling effort by considering the free gifts offered to customers as an "improvement" in the quality of the total package offered for sale (in exchange for the money price being asked.) This suggests the symmetrical treatment of the buying effort which took the form of improving working conditions for employees. Such improvements can be considered as altering the worker's view of what he is

64. We should notice that this view of selling effort (which we have not been following in this chapter) is *not* Chamberlin's view. Chamberlin's view of pure selling effort requires him to restrict it to cases where *no* direct utility is thereby provided to customers besides that of "the" product.

being asked to sell for the money wages. In this view, the worker sees improved working conditions not as higher wages for a given quality of labor service, but as a reduction in the sacrifice that he, as seller, is called upon to make for given wages. He sees himself as working less dangerously, or in less disagreeable surroundings. The employer has sought to win him away from other employers by offering him the opportunity of *selling a different kind* of labor. From the employer's point of view, in this way of seeing things, we must treat the expenditures devoted to achieving the improvements in working conditions as a deduction from the gross revenue product made possible by his labor force. He has chosen to buy a lower "net" revenue product (i.e., lower than the revenue product from the same number of man hours would have been without the expenditures upon these improvements in working conditions) by choosing to buy a "different quality" of labor. The employer has selected that quality of labor which, in his entrepreneurial estimation, will provide him the greatest surplus of net revenue product over wage bill. His buying effort has succeeded in entrepreneurially "differentiating" that which he buys, in exactly the same way as selling effort "differentiates" entrepreneurially that which a producer offers for sale. Although this way of viewing buying effort is not necessarily "better" than that considered in the preceding paragraph, it does preserve the symmetry with the treatment of selling costs adopted in this chapter (at the same time sharing with the alternative treatment of the preceding paragraph the merit of not being bound by the classic Chamberlinian judgment that selling effort — and, by symmetry, buying effort — leaves unaltered the character of the opportunity being offered for sale [or asked to be sold]). And it should be apparent, once we have thus clarified how *this* kind of buying effort (that clearly provides utility to the seller) is to be treated, that we have no reason to treat *any* kind of buying effort differently. The same logic which showed us how arbitrary it was to treat selling effort as merely shifting the demand curve without providing utility to the consumer is sufficient to convince us that we have no right, without exercising arbitrary judgments of value, to treat buying effort which shifts supply curves to the right as not providing utility to sellers.[65]

Our discussion thus far further illuminates the quality-determining dimension of the entrepreneurial competitive process. It turns out, we have discovered, that the entrepreneur's role as buyer in the factor market is wholly symmetrical with his role as seller in the product market. In both markets he "constructs" the opportunities he places before the other (Robbinsian) mar-

65. The choice between the view of buying and selling effort adopted here and that described in the preceding paragraph does not involve any "real" difference. The choice arises from an ambiguity always present when we consider an opportunity available to an individual which necessitates certain sacrifices that are inseparable from his enjoyment of the opportunity. If "one pays fifty cents for the privilege of sitting on a hard chair (with the hardness viewed as a necessary evil), one may . . . alternatively say that one is sacrificing fifty cents plus the discomfort of sitting on a hard chair, for the privilege of sitting on a chair at all" (I. M. Kirzner, *An Essay on Capital* [Clifton, N.J.: A. M. Kelley, 1966], p. 100 n). Thus the utility provided to buyers in the form of selling effort can be viewed either (*a*) as lowering the net price, or (*b*) as increasing the utility of the commodity purchased. From the seller's point of view these alternatives mean (*a*) a reduction in net revenue received for the commodity, or (*b*) an addition to production costs. (See on this the literature cited above, chap. 4, n. 61). Similarly, the utility provided to sellers by buying effort can be viewed either (*a*) as increasing the "price" received by the sellers, or (*b*) as reducing the sacrifice sellers are being asked to make. These alternatives, from the side of buyers, appear as (*a*) an increase in factor outlay, or (*b*) a deduction from the factor revenue product. All this is highly relevant to the difficulties, noted in the literature (but by no means cleared up), that surround the task of defining a commodity. On this problem see G. J. Stigler, "A Theory of Oligopoly," *Journal of Political Economy* 72 (February 1964): 44 f; N. Georgescu-Roegen, "Chamberlin's New Economics and the Unit of Production," in *Monopolistic Competition Theory: Studies in Impact*, ed. R. E. Kuenne (New York: John Wiley, 1967), pp. 33–34; R. Triffin, *Monopolistic Competition and General Equilibrium Theory* (Cambridge: Harvard University Press, 1940), pp. 90 ff., 95; W. Nutter, "The Plateau Demand Curve and Utility Theory," *Journal of Political Economy* 63 (December 1955): 525–28; Clark, *Competition as a Dynamic Process*, pp. 98 f.

ket participants by shrewdly selecting among the opportunities which he perceives to be available, in each of these markets, to *him*. In both markets he competitively selects the opportunities he should construct. That is, he selects the price and quality dimensions of the opportunities he makes available to the others so they appear just more attractive than the opportunities he believes are made available by other entrepreneurs. The entrepreneur-producer discovers that in this way he can simultaneously offer opportunities in the factor market and in the product market, at terms that leave him with a profit. This consists in selecting a combination of *chosen* factor services to produce a *chosen* consumer product. These selections of factor quality and of product quality are made entrepreneurially and competitively; they involve the alertness needed to discover where factor services of the "right" quality are to be cheaply procured, and how they can be translated into the "right" product quality.

Moreover, the symmetry between the entrepreneur's roles in the product and factor markets extends further. In the product market, we found, the entrepreneurial function consists not merely in laying an opportunity before the consumer, but in ensuring his awareness of it. This accounted for competitive producer effort in communicating with the consuming public. In the factor market, too, the entrepreneur's function must surely include making factor owners aware of the opportunities to sell which he is prepared to offer them. Thus there is nothing so far to suggest that buying effort by entrepreneur-producers should necessarily be less vigorous than their selling effort.

(On the other hand, however, our discussion does suggest that buying effort by final consumers may well assume considerably more modest proportions. If one believes that producers have in fact assumed the major entrepreneurial role in the market [so that the analytical treatment of consumers and factor owners as Robbinsian is not wholly unrealistic], then the kind of entrepreneurial buying effort just described may be expected in factor markets, not in product markets.) [66]

My emphasis upon the symmetry of the entrepreneur's initiative in the market in which he buys and in the market in which he sells, and upon the corresponding symmetry in the way both product quality and factor service quality are determined by this competitive-entrepreneurial initiative, has been motivated in part by an apparent failure of the literature to acknowledge this symmetry.

In reviewing the Chamberlinian excess-capacity doctrine, Rothschild drew attention to the point made by Chamberlin himself, that, to the extent that consumers *prefer* extensive product differentiation, it is not legitimate to pronounce excess capacity waste. But on the other hand, Rothschild continues, where excess capacity arises from an employer's facing a supply curve of labor which is not infinitely elastic, "no modifying remarks are necessary when we characterize the resulting under-employment and under-production as waste." [67]

The truth, as we have seen, is that rising supply curves facing employers may involve "factor differentiation" in exactly the same way as do downward sloping demand curves facing producers. To the extent that workers prefer absence of uniformity in working conditions, say, it is as illegitimate to ignore these preferences as it would be to ignore consumer tastes for variety.

Moreover, the complete refutation of Chamberlinian excess-capacity doctrine that follows as soon as selling costs are properly incorporated into the analysis can be carried through, with complete symmetry, to cover cases where it might be asserted that excess capacity is generated by rising supply curves. As soon as buying costs are properly incorporated into the analysis, the necessity of excess capacity dissolves. The diagrams with

66. For further valuable discussion of the role of buyer initiative in product and factor markets, see Heflebower, "The Theory and Effects of Nonprice Competition," pp. 178–84.
67. Rothschild, "Wastes of Competition," p. 305.

which Professor Demsetz refuted the excess-capacity doctrine [68] by consistently adding selling costs to production costs) can be used, with appropriate symmetrical modification, to dispel the necessity of excess capacity following from rising factor supply curves (by deducting buying costs from revenue product).[69]

68. See H. Demsetz, "The Nature of Equilibrium in Monopolistic Competition," *Journal of Political Economy* 67 (February 1959):21–30, and idem, "Welfare and Empirical Implications of Monopolistic Competition." See also D. Dewey, "Imperfect Competition No Bar to Efficient Production," *Journal of Political Economy* 66 (February 1958): 24–33.

69. Of course the reservations expressed above, chap. 4, n. 61, to the diagrams used by Demsetz would apply with equal force to their analogues in the factor market.

|5|
The Long Run and
the Short

IN THIS CHAPTER WE TAKE UP AN ASPECT OF THE COMPETITIVE-entrepreneurial process to which I have so far alluded only briefly — the possibility of alternative long-run and short-run interpretations. This possibility, we shall discover in the next chapter, will be of great importance in the normative evaluation of the process. In addition, it provides fresh insights into the nature of the competitive-entrepreneurial process which are valuable in themselves. These follow naturally from the ideas developed in the preceding chapters and are complementary to them. The fact that in pursuing these insights we shall be forced to sharply criticize the orthodox position on the significance and the interpretation of the long-run–short-run distinction both justifies and calls for a careful statement of the issues involved.

THE LONG RUN AND THE SHORT RUN IN THE LITERATURE

Several quite different ideas have been represented in the literature under the description of "long run." Each of these uses of the term focuses attention on some more or less important aspect of microeconomic decision-making or the market adjustment process. Since in this chapter I will emphasize an *additional*, little-noticed aspect of the market for which the term "long run" seems appropriate, it is necessary to clearly review the existing uses of this term, so that the reader can perceive without ambiguity what I wish to emphasize in my own treatment.

1. The most common understanding of the term "long run" is that it refers simply to a time span of long duration. And economists have indeed frequently used the term in this sense. It will not be forgotten that in the long run, Keynes assured us, we are all dead. More important is that by the long-run consequences of a given policy or decision or event one means, in this usage, the consequences as they unfold over an unlimited time span. Short-run consequences, by contrast, refer to those consequences which reveal themselves within a relatively short period after the relevant decision or event.[1] It is according to this terminology, for example, that Stigler distinguishes between a short-run demand curve and a long-run demand curve, with the latter reflecting the responses to alternative prices, given all the time needed for full adjustment to these different prices.[2] For Marshall the meaning of the doctrine that "the normal . . . value of a commodity is that which economic forces tend to bring about *in the long run*" is that this is "the average value which economic forces would bring about if the general conditions of life were stationary for a run of time long enough to enable them all to work out their full effect."[3]

2. Closely connected with the preceding use of the term is the widespread distinction between long-run profits and short-run profits. Long-run profits are those calculated by an entrepreneur with a very long horizon, taking into account the full

1. Mises has pointed out that in working out the long-run consequences of changes in the data, shorter-run consequences are inevitably taken account of. "The long run analysis necessarily always fully includes the short run analysis" (*Human Action* [New Haven: Yale University Press, 1949], p. 649).

2. G. J. Stigler, *Theory of Price*, 3d ed. (New York: Macmillan, 1966), pp. 26 ff.

3. A. Marshall, *Principles of Economics*, 8th ed. (London: Macmillan, 1920), p. 347.

profile of receipt and outlay flows throughout this long prospective period. Short-run profits are those computed prospectively by ignoring all receipts and outlays that are anticipated only after some relatively far-off future date. It is around these concepts that the controversy concerning the realism of the profit-maximization hypothesis has revolved.[4] It is in terms of these concepts that writers have discussed alternative possible strategies for competing firms.[5] And it is the relevance of this distinction between the long-run goals and the short-run goals of the firm which Alchian has so severely criticized as eliminating "capital theory from the theory of the firm and from much of price theory."[6]

3. Another use of the term "long run," which is also closely related to the length of the time span permitted for adjustments to work themselves out, is in the traditional notion of "long-run costs." Whereas the traditional use of the notion depends heavily on the distinction between "fixed factors" and "variable factors," this distinction is expressed in terms of length of the period during which the producer is imagined to make his adjustments.[7] For Viner's cost curves the "short run" is a "period which is long enough to permit of any desired change of output technologically possible without altering the scale of plant, but which is not long enough to permit of any adjustment of scale of plant."[8] The "long run" is "a period long enough to permit each producer to make such technologically possible changes in the scale of his plant as he de-

4. See, e.g., F. Machlup, *The Economics of Sellers' Competition* (Baltimore: Johns Hopkins University Press, 1952), pp. 426 ff.

5. See, e.g., H. R. Edwards, *Competition and Monopoly in the British Soap Industry*, p. 51, and his reference to J. R. Hicks, "The Process of Imperfect Competition," *Oxford Economic Papers* 6 (February 1954): 45.

6. A. Alchian, "Costs and Outputs," in *The Allocation of Economic Resources*, ed. Abramovitz et al. (Stanford: Stanford University Press, 1959), p. 37.

7. On this see F. Machlup, *Essays in Economic Semantics* (New York: W. W. Norton, 1967), p. 52.

8. J. Viner, "Cost Curves and Supply Curves," *Zeitschrift für National-Ökonomie* 3 (September 1931): 26.

sires."[9] By using this notion of "long run" to qualify "costs," one is not referring to a more distant prospective horizon (as in "long-term profits"), nor to consequences that unfold as longer periods of time are permitted to elapse (as in "long-term demand"); one is referring, rather, to the range of options facing a producer who is assured of all the time needed to make any adjustment he might wish to introduce.

4. This traditional distinction between long-run costs and short-run costs in terms of fixed and variable factors has been strongly attacked by Alchian. "In fact," Alchian argues, "there is no such fixed factor in any interval other than the immediate moment *when all are fixed*. . . . There are no technological or legal restraints preventing one from varying any of his inputs. . . . The fact is that the costs of varying the inputs differ among inputs, and the ratios of these costs vary with the time interval within which the variation is to be made."[10] Alchian therefore proceeds to construct a distinction between short-run and long-run costs not on the basis of time periods during which some factors are fixed, but on the basis of the different costs a producer is called upon to incur as the time available for preparing to meet the new demand is varied.

5. Hirshleifer has proposed to preserve the conventional distinction between short-run costs and long-run costs by interpreting the fixity of inputs in the short run in a way Alchian has not considered. "What 'fixes' a fixed factor is not that you *cannot* vary it immediately if you desire, but that you do not *want* to vary it in response to only a temporary fluctuation in demand. . . . The more permanent a shift in demand is expected to be, the more "unfixing" of factors becomes rational and takes place."[11] In this usage the term "long-run costs" refers,

9. Ibid., p. 28.

10. Alchian, "Costs and Outputs," p. 33. See also L. DeAlessi, "The Short Run Revisited," *American Economic Review* 57 (June 1967): 450–61; R. E. Lucas, "Adjustment Costs and the Theory of Supply," *Journal of Political Economy* 75 (August 1967): 321–34.

11. J. Hirshleifer, "The Firm's Cost Function: A Successful Reconstruction?" *Journal of Business* 35 (July 1962): 250.

then, to the options as they appear to a producer who expects given market conditions to persist for a long time. (Hirshleifer's interpretation of the conventional distinction between long-run costs and short-run costs seems to coincide with that detailed a decade earlier by Machlup.) [12]

There can be no doubt that each of these uses of the long-run–short-run distinction draws our attention to significant aspects of market decisions and of their interaction in the marketplace. In drawing attention, during the remainder of this chapter, to a neglected distinction that might seem to fit naturally a terminology based on the "length of run," I am primarily criticizing earlier writers for failing to notice a significant aspect of the market process. At the same time, however, I will also be arguing that the "conventional" distinction between long-run costs and short-run costs seems to call out for a reformulation in terms of this other, neglected distinction.

ON SUNK COSTS AND THE SHORT RUN

The distinction I wish to emphasize can best be introduced in terms of the widely accepted concept of *sunk costs*. Sunk costs, it is recognized, are not costs at all from the point of view of the present. That is, where past, irretrievable expenditures were made, these expenditures should not and do not affect in the least any decisions being made now. Because bygones are bygones, sacrifices assumed in the past, which cannot be avoided by any course of action currently available, simply do not affect present choices between those alternative courses of action which are now available.

It follows, therefore, that where a firm finds itself with a given plant for which unavoidable obligations have been incurred, its present production decisions need (and ought) not take these obligations into account. Even if these obligations call for present money outflows from the firm, these outflows can in no way be considered costs in the "short run." That is,

12. Machlup, *Economics of Seller's Competition*, p. 40.

from the point of view of the firm with its given plant, efficiency in making decisions to produce does not require that these outlays now be taken into account. In terms of the economic concept of cost, these outlays are not costs at all; from this point of view, they involve no opportunity sacrifice whatsoever.[13]

Suppose, now, that one takes a unit of the final product produced by a firm and asks how much was sacrificed so it could be produced (either on an average or on a marginal basis). It should be apparent that at least two quite different answers can be given; that each of these answers is completely valid; and that in fact it is the ambiguity of the *question* which is responsible for the multiplicity of answers. To ask how much was sacrificed to produce a product is to refer to a point in time when the decision was made to undertake its production. But a product may have been produced through a *sequence* of decisions, the later decisions being made possible by the decisions already made. If so, it is entirely appropriate to ask, *with respect to each decision separately*, what the producer planned to sacrifice to obtain the product *at the time when that decision was made*. Thus, for any given product, an entire series of questions can validly be asked about the cost at which the product has been produced. And an entire series of different, equally valid answers to these questions must be given.

This multiplicity of cost measures is entirely appropriate to the purposes for which economists are concerned with costs in general. We are interested in cost of production, after all, in order to understand the alternative options facing prospective producers contemplating production decisions.[14] Each of these

13. See P. A. Samuelson, *Economics*, 8th ed. (New York: McGraw-Hill, 1970), p. 443; A. Alchian and W. R. Allen, *University Economics* (Belmont, Calif.: Wadsworth, 1964), p. 283; M. Friedman, *Price Theory* (Chicago: Aldine, 1962), p. 98; I. M. Kirzner, *Market Theory and the Price System* (New York: Van Nostrand, 1963), pp. 190 f.

14. For a discussion of the various possible approaches to the role of costs in economic theory see J. M. Buchanan, *Cost and Choice* (Chicago: Markham, 1969), especially chaps. 1–3.

options presents itself as an opportunity to receive revenue by
making the sacrifice required for production. To understand
the decision a producer makes at any given time, we must take
account of the relevant sacrifice involved. To explain the decisions made early in a lengthy process of production, (e.g., to
account for a decision to build a new shoe factory), one must
presume that the prospective flow of revenue from shoe sales
over the expected life of the factory is considered to more than
justify the present and prospective sacrifices (including, especially, the cost of factory construction) that the builder believes must be undertaken to produce that revenue flow. On
the other hand, to explain the decisions made much later in
the lengthy process of production (e.g., to account for the decision to operate the factory at a certain level of output), we
must presume that the relevant prospective revenue flow is considered to more than justify the sacrifices required for production once the factory is already constructed. The latter cost figure, as discussed, does not include the construction cost of the
factory.

It seems entirely natural to label the costs of production,
from the point of view of a prospective producer who has so
far taken *no* steps on the long road of production, as "long-run
costs." These costs, from his perspective, include all the sacrifices he sees himself as called upon to undertake, from the present until he has finally achieved his production goals. By contrast, it seems appropriate to label as "short-run costs" those
sacrifices which a producer sees himself as called upon to make
(in order to achieve his product) when he finds himself already
equipped with a factory. What makes these latter costs "short-
run costs," it will be observed, is not that the producer is not
free to "vary" his factory. As Alchian has argued, there is nothing to stop the producer from altering his plant input. And,
again, these are short-run costs not because of any pattern of
expectations that happen to be held by the producer, but because, with a portion of the lengthy process of production

already accomplished, the remaining distance until the final goal is that much shorter.[15] In fact, *each* stage at which decisions must be made during a long sequence of production decisions provides a different "run" of costs. The closer the decision is to the final output goal, the shorter the run of the relevant costs.

Our interpretation of the distinction between costs of shorter and of longer run is not unrelated to the common usage (cited above under point 1) in which the term long run refers to a span of time sufficient for all adjustments to take effect. As a matter of empirical fact, it is likely that the earlier steps in the sequences of production decisions (such as the construction of plant) will be undertaken relatively infrequently — precisely because once a factory has been constructed, it represents a costlessly available resource. Thus the effect of a change in long-run costs, such as an increase in plant construction, will be felt in the market only as longer and longer periods of time are considered. In the short run, only changes in short-run costs will manifest themselves in the form of changed output and price patterns.

It will be observed, moreover, that this interpretation of the distinction between long-run and short-run costs is in some respects similar to the common usage (cited in the preceding section under heading 2) distinguishing between long-run and short-run profits. In both usages, "long run" considerations require attention to the relevant magnitudes for the entire length of a prospective long period of time. However, it will be noticed that the "shortness" relevant to "short-run profits" is of a different kind from that relevant to "short-run costs." In the case of short-run profits it is imagined that, for some unexplained reason, the horizon of the firm is so near that the only receipts and outflows relevant to the calculation of profit are those anticipated in the near future. In the case of our short-

15. For a formulation of the long-run–short-run distinction in terms similar to these, see Alchian and Allen, *University Economics*, pp. 338–40.

run costs, on the other hand, the explanation for confining attention to the sacrifices anticipated during the near future only is a simple one — namely, that the production goal can in fact be achieved in the near future, since all necessary earlier steps have already been taken and call for no present sacrifice.

That earlier writers have generally overlooked this kind of distinction between long-run costs and short-run costs seems to reflect an unwillingness to accept the possibility of more than one answer to the question: "What did it cost to produce a given product?" Consequently, the difference between the long-run cost of producing a given product and its short-run cost has been sought in the different circumstances under which the product may be produced, such as the time available for production, or the kinds of expectations held when production is undertaken. For my part I have found it entirely understandable that the cost of producing a given product turns out to be of one magnitude when referred back to the earliest in a long past sequence of decisions and of a different magnitude when referred back to another decision in that sequence.

I will now try to show that the long-run–short-run distinction which we have identified in the context of costs is merely an example of a general and profoundly important aspect of the entrepreneurial-competitive process which has been almost completely ignored in the literature.

COSTS, PROFITS, AND DECISIONS

We can see the generality of the long-run–short-run distinction to which I have drawn attention by considering more carefully what is involved in a project that calls for a sequence of decisions (in which the earlier decisions are prerequisites for the later ones).

As has been discussed, the earlier decisions (insofar as they are made with an eye to the consequences of the entire sequence of future decisions which these earlier decisions make possible) call for comparing all the future positive consequences with all the future relevant sacrifices. For later decisions, the flows of positive consequences and sacrifices to be compared are short-run flows. When, in the course of time, the "profitability" of the project is being assessed, it is necessary to examine once again the comparative significance of the gains which have accrued from the project and of the sacrifices which were undertaken for its sake. And here we encounter in the context of profits what we have already discovered in the case of costs — that they cannot be treated in abstraction, but must be referred back to specific decisions.

Beginning students in the theory of the firm learn that in the short run it may be in the firm's interest to continue to produce even if revenues do not cover both "fixed" costs and variable costs. So long as revenue can more than cover variable costs, students are taught, the firm is better off producing. Sometimes this is explained by the statement that although the firm is indeed taking losses (because its revenues fall short of the sum of its fixed and variable costs), it would be suffering even larger losses were it to forgo the surplus of revenue over variable costs that is made possible by producing.

It should be apparent that this is not the most helpful way to explain why, so long as revenues exceed variable costs, it is advantageous to continue production. The truth, as we have seen, is that for the firm with given plant the "fixed" costs associated with the plant, are not present costs at all, since these outlays were unavoidably incurred in the past. For current, "short-run" decision-making they are not relevant sacrifices at all. From the point of view of such short-run decision-making it is *profitable* to produce, for the simple reason that prospective revenues from the sale of output promise to exceed the relevant short-run costs of production. It is at the same time true that this process of production must be judged to have been unprofitable from the point of view of the "long-run" decision made in the past to build the plant in the first place. From a "long-run" point of view (in which it is long-run costs that are to be compared with revenue) a particular batch of products may be seen as generating a revenue insufficient to cover costs; at the same time a shorter-run point of view (in which only short-run costs are relevant) may see the same revenue, generated by the same batch of products, as more than justifying the corresponding costs. The same project that is now seen as a losing proposition from the long-run point of view was profitable from the short-run perspective. Once we recognize that the profitability of a project can be assessed only in terms of the date of the decision setting that project into motion, it becomes entirely understandable that, where more than one decision was needed to complete the project, its "profitability" depends on the particular decision singled out for evaluation. The very same receipts that appear as surplus over costs, when costs are assessed from one vantage point, turn out to be needed (and possibly insufficient) to cover costs, when these are assessed from another vantage point.[16]

To sum up, we have discovered that, for profits as for costs, the very same events may qualify for quite different labels, depending on the point of view from which they are appraised. The possibility of events' being appraised from more than one point of view arises, we have seen, from the circumstance that these events are the outcomes not of a single decision, but of a sequence of indispensible decisions. Because each decision in the sequence was a prerequisite for the final outcome, the economic significance of that outcome can be evaluated in terms of each of these decisions separately. The outcome depended, indeed, on each of these decisions; each is seen to be "responsible" for the outcome and thus provides a legitimate and perhaps highly interesting vantage point from which to appraise what was accomplished.

I will now show how this same phenomenon — that the very

16. Clearly the distinction between long-run profits and short-run profits emphasized here must be sharply distinguished from that discussed above, pp. 188–89.

same events can be interpreted in quite different ways, depending on the "length of run" of the interpretation — extends to the competitive-entrepreneurial process generally. I will show that because market phenomena frequently represent the outcomes of long chains of decisions (each one a prerequisite for the later decisions), a market process which is seen as competitive from one point of view may turn out to be monopolistic when evaluated from a different vantage point. This highly important insight is the real purpose of this chapter, and the discussions thus far are to be viewed as introductory.

ENTREPRENEURIAL DECISIONS, THE LONG RUN AND THE SHORT RUN

For this discussion I will, then, without apology use the terms long run and short run in the sense suggested by my treatment of costs and profits. A longer-run view will be one taken from the perspective of an earlier decision in a sequence (in which earlier decisions are prerequisites for later ones); a shorter-run view will be one taken from the perspective of a decision later in the sequence. With this terminology, and with the insights of the preceding sections in mind, let us now examine once again the nature of entrepreneurial decision-making.

It will be recalled that "pure" entrepreneurship involves a decision to buy in one market with the intention of reselling at a higher price in a second market. We have here a sequence of decisions in which the first, that to buy, is a prerequisite for the subsequent decision to sell. Clearly then, every completed entrepreneurial sequence can be appraised from a long-run point of view (i.e., from before the decision to buy) or from a short-run view (from the time just before the decision to sell). Where the entrepreneurial purchase and sale have been in the form of an arbitrage transaction, in which the commitments to buy and to sell are simultaneous, these two points of view will coincide completely. But where the final selling commitment has been made only *after* the decision to buy, there is scope in general for *different* interpretations of the entrepreneurial decision sequence, depending on whether one is adopting a long-run or a short-run perspective.

It will be recalled further that in a world of imperfect knowledge the activities of producers are almost invariably entrepreneurial. The decision to produce involves a decision to buy inputs in the factor market in order to sell the output (forthcoming from these inputs) at a profit in the product market. So long as entry is free, as we saw in chapter 3, an entrepreneur-producer is subject to the competition of other entrepreneur-producers. Only if the producer happens to be the sole owner of a necessary resource, so that entry by other entrepreneurs into his line of production is ruled out, is he able to monopolize his particular productive activity. The fact that he is the monopolist-owner of the essential resource, we found, diverts entrepreneurial activity into the production of other products (or at any rate into other methods of production). Let us consider now the possibility (mentioned toward the end of chapter 3) that a producer who is the unique owner of a particular resource won his monopoly position by buying up all the rights to that resource. Whereas during most of chapter 3 I considered monopolist-producers who "found themselves" unique owners of particular resources as a result of the initially "given" distribution of resources, I now wish to treat the case of a producer who has become the monopolist owner of a resource by virtue of his own entrepreneurial activity as resource buyer. Here we have a case where the possibility of different short-run and long-run interpretations of entrepreneurial activity becomes directly relevant.

The case I wish to consider is that in which an entrepreneur has bought all the available supply of a resource and then, having thus established himself in a monopoly position, proceeds to exploit that position through his production and product-pricing decisions. When one seeks to describe this entrepreneur's production and pricing decisions *from the point of view which takes his monopoly ownership of the resource as given,* one must describe them simply as the decisions of a monopolist. The producer's unique ownership of the resource provides him with some protection against the competition of other entrepreneurs who might seek to produce what he wishes to produce. Because entry into this particular productive activity is thus blocked to competing entrepreneurs, their competitive-entrepreneurial activity is diverted into other channels. The monopoly resource ownership of the producer has thus distorted the competitive market process. Because the resource monopolist is, to the extent made possible by his monopoly ownership position, protected against the competition of others, he may find it possible to secure a monopoly profit by restricting the utilization of his monopolized resource. All this seems the completely normal description of a monopoly situation, as analyzed in chapter 3.

But, our discussions earlier in this chapter have alerted us to the possibility that the very same events can be described in quite different terms, depending on the vantage point in time. In our present case, it should be apparent, we have before us yet another example of this possibility.

If we attempt to categorize the case in hand from the long-run point of view, that is, as of a date before the *acquisition by our "monopolist" of the entire supply of the essential resource,* things appear in a quite different light. Before our producer acquired unique control of resource supply, he was in no sense a monopolist. He was in no better position to make the desired product than any other potential entrepreneur-producer. Other producers could, if they wished, have purchased some (or all) of the resource supply and proceeded to make the product. Their failure to do so presumably reflects their failure to perceive the profitability of this line of production (i.e., they apparently not only did not see profit in producing part of the product supply, they did not even anticipate profit from uniquely controlling the supply). Our own producer, who wisely or unwisely bought up the entire resource supply, believed that its use in producing the product promised sufficiently high profits to make the venture worthwhile, at least as long as no one else possessed the resource. His entrepreneurial alertness in acquiring this resource ahead of his competitors is thus the basis of the subsequent course of events. Certainly his acquiring the resource, in a field which was freely open to all entrepreneurs, was a normal step in the undistorted competitive-entrepreneurial process. His subsequent unique position in the product market, when appraised from the point in time before he acquired the resource, appears exactly like the results of any other successful entrepreneurial step. The profits our producer is able to secure by exploiting his unique position appear, from *this* vantage point, to be entrepreneurial profits grasped in a competitive market by the most alert entrepreneur. The very same receipts which from the short-run point of view (taking its perspective from *after* the resource acquisition) appear as monopoly rents acquired by exploiting a unique resource ownership position turn out to be pure entrepreneurial profits (with *no* connection with the ownership of any resource) when traced back, from the long-run perspective, to the original entrepreneurial decision to which they must be attributed (i.e., the decision to purchase the resource). From the short-run viewpoint the producer's profits arise from his monopoly of the resource; from the long-run point of view these profits arise not from resource ownership but from the decision to acquire the resource.[17] Neither description is less

17. It must of course be emphasized that the long-run profits that provide this incentive for competitive entrepreneurship will be forthcoming only through the perceived possibility of monopolistic restriction. Thus it is this possibility that directs entrepreneurial attention to this particular opportunity. It might appear, moreover, that the entrepreneurial process should generate a tendency toward (profitless) resource monopoly, with competing entrepreneurs, intent upon capturing the monopoly position, bidding up the price (for the entire resource supply as a unit) to reflect the full value of the future monopoly profits. What operates to offset this tendency, of course, are the transactions and policing costs involved in

"true" than the other; from its own perspective each description is the only correct and relevant one.

It is instructive to compare the case just discussed with the case of an entrepreneur who, with no unique resource ownership and with entry into his line of production freely open, is yet the only producer of his product. In chapter 3 we insisted on withholding the monopolist label from this entrepreneur. I pointed out that the only reason for this entrepreneur's being the only producer of his product is the difference between his own entrepreneurial judgment and the judgments of other entrepreneurs. Others see no profit in his line of production; the producing entrepreneur, rightly or wrongly, believes that he has discovered a profitable activity. That the producing entrepreneur is the only seller of his product, that the demand curve which faces him is that of the entire market for the product, did not in any way qualify his activity as that of a monopolist. He is an entrepreneur who, in a wide-open competitive field, has perceived as profitable an activity which others have not so perceived.

It will be observed that in *that* case (the case of the entrepreneur who is the sole producer of a product *without* monopoly ownership of a resource) his activity is wholly competitive, not only from the long-run viewpoint but also from the short-run viewpoint. Not only was the entrepreneur facing open competition when he made the decision to acquire the resources for his product, he continues to face the same competition even after he has acquired the resources, since he has not acquired unique control over the entire resource supply. Should his activity turn out to be profitable, we can expect that

assembling and maintaining complete control over a resource with a widely scattered ownership. For a discussion of the inherent instability of cartels, see, e.g., Machlup, *Economics of Sellers' Competition*, pp. 477, 518 ff. See also D. Dewey, *Imperfect Competition: A Radical Reconstruction* (New York: Columbia University Press, 1969), pp. 119 ff.

sooner or later other entrepreneurs will enter the field and erode his entrepreneurial profits.

What distinguishes this latter case, then, from the case of the monopolist resource owner previously discussed is the possibility of future erosion of profits. With a resource monopolized for all time, the monopoly profits made possible by resource ownership cannot be whittled away by any competitive process. Although, as we have seen, the activity of the producer (with monopoly resource ownership) is to be described as wholly competitive from the long-run point of view, this does *not* mean that if we permit enough time to elapse his profits will be wiped out through any "long-run" process of competition. In this case, his superior entrepreneurial judgment will *not* lead to his decisions' being emulated, because this judgment has caused him to block others from duplicating his activity. All we can mean by describing the activity of the producer with unique resource ownership as wholly competitive from the long-run point of view is that there was nothing in the state of the market before he acquired the resource that inhibited the normal course of the entrepreneurial-competitive process (and that, indeed, his acquiring the resource was entirely consistent with that process). Of course, if the supply of the resource thus acquired can be expected to be periodically renewed (so that the producer has acquired only a temporary monopoly), then the freedom of entry which entrepreneurs have to the market for this resource will tend, given sufficient time, to eliminate all profits from this line of production (as for all lines of entrepreneurial endeavor.) It still remains true, however, that for the duration of the producer's resource monopoly he will be able to exploit his unique position without fear of competition from others producing exactly what he is producing, even though from the long-run point of view his profit is seen to be entrepreneurial profit won in a wholly competitive market.

A special case arises where entrepreneurial competition

in the resource market forces the price of the resource up to the point where its market value fully reflects the capital value of the stream of monopoly revenues to be obtained from its exploitation (so that, in spite of the successful bidder's acquisition of the total resource supply, his monopoly position no longer generates profits, as viewed from the long-run view).[18] We may think of a line of production characterized by pronounced economies of scale, so that production would be carried on most economically if a single firm produced for the entire market. Then vigorous entrepreneurial competition in the resource market might treat the entire resource supply as an indivisible unit and thus tend to bid up its price to eliminate subsequent profit. But the successful bidder would, once he has acquired the entire resource supply, still make his production decisions "monopolistically" — that is, in a manner restricting use of the monopolized resource so as to maximize the surplus of revenues over the outlays for the nonmonopolized resources used. (Were he *not* to do this, he would not only not be winning profits, in the long-run sense, he would actually be *losing* money, since the competition in the resource market has bid up the outlay for the monopolized resource to anticipate such a maximum surplus.)

This special case should be contrasted with that in which entry into a line of production characterized by powerful scale economies does *not* depend on prior possession of a particular resource. (We may think of a line of production that requires only resources available in such abundance throughout the market that they cannot be monopolized.) In such a case vigorous entrepreneurial competition can once again be expected to tend toward the emergence of a single producer. But in *this* case, the competition will not only tend toward the elimination of profit, it will do so without any of the resource underutilization that may be associated with resource monopoly.[19]

18. See also chap. 5, n. 17.
19. Demsetz has, in effect, criticized the "natural monopoly" argument

FURTHER OBSERVATIONS ON LONG-RUN COMPETITION AND
SHORT-RUN MONOPOLY

The literature does not often refer to the possibility that the activity of a monopolist producer may, from a longer-run point of view, be seen as wholly competitive. However, it has been noticed that a monopoly position may be won through competition and entrepreneurship. And it is interesting to observe how writers who have remarked on this have dealt with the phenomenon. Long ago, in a somewhat confusing passage, Schumpeter discussed the case in which a new entrepreneurial combination consists of a trust protected against outside competition. "The carrying out of the monopolistic organization is an entrepreneurial act and its product is expressed in profit. Once it is running smoothly the concern in this case goes on earning a surplus, which henceforth, however, must be imputed to those natural or social forces upon which the monopoly rests — it has become a monopoly revenue. Profit from founding a business and permanent return arc distinguished in practice; the former is the value of the monopoly, the latter is just the return from the monopoly condition." [20] This passage seems to distinguish between what happens at the time the trust is formed and what happens afterward. The formation of the trust is a profitable entrepreneurial act producing an immediate profit (which is the capitalized value of the future

for the regulation of utilities for overlooking this case (see H. Demsetz, "Why Regulate Utilities?" *Journal of Law and Economics* 11 [April 1968]: 55–66). As Demsetz points out (p. 58), his demonstration of the possibility of a single producer's emerging with prices no higher than costs of production assumes (as I have shown here in the text) free access to all necessary inputs. Where it takes time to duplicate a plant, a single producer possessing a plant is temporarily in a favored position. Thus the case of utilities may, at least for the short run, be judged more similar to the case considered in the preceding paragraph than to that discussed here.

20. J. A. Schumpeter, *The Theory of Economic Development* (Cambridge: Harvard University Press, 1934), p. 152. Triffin interprets this passage as making a distinction between "monopoly profit" and "monopoly revenue" (R. Triffin, *Monopolistic Competition and General Equilibrium Theory* [Cambridge: Harvard University Press, 1940], p. 163).

stream of monopoly revenues forthcoming from the trust). The later flow of monopoly revenues is simply the normal return on the resources and the social arrangements which have made these revenues possible. Writing much later, Schumpeter refers to the possibility of "an element of genuine monopoly gain in those entrepreneurial profits which are the prizes offered by capitalist society to the successful innovator." [21] But here he seems to refer to a *portion* of the total entrepreneurial profit as arising out of monopoly position (made possible by patented innovation). Samuelson, on the other hand, seems to have recognized that where there is freedom of entry to the possibility of securing monopoly profits (through patented innovation), the gains received, ex post, as monopoly profits, are from the ex ante view simply an inducement to creative entrepreneurial innovation.[22]

A particularly clear perception of the role of entrepreneurial competition in securing unique (if not monopolistic) positions is that presented by Heflebower. In his discussion of the differential market positions acquired by firms, Heflebower emphasizes that a firm's position defines the kinds of activity it is able to engage in, and that it encompasses differential attributes acquired by past skill and luck.[23] "Once a strong position as a differentiated seller has been achieved, it is like a well-designed fortification; if maintained and adapted to developments in usable means of defense, those challenging it . . . must have a far larger attacking force."

What emerges, then, from our discussions of long-run and short-run interpretations of monopoly, as well as from the references in the literature to the competitive acquisition of

21. J. A. Schumpeter, *Capitalism, Socialism, and Democracy* (New York: Harper and Row, 1962), p. 102.

22. P. A. Samuelson, "Intertemporal Price Equilibrium: A Prologue to the Theory of Speculation," *Weltwirtschaftliches Archiv* 79 (December 1957): 210.

23. R. B. Heflebower, "The Theory and Effects of Nonprice Competition," in *Monopolistic Competition Theory: Studies in Impact*, ed. R. E. Kuenne (New York: John Wiley, 1967), pp. 188–90.

superior positions, is a significantly enriched insight into the character of the entrepreneurial-competitive market process. At any given time the market presents an array of consumer tastes, a pattern of resource ownership, and a body of technological possibilities (by which resources can be utilized to satisfy consumer desires). With imperfect knowledge it is inevitable that in any given period of time the pattern of transactions and production processes being initiated in the market fails to fully reflect the realities of the market. The disappointments and regrets generated by experience in the market (as production and consumption plans are forced to confront the true facts of the market) force changes in these plans. The course of plan changes thus forced upon market participants is led by the alertness of entrepreneurs as they become aware of the existence of profit opportunities as yet untapped or of the loss potential of some of the existing patterns of activity. So long as entry is free, this competitive-entrepreneurial activity results in continually shifting qualities of products, methods of productions, and resource-hiring patterns, through the medium of changing prices bid and asked by entrepreneurs.

As was made clear in chapter 3, this market process is competitive in the sense that each opportunity, for buying or for selling, that a decision-maker makes available to the market is offered with full "entrepreneurial" awareness that it must be somewhat more attractive than the opportunities likely to be offered by others. With free entry to all resources, we found, the course of the market process generated by entrepreneurial competition will be governed by the speed with which the various alert entrepreneurs learn of the rival opportunities they must outstrip. As a special situation, we discussed the distortion introduced into this process by monopoly ownership of a resource. We explored the way such ownership may generate a pattern of production that deliberately underutilizes the monopolized resource, diverting the course of rival entrepreneurial activity into other channels.

The Long Run and the Short

Recognizing the need to examine monopoly situations not only from the short-run point of view but also from the long-run helps us to better understand this competitive-entrepreneurial process. In chapter 3 we saw monopoly situations as a consequence of the "given," not-to-be-explained natural distribution of resource ownership. Now we see that the course of entrepreneurial competition itself may again and again generate at least temporary patterns of resource ownership *preventing* subsequent entrepreneurs from immediately duplicating what the most alert entrepreneurs have discovered it is profitable to produce. Where, as will usually be the case, the monopoly resource ownership thus won is only temporary, the long-run view presents a wholly competitive picture, with the temporary profits won by the alert entrepreneurs sure to attract emulation that will sooner or later squeeze away all profits. (From the short-run view this case presents the alert entrepreneur as the beneficiary of a temporary monopoly position [24] which he can exploit for as long as his uniqueness lasts.) Where alert entrepreneurship has acquired *permanent* control of the rights to the entire supply of a resource, then we have the possibility of permanent resource monopoly (with permanent monopoly of relevant production processes) that, although immune to the profit-eliminating emulation of competing entrepreneurs, must yet be recognized as the consequence of freely competitive entrepreneurship. From both the positive perspective and (as we shall discuss in the succeeding chapter) the normative viewpoint, therefore, it is necessary to bear in mind the multifarious facets presented by market phenomena, as determined by the "length of run" of the vantage point adopted.

All this underlines the essential feature of the process of rivalrous competition (as opposed to the "competitive state" of orthodox equilibrium theory). The essence of this process is

24. In the literature temporary monopolies are sometimes identified as "short-run monopolies." See, e.g., Schumpeter, *Capitalism, Socialism and Democracy*, pp. 99, 102.

the entrepreneurs' perception of temporarily advantageous positions which are available for the snatching (through reallocating the utilization of resources). The "temporariness" of the advantage offered by any prospective entrepreneurial opportunity may, however, vary over a wide range. At one end of the spectrum of "temporariness" is the fleeting profit opportunity which, once perceived and exploited, almost immediately is copied by a mass of other entrepreneurs, so that its "advantage" is squeezed away almost instantly. With no resource "controlled" (for a period longer than that needed by other entrepreneurs to see what is going on) the process reveals no element of monopoly whatsoever.[25] Advantageous positions of somewhat lesser impermanence can be imagined as the time necessary to assemble the resources required for emulation lengthens. Depending on the technology of production, the market conditions surrounding resource acquisition, and the psychology of consumer demand, competing entrepreneurs may discover that even after they have discovered the secret of the pioneer entrepreneur's success his start has rendered him immune from their imitation for periods of various lengths. Sooner or later the entrepreneurial process will work its way; profits will sooner or later tend to dwindle. In these cases, what we have termed short-run monopoly positions turn out also to be merely temporary. Only at the other extreme of the spectrum, where the advantage secured by an alert entrepreneur can be imagined to give him *permanent* control over a needed resource, can what we have termed short-run monopoly also be conceived of as permanent. Rivalrous competition consists of exploiting temporary advantages. The staggering variety of possible situations, accompanied by entrepreneurial positions with advantages of so many different degrees of impermanence, is able to account for the complexity of the real world of produc-

25. Contrast the statements in the literature associating every entrepreneurial innovation with monopoly, e.g., F. H. Knight, "An Appraisal of Economic Change: Discussion," *American Economic Review* 44 (May 1954): 65. See also above, chap. 3, n. 26.

tion. Perceiving the workings of entrepreneurial competition through these complexities requires an awareness not only of the temporariness of entrepreneurial advantage, but also of the difference between short- and long-run comprehension of the market process.

This discussion thus further supports my unhappiness with the treatment orthodox price theory (especially where derived from the theory of monopolistic competition) accords to such phenomena as advertising, product differentiation, and role of capital requirements as blockages to entry. As I have noted in earlier chapters, these phenomena have almost invariably been identified as monopolistic elements in the market. We have insisted on recognizing that advertising and product differentiation are strategic weapons in the competitive arsenal of rivalrous entrepreneurs. The acquisition of advantageous entrepreneurial position through advertising or other techniques of product differentiation is undertaken without any *prior* advantageous position, and is thus wholly competitive. The temporary advantage thus secured is not merely competitive in this "longer-run" view of the process; it is further competitive in the sense that competitors, as soon as they learn of the opportunities to be gotten through these techniques, are free to move in immediately to share these possibilities — and thus eliminate them. (Where, moreover, earlier investments have been made in inventory, or specialized productive equipment, selling activity may be seen as "short-run" exploitation of the sunk capital so represented.)

Large-scale capital requirements are frequently cited as a blockage to entry and thus a powerful cause of monopoly.[26] For us such requirements are temporary advantages held by existing firms as a result of the costlessness of sunk capital and the time necessary to accumulate competing capital complexes. Further,

26. For discussion see J. Bain, *Barriers to New Competition* (Cambridge: Harvard University Press, 1956), chaps 3, 5. See also G. J. Stigler, "Imperfections in the Capital Market," *Journal of Political Economy* 75 (June 1967): 287–92.

we insist on remembering that the incumbent firms, who at one time undertook to assemble the capital sunk, did so without prior advantage. Not only will competition of new firms (even with powerful economies of scale) force the incumbent firms, sooner or later, to follow policies geared toward eliminating profits, but even the temporary advantage enjoyed by the pioneer firms is to be recognized (from the long-run view) as originating in wholly competitive entrepreneurship exercised by farsighted pioneers. We will return in chapter 6 to a normative examination of some of the issues raised by the insights of the present chapter.

|6|
Competition, Welfare, and Coordination

THE EARLIER CHAPTERS HAVE BEEN DEVOTED TO THE POSITIVE
theory of the competitive-entrepreneurial process. The major
theme has been the identification of this process as the central
characteristic of the market economy. To understand the operation of a market economy, we have argued, it is necessary to
pay attention not to the conditions required for market equilibrium but to the systematic changes we can expect to be
generated in a market in which these conditions are not fulfilled. Emphasis on the market process rather than on market
equilibrium has enabled us to perceive the role of entrepreneurship and to recognize the essentially competitive character of
the market process. By pursuing this line of thought we have
gained fresh insight into a number of important features of the
market system. But our discussions have so far not sought to
do more than depict the positive aspects of the market process;
no attempt has been made to evaluate it in terms of the norms
usually adopted by economists, such as the system's ability to
"allocate social resources efficiently" or to "maximize the welfare of society" and the like. In this chapter I will evaluate
normatively the competitive-entrepreneurial process which I
have shown to characterize the market economy. We shall
discover that our emphasis on the market process rather than
on the conditions for market equilibrium suggests a similarly

unorthodox approach to the task of evaluating the market economy. And it is the fact that my dissatisfaction with the approach adopted by orthodox welfare theory stems from an awareness of the importance of the market process which justifies the inclusion of this present chapter.

THE FUNDAMENTAL FLAW IN WELFARE ECONOMICS

The basic weakness inherent in the orthodox approach to the analysis of welfare was pointed out with complete clarity by Hayek over a quarter of a century ago. A careful examination of Hayek's criticism — a criticism that unfortunately has remained virtually unnoticed — will help us relate his central point to the theme of this book.

In the standard approach to welfare theory, Hayek explains, the problem to be solved is finding the best use of available resources *on the assumption that we possess all the relevant information concerning the given system of preferences and the various means available.* This problem is a purely logical or mathematical one; its solution is implicit in the assumptions that identify it. And it is this identification of the problem which, Hayek argues, renders the entire approach almost wholly unhelpful.

This . . . is emphatically *not* the economic problem which society faces . . . the "data" from which the economic calculus starts are never for the whole society "given" to a single mind which could work out the implications and can never be so given. . . .
The peculiar character of the problem of a rational economic order is determined precisely by the fact that the knowledge of the circumstances of which we must make use never exists in concentrated or integrated form but solely as the dispersed bits of incomplete and frequently contradictory knowledge which all the separate individuals possess. The economic problem of society is thus not merely a problem of how to allocate "given" resources. . . . It is rather a problem of how to secure the best use of resources known to any of the members of society, for ends whose relative importance only these indi-

viduals know. Or, to put it briefly, it is a problem of the utilization of knowledge which is not given to anyone in its totality.[1]

From Hayek's critique of orthodox welfare economics must flow, almost directly, sharp disagreement with the way it perceives the market, or for that matter any social system of economic organization (and thus the terms in which its performance is evaluated). To orthodox welfare economics, with its attention focused upon the mathematical solution to the social allocation problem with all information given, the market's social role is a social computational device. Its success is measured by the closeness with which it yields the correct solutions to the equation system identifying optimum allocation.[2] For Hayek, on the other hand, "if we want to understand [the market's] real function," it is necessary to see it not as a computer, but as "a mechanism for communicating information"[3] — as a social instrument for mobilizing all the bits of knowledge scattered throughout the economy.

Hayek's critique of the market-as-computer view is thus directed at its total unawareness of the very existence of the problem of social mobilization of knowledge. Much of this chapter will be devoted to the role of the competitive-entrepreneurial process in marshaling the information scattered through society. Again and again we will discover that orthodox welfare analysis calmly assumes that the critically important social task of making all the scattered bits of information available to those making decisions has already been performed. In particular, we will discover, orthodox price theory's consistent lack of attention to the role entrepreneurship plays in the positive analysis of market operation is matched by orthodox welfare

1. See F. A. Hayek, "The Use of Knowledge in Society," *American Economic Review* 35 (September 1945): 519–30; reprinted in his *Individualism and Economic Order* (London: Routledge and Kegan Paul, 1949), pp. 77–78.

2. On the literature reflecting this view of the market as a "computer," see also J. M. Buchanan, "What Should Economists Do?" *Southern Economic Journal* 30 (January 1964): 213–22.

3. Hayek, "Use of Knowledge in Society," p. 84.

economics' parallel obliviousness to the function of the entrepreneurial process in mobilizing available information.

At the same time, the orthodox welfare view of the market as computer has, at least by implication, been sharply criticized from a quite different angle. In appealing for economists to adopt a "catallactic" view, rather than their present allocation-of-resources perspective, Buchanan has pointed out that the latter perspective "prejudges the central issue that has been debated in theoretical welfare economics," assuming the legitimacy and meaningfulness of the notion of "social welfare." [4] The notorious (and inevitable) failure of modern welfare economics to overcome the problems raised in interpersonal comparisons of utility has, quite simply, invalidated all attempts to evaluate the market in terms of resource-allocation norms. And it is here, as we shall see, that the economic problem identified by Hayek offers a scope for normative discussion that is not vulnerable to this kind of criticism. And, although the "catallactic" alternative urged by Buchanan (instead of the orthodox allocation-of-resources point of view) does not explicitly raise the question of the social mobilizing of available information, we shall discover that it can be interpreted in a manner that renders Hayek's "economic problem" directly relevant.

KNOWLEDGE, COORDINATION, AND ENTREPRENEURSHIP

In accepting any existing distribution of assets as a basis for subsequent normative discussion, it is fundamental that any exchange freely entered into between two parties will, in the best prospective judgment of the parties concerned, "improve" the position of each. Now for an exchange transaction to be completed it is not sufficient merely that the conditions for exchange which prospectively will be mutually beneficial be present; it is necessary also that each participant *be aware* of his opportunity to gain through the exchange. In standard welfare

4. Buchanan, "What Should Economists Do?" p. 215.

economics an Edgeworth box-diagram is used to show that wherever the indifference curves of the two parties intersect, scope for mutually beneficial exchange is present. It is usually assumed without further discussion that where such scope is present, exchange will in fact occur (barring obstacles arising from the possible range of indeterminacy). In fact, of course, exchange may fail to occur because knowledge is imperfect, in spite of the presence of the conditions for mutually profitable exchange.

We notice immediately that where the conditions for exchange in fact exist but are not exploited owing to ignorance there now exists scope for profitable entrepreneurship. If A would be prepared to offer as much as twenty oranges for a quantity of B's apples, and B would be prepared to accept, in exchange for his apples, any number of oranges greater than ten, then (as long as A and B are each unaware of the opportunity presented by the attitude of the other) entrepreneurial profit can be secured by buying B's apples at a price (in oranges) greater than ten and then reselling them to A for a price less than twenty.

We notice further than where an unexploited mutually beneficial exchange opportunity for A and B exists, the resulting "inefficiency" can be described as an *absence of coordination*. That is, we need not say that failure of exchange to occur is responsible for a failure to increase social welfare (as defined, say, in terms of Pareto-optimality criteria). We need not say anything about social welfare at all. We can simply say that an absence of coordination, arising out of ignorance, characterizes the actions of A and B. By A's not buying B's apples, and by B's not selling them to A, each party is, because of ignorance of the other's "existence," acting as if the other did not in fact exist. A knows his own taste and assets; B knows *his*. But because these bits of *knowledge* are not coordinated, the *actions* taken by A and B are uncoordinated. *It is possible to evaluate a system of social organization's success in promoting the coor-*

dination of the decisions of its individual members without invoking any notion of social welfare at all.

In a market economy at any given time, an enormous amount of ignorance stands in the way of the complete coordination of the actions and decisions of the many market participants. Innumerable opportunities for mutually beneficial exchange (including production as an avenue for exchange) are likely to exist unperceived.[5] Each of these opportunities also offers an opportunity for entrepreneurial profit. Each of the potential parties to each of these unexploited exchange opportunities is, as a result of the imperfection of knowledge, losing some possible benefit through the absence of coordination represented by this situation. The normative question raised by Hayek is how well the market succeeds in bringing together those uncoordinated bits of information scattered throughout the economy. Successful coordination of these bits of information cannot fail to produce coordinated activity — exchange — benefiting both parties.

Orthodox price theory is unable to help with this normative question. By setting up its analytical apparatus on the assumption of perfect knowledge, with consumers aware of all purchase possibilities, with resource owners aware of all selling possibilities, and with firms aware of all possible cost and revenue conditions, orthodox price theory has assumed away those circumstances in which this kind of normative evaluation is possible. The world of market equilibrium cannot be judged on its success in coordinating scattered driblets of information; ignorance is simply assumed not to exist. For such a world it is only natural to expect welfare analysis to be confined to an appraisal of how closely it approximates the conditions for optimality. Such a world exhibits no ignorance, no absence of coordination, no opportunities for entrepreneurial profit, and,

5. The possible arrays of such unexploited opportunities make relevant, of course, the welfare analysis of Pareto-optimality. The role of such analysis, and the difference between it and the normative approach advanced here, have been made clear in the text.

in fact, no entrepreneurs at all. It has been the purpose of this book to liberate the theory of price from the unrealistic confines of such an artificially restricted world. My task is therefore not complete without a discussion of the normative implications of the entrepreneurial process; for this discussion the success of a system is to be measured by its capacity to coordinate the innumerable individual decisions, plans, and actions that will be made independently in society during a given period of time.

THE COORDINATING PROCESS

We may approach our task of evaluating the success of the entrepreneurial market process in coordination by recalling the relationship between the state of equilibrium and the perfection of knowledge. "It appears," Hayek taught us long ago, "that the concept of equilibrium merely means that the foresight of the different members of the society is . . . correct in the sense that every person's plan is based on the expectation of the same set of external facts. . . . Correct foresight is then not, as it has sometimes been understood, a precondition which must exist in order that equilibrium may be arrived at. It is rather the defining characteristic of a state of equilibrium." [6] In other words, the state of equilibrium is the state in which all actions are perfectly coordinated, each market participant dovetailing his decisions with those which he (with complete accuracy) anticipates other participants will make. The perfection of knowledge which defines the state of equilibrium ensures complete coordination of individual plans.

It follows that the movement from disequilibrium to equilibrium is at once a movement from imperfect knowledge to perfect knowledge and from uncoordination to coordination. We have seen that the movement from disequilibrium to equilibrium is nothing but the entrepreneurial-competitive pro-

6. F. A. Hayek, "Economics and Knowledge," *Economica* 4 (February 1937): 33–54; reprinted in his *Individualism and Economic Order*, p. 42.

cess, which is a process of communicating information. Now the price system in a state of equilibrium, too, is often described as a system of communication — as a signal system. When we describe the market *process* as communicating information, however, we mean something quite different. The price system in equilibrium presents each decision-maker with a fully coordinated set of signals which, if followed, will permit all plans to dovetail. In the market process, on the other hand, these price signals themselves are *developed* through a process of learning that is governed step by step by the interim sets of prices; it is the latter process to which we refer as a process of communication of information.

This learning process at the same time nudges individual plans into closer and closer coordination. The rule is simple and obvious: coordination of information ensures coordination of action. As soon as a single mind becomes aware of the situations and attitudes of two separate individuals between whom exist the conditions for mutually beneficial exchange, so that he perceives the opportunity so presented — as soon, that is, as the previously isolated pieces of information have become coordinated in the mind of a single human being — we are assured of action to coordinate the decisions, plans, and actions of the individuals concerned.

The entrepreneurial-competitive process becomes visible now not merely as generating a tendency toward equilibrium, but as discovering and correcting discordant individual plans and decisions. We can observe this both in the simplest of market contexts and in the most complex.

Let us, for example, limit ourselves initially to a simple market for a single, undifferentiated product of standard quality. Let us call it "milk." Disequilibrium in this market means that (*a*) numerous milk prices prevail in the market, or (*b*) milk prices are, on the average, either above or below that price at which prospective sellers would find their selling plans in aggregate exactly matched by the aggregate buying plans of prospective buyers, or both. Only widespread ignorance concerning the true willingness of the various market participants to buy and sell milk can account for these disequilibrium market phenomena. Because of this ignorance, numerous possibilities for milk sales (that would be naturally beneficial to both sellers and buyers) are not being exploited. Thus many prospective sellers (aware only of the lower prices prevailing in the market and considering these too low to be worthwhile) forgo sales altogether because they are not aware that higher prices can be obtained; other sellers (aware of the higher prices prevailing, and seeing no reason why they should sell for less) find that they have missed sales at lower prices when they discover that there are *not* in fact sufficient buyers ready to pay these higher prices. Similarly, many prospective buyers (aware only of the higher prices, and considering these too high) miss purchase opportunities at lower prices; other buyers (aware of the lower prices and therefore refusing to buy for more), turn out to have missed these purchase opportunities available at the higher prices when it becomes evident that in fact there are not sufficient sellers prepared to sell at the lower price all that buyers would be prepared to buy.

In this simple market, with the attitudes and tastes of prospective buyers and sellers unchanging, the entrepreneurial-competitive process gradually introduces fuller general awareness of the temper of prospective buyers and sellers. The many prices for milk gradually converge toward a single price throughout the market, and this single price tends, moreover, to be the one capable of clearing the market. Each step in this process of convergence toward equilibrium is, we have seen,[7] an entrepreneurial one — in the sense that each step requires that market participants change their buying or selling plans because they now realize that the array of opportunities before them is different than they had believed. Each step in the equilibrating process, that is, reflects information learned through earlier

7. See above, pp. 69–72.

experiences in the market. These experiences revealed the absence of coordination that had characterized the market — the opportunities to buy (sell) that had been deliberately passed up in the overly optimistic belief that lower (higher) prices were possible, and the opportunities to buy and sell that had been unwittingly passed up because they simply were not recognized. "Entrepreneurship" — alertness to new information thus revealed — is what leads to revised plans nudging milk prices into a narrower and narrower band, a band that is itself nudged closer and closer to the market-clearing price. Each such entrepreneurial step — the abandoning by prospective buyers (sellers) of unrealistically low (high) buying (selling) offers, the initiation of offers to buy (sell) that were hitherto thought to be unrealistically unattractive to sellers (buyers) — is a replacement of plans that were revealed as more or less discordant by plans which, it is now believed, will be more completely coordinated.

The coordinating process which is thus revealed within the equilibrating entrepreneurial process in the simple market for the single commodity can be shown to be present wherever successful entrepreneurship is exercised. In earlier chapters we saw how entrepreneurship manifests itself not only in price movements for given products and resources but, perhaps even more important, also in changing patterns of product quality (interpreted broadly enough to include selling effort). The complex equilibrating process that is relevant to general equilibrium discussion, with this process determining at each step the entire set of opportunity specifications being made available, is, as we know, entrepreneurial. Its course is governed by entrepreneurial discovery of information — concerning new sources of resources, new technological opportunities, new possible combinations of product specifications, new patterns of consumer tastes — that generates entrepreneurial production plans that change the prices of resources and the quantities produced of the various varieties and qualities of products.

Each entrepreneurial discovery represents alertness to a hitherto unperceived interpersonal opportunity — an opportunity that depends on the coordinated plans of two separate individuals. As this "general" equilibrating process proceeds by competitive-entrepreneurial alertness, it identifies more and more uncoordinated situations, at the same time spreading the information perceived by entrepreneurial alertness among wider and wider circles in the market.

THE ROLE OF PROFITS

In this entrepreneurial coordinating process we must be careful to recognize the role of profits. Pure entrepreneurial profits are obtainable where there is more than one price for a given commodity in the same market (or where there is one price for the bundle of resources required to produce a given commodity and a different price for that commodity itself). But this means that entrepreneurial *profit opportunities exist wherever there is scope for more complete coordination of individual plans.* Where there is more than one price for the "same" thing (with the bundle of necessary inputs treated, for this discussion, as the "same" as the output they make possible), it is clear that discordant plans have been made. Those who have sold for the low price have clearly not coordinated their plans with those who have bought for higher prices (or with those who did not buy at all because they were aware only of the higher prices).

It follows therefore that to identify absences of coordination among the plans of market participants it is sufficient to identify profit opportunities. And it is here, of course, that we have the source of entrepreneurial alertness. Alertness toward new opportunities is stimulated by the heady scent of profits. Profits are to be found where available bits of information have not yet been coordinated. The exploitation of profit opportunities consists in identifying and correcting uncoordinated groups of plans. And, of course, as the process of correction proceeds the profit opportunities themselves dwindle away. At best, the capacity of men to notice what is happening (and, a fortiori, what is likely to happen) is highly imperfect. The lure of profits and fear of losses can be counted upon, in some measure, to attract at least some entrepreneurs. And as these pioneers act, their actions confront other, less alert entrepreneurs with information which it is less and less possible to overlook.

The essence of the "profit incentive" (and in particular its significance for normative economics) is thus not to be seen as motivation to work harder or to allocate resources more efficiently. The profit incentive (including, of course, the disincentive of loss) operates most significantly by sparking the alertness of entrepreneurs — by encouraging them to keep their eyes open for new information that will lead to new plans.[8] And its powerful effect in this regard acquires normative significance because of the market's prior failure to coordinate sets of decisions.[9]

When pure entrepreneurial profit arises from speculative foresight the situation is no different. If a generally unexpected crop failure causes a rise in grain prices, grain speculators profit. The difference between the old grain price and the new higher price reflects an absence of "coordination" (across time) among the consumption plans of individuals. Many who consumed or sold grain when its price was low would not have done so had they been aware that others (or they themselves) would shortly be willing to pay much higher prices. Had some entrepreneur correctly forecast the crop failure, he would have been able to prevent this lack of coordination. The fortunate grain speculator's profits have arisen in precisely this way.

In a paper concerned with the theory of speculation, Sam-

8. See further below, p. 229.
9. On the relationship between the inefficiency signalled by the existence of profit opportunities and what H. Leibenstein calls "x-inefficiency," see above chap. 2, n. 11.

uelson denies that competition among speculators can wipe out such speculative grain profits. These profits "are created by the changed conditions." [10] This is true only to the extent that previous competition among speculators has failed to anticipate the failure. Thus it is not so much the changed conditions themselves which have generated these profits as the earlier market ignorance of these future conditions.

Samuelson also points out that it is impossible to declare that profits are "deserved" by the entrepreneur (in the sense that he alone has "produced" something which society values at the amount of the profits). The advantage society derives from the market's discovering a crop failure a few seconds earlier must, for example, be quite small. Yet the entrepreneur who discovers the failure a few seconds earlier than his competitors wins a fortune.[11] Here Samuelson appears to be arguing that there is no relation between the incentive offered to the entrepreneur and the social function he performs. Here too Samuelson's remark may lead to misunderstanding.

It is of course true that pure entrepreneurial profit is not to be interpreted as a productivity return (so that Samuelson's reference to "a Clarkian naive-productivity theory of ethical deservingness" is hardly relevant). But it is not necessary to resolve the question of the ethical deservingness of profits in order to recognize the social function performed by profits and the correspondence between the value of this service and the size of the profit incentive. If a commodity is being sold at ten, when elsewhere (or at a future time) a buyer would be prepared to pay fifty, the gap in the price reflects the difference in valuation of the commodity by the two buyers (and thus the seriousness of the absence of coordination between the decisions being made in the market). The profit opportunity thus presented offers, therefore, an incentive for entrepreneurial

10. P. A. Samuelson, "Intertemporal Price Equilibrium: A Prologue to the Theory of Speculation," *Weltwirtschaftliches Archiv* 79 (December 1957): 209.

11. Ibid.

correction that faithfully reflects the degree of uncoordination. It is this incentive upon which the market relies to set competing entrepreneurs ("speculators") running to close the gap. It seems not at all inappropriate, therefore, for the winning entrepreneur to take all. It is true that even if the "winning entrepreneur" did not exist, and thus did not win his fortune, the others would arrive only a few seconds later; it is *not* necessarily true that these others would come forward as rapidly (or at all) were no fortune available for the winner.

RESOURCE MISALLOCATION, TRANSACTION COSTS, AND ENTREPRENEURSHIP

The theme of this chapter can perhaps be brought into clearer focus by relating it to some recent critical discussions concerning orthodox welfare economics. In welfare economics, Pareto-optimality sets well-known marginal conditions to ensure that there is no alternative assignment in which a unit of resource or product might make a more valuable marginal contribution to welfare. If these conditions are not satisfied we have, in Paretian terms, an inefficient pattern of resource allocation. On the other hand, it has been argued, in a vigorous literature stemming from a pioneering article by Coase,[12] (*a*) that if the transactions required for resource reallocation are costless, the market will eliminate all resource misallocation; and (*b*) that if the transactions required for reallocation are themselves costly, it may be incorrect to describe a violation of the Paretian conditions as inefficient (since the cost of "correction" may be so high that the improvement is outweighed by its cost). It is the first of these propositions that I now wish to examine critically.

Coase describes the nature of transaction costs as follows:

In order to carry out a market transaction it is necessary to discover who it is that one wishes to deal with, to inform people that one wishes to deal and on what terms, to conduct negotiations leading up to a bargain, to draw up the contract,

12. R. H. Coase, "The Problem of Social Cost," *Journal of Law and Economics* 3 (October 1960): 1–44.

to undertake the inspection needed to make sure that the terms of the contract are being observed, and so on. These operations are often extremely costly.[13]

But were transactions costless, Coase showed, bargaining would proceed until no further bargain could improve the allocation of resources. Calabresi has presented clearly the results of Coase's analysis:

Thus if one assumes rationality, no transaction costs, and no legal impediments to bargaining, *all* misallocations of resources would be fully cured in the market by bargains. . . . A misallocation exists when there is available a possible reallocation in which all those who would lose from the reallocation could be fully compensated by those who would gain, and, at the end of this compensation process, there would still be some who would be better off than before.

This and other similar definitions of resource misallocation merely mean that there is a misallocation when a situation can be improved by bargains. If people are rational, bargains are costless, and there are no legal impediments to bargains, transactions will *ex hypothesi* occur to the point where bargains can no longer improve the situation; to the point, in short, of optimal resource allocation.[14]

The proposition thus stated in terms of resource misallocation can be translated into the "coordination" terminology which we have adopted here. Where there is absence of coordination among the decisions, plans, and actions of individuals in a market, then, if transactions are costless and legally unimpeded, transactions will occur until complete coordination among all individuals has been achieved. It is my position that this statement may be misleading, and that it has been used to infer conclusions which may be invalid.

My central theme has been to explore the implications of the insight that even where transactions are costless and other-

13. Ibid., p. 15.
14. G. Calabresi, "Transaction Costs, Resource Allocation, and Liability Rules: A Comment," *Journal of Law and Economics* 11 (April 1968): 68. See also H. Demsetz, "The Cost of Transacting," *Quarterly Journal of Economics* 82 (February 1968): 33–34.

wise unimpeded, attainment of the state of equilibrium is by no means "assured" and is in any event certainly not instantaneous. This insight, which draws attention to the delicate role of the entrepreneurial process in bringing about a tendency toward equilibrium, seems to be absent from the statements cited in the preceding paragraphs. That literature seems, as we shall see, to accept the idea that the assumed condition of unimpeded transactions at zero cost is sufficient to ensure immediate, automatic, and frictionless elimination of all resource misallocation.

Among the transaction costs relevant to the cited statements is the cost of obtaining the information necessary to enter into and complete bargaining negotiations. With zero transaction costs, therefore, we have the case where all desired information can be obtained costlessly. The cited statements seem to assert, and I deny, that, since transacting is costless and since all information is available at no cost, nothing can conceivably delay the completion of all possible transactions that can be shown to be mutually beneficial. For a market displaying numerous opportunities for improved resource allocation, complete optimality will be attained as soon as the transactions can be physically completed. I deny this on the grounds that *the possibility of costlessly acquiring information concerning available desirable opportunities is by no means sufficient to ensure that these opportunities will ever be grasped*. To have costless access to an item of information is not yet *to know* that information, since one may still not be aware of it.

To take advantage of available opportunities one must first *perceive* them. To "learn" free information, one must perceive the opportunity to do so. To complete a mutually profitable transaction one must not merely have free access to the requisite information, but must perceive its availability (and thus the possibility of the profitable transaction). Zero transaction costs do not of themselves guarantee that transaction opportunities will be discovered. Even in a world of zero transaction

227

costs (including zero cost of obtaining all necessary information), a tendency toward equilibrium can exist only if the competitive-entrepreneurial process communicates steadily improved flows of information to market participants. There will be absence of coordination in a zero-transaction-cost market (as in more realistic markets) until it is gradually eliminated by successive entrepreneurial steps. Assurance that such steps will be taken requires not merely that desirable transactions be available (even costlessly), but that profit-motivated entrepreneurs be alert to them and thereby set in motion a process spreading such knowledge throughout the market. (I stress the *process* of spreading knowledge. Were the entrepreneurial process accomplished in one step, my disagreement with the zero-transaction-costs literature would be trivial. But we know that this process is a gradual one, in which entrepreneurs gradually feel their way toward the true temper of the market, while the course of price movements gradually communicates more and more accurate information to more and more market participants.)

My insistence that the entrepreneurial process is needed even in a world of zero transaction costs can be expressed in terms of the incentive provided by profit opportunities. Writers who have emphasized that the market (if unimpeded by transaction costs) can eliminate inefficiency in resource allocation have recognized the importance both of information and of incentives. Thus Demsetz writes: "There are two tasks which must be handled well by any acceptable allocative mechanism. These are, firstly, that information must be generated about all the benefits of employing resources in alternative uses, and secondly, that persons be motivated to take account of this information." [15]

Now, we can distinguish *two* levels at which incentives are needed to motivate decision-makers to grasp opportunities.

15. H. Demsetz, "The Exchange and Enforcement of Property Rights," *Journal of Law and Economics* 7 (October 1964): 16.

First, incentives are needed *when this opportunity has already been perceived.* (Thus in the theory of the "Robbinsian" firm, with revenue and cost curves already known, we talk of the profit motive as the incentive for the profit-maximizing price-output decision.) But a second level of incentive is needed to motivate alertness to the possibility of as yet unperceived opportunities that may be lurking around the corner. The writers on zero transaction costs certainly recognize the crucial role of the first kind of incentive. But they seem to take the second entirely for granted, assuming that if useful information is freely available it will immediately become known — every bit of it — in one instantaneous step. My position, on the other hand, emphasizes the role of the entrepreneurial process, which is explicitly founded on the second kind of incentive — that is, on the entrepreneurial capacity to smell profits. We need this incentive — imperfect a mechanism as it is — to explain why entrepreneurs try new ventures, why they experiment with new prices and new qualities of product, why they search for something they are not sure exists. Most important, we need it to show how pioneering changes in prices and product qualities systematically communicate to less alert imitators the information which their own entrepreneurship has not yet discovered.

In the light of my remarks on the incentive role of entrepreneurial profits, it becomes particularly evident that the cited proposition of the zero transaction-cost-writers has led them to doubtful conclusions. We can see this in the way they have compared the market and government as alternative social devices for allocating resources. If, as these writers argued, a market's violation of Pareto-optimality conditions is to be attributed solely to the costs of resource reallocation (transaction costs), then this violation may not signify inefficiency (since efficiency requires that transaction costs too be economized). However, they point out, a conclusive judgment cannot be made without examining the resources required to achieve the relevant resource reallocation through social devices, such as government, alternative to the market. Thus, if a government reallocation of the "misallocated" resources can be achieved at a cost low enough to make it worthwhile, then a laissez-faire situation which (because of high market transaction-costs) has not produced this reallocation must be pronounced inefficient.

My objection to this conclusion can be stated briefly. For government decision-making as for market decision-making, it is not enough that a worthwhile opportunity be available; it must be *perceived* as available. A comparison between the efficiency of market resource allocation and that of government cannot, therefore, be made simply on the basis of the cost of market transactions as compared with the cost to government of reallocation. The crucial question for government-market comparisons must concern the capacity of each of the two systems *to bring available opportunities to the attention of decision-makers.* Even if the costs to government of reallocating resources were zero, and even if this included the costs of acquiring information, it would not follow that in a government-directed economy resources would inevitably be optimally allocated. To make this conclusion valid we would have to assume not merely that government could acquire information costlessly, but that government was already omniscient. A market relies on the incentive of profit to set in motion the entrepreneurial process. It is solely because of the desire to obtain profits that we can, in any degree, "rely" on entrepreneurial discovery of where profits are to be had. Under government direction, it is not at all clear what substitutes for the profit incentive are available, in the absence of omniscience — not merely to spur the exploitation of socially desirable opportunities, but to direct attention to their very existence. Only if we ignore the role played in the market by this entrepreneurial element can we fail to raise the question of a corresponding role in the government-directed economy. (My criticism in this regard is thus parallel to Hayek's position in the classic debate concerning the possibility of economic calculation under socialism. The writers who affirmed this possibility, Hayek showed,[16] apparently did so on the assumption that the central planning authorities would already possess all necessary information. But of course it is precisely the mobilization of information which is under debate.)

NIRVANA, TRANSACTION COSTS, AND COORDINATION

It will be recalled that we have eschewed the orthodox approach to welfare analysis and have adopted instead the notion of *coordination* as the norm for evaluation. Our dissatisfaction with the orthodox welfare framework was twofold. First, that framework assumes, as Hayek has pointed out, that all relevant information is already possessed — an assumption which begs the real question we wish to answer. Second, that framework must adopt the doubtful presumption that a meaningful notion of "social welfare" can be distilled from the separate sets of values displayed by the individual members of society. By setting up "coordination" as the standard, we were able to escape both these sources of dissatisfaction. It may be useful now to observe how the coordination approach helps avoid a further difficulty that has frequently clouded applications of the orthodox welfare analysis. Demsetz has pointed out the danger as follows: "The view that now pervades much public policy economics implicitly presents the relevant choice as between an ideal norm and an existing 'imperfect' institutional arrangement. This *nirvana* approach differs considerably from a *comparative institution* approach in which the relevant choice is between alternative real institutional arrangements." [17] The nirvana approach is likely to mislead, in particular, because a situation which appears ideal once it has been attained may be far from an ideal goal if it can be attained only at a high cost (of transactions, reallocations, mobility, and the like).

16. See Hayek, *Individualism and Economic Order*, pp. 201–2.
17. H. Demsetz, "Information and Efficiency: Another Viewpoint," *Journal of Law and Economics* 12 (April 1969): 1.

This danger applies because orthodox welfare economics concentrates upon the state of affairs that is optimal *once it has been attained* rather than upon the *process* by which less-than-optimal states can be improved. (As was noted earlier, this corresponds closely to the way orthodox price theory is preoccupied with states of equilibrium rather than with the process by which a tendency toward equilibrium takes effect.) By contrast, a normative approach cast in terms of the degree of coordination among the actions of individual market participants (and among the pieces of information underlying these actions) can more easily escape the danger of a nirvana approach. Questions concerning coordination do not (like the questions treated by orthodox welfare economics) take for granted given sets of data which of themselves imply an "ideal." Questions on coordination concern the actual decisions being made by market participants, seeking to assess the extent to which such decisions are mutually "incompatible" (in the sense that they would not have been made had the decision-makers been aware of the others' decisions). A pair of decisions by two market participants are "discordant" not because they diverge from some "ideal" set of decisions but because if either were aware of what the other meant to do he would decide differently. Phenomena as important as transaction costs can be overlooked in orthodox welfare theory because it emphasizes the state of affairs in which marginal adjustments offer no net promise of improvement. Thus it tends to dismiss other situations as inefficient without remembering to count the costs of reallocation itself. Focus upon coordination, on the other hand, is concerned with what market participants would themselves decide to do, and thus makes it more difficult to ignore such elements as the transaction costs which the market participants themselves take into account.

In general, the emphasis on the entrepreneurial process central to our approach is ill suited to the nirvana approach so incisively identified by Demsetz. Our focus of interest is never the optimality of an existing pattern of decisions; it is always the desirability of the direction in which this pattern of decisions is changing. The elimination of uncoordination between existing decisions provides a yardstick (for measuring the desirability of such change) eminently suited for a normative approach not vulnerable to the danger of nirvana thinking.

The analysis of externalities, which has spurred much of the interest in transaction costs (and has underlined the role of the nirvana approach in orthodox welfare theory) offers examples supporting the assertions of the preceding paragraphs. Suppose a factory belches smoke which causes damage to surrounding houses, and no legal responsibility for this damage falls upon the factory owner. Orthodox welfare analysis is quick to conclude that factory output will be such that social costs at the margin outweigh relevant social benefits, since the damage to the houses does not enter the cost calculations of the producer. More careful analysis warns of an error here; were it not for the transaction costs hampering deals between homeowners and the producer, the damage might indeed enter the cost calculations of the producer (in the form of forgone revenues, offered by the householders to persuade him not to inflict the damage).

An approach based on coordination, on the other hand, is unlikely to fall into this error. We would not ask whether the marginal benefits to society, in the factory case, outweighed the corresponding costs (including smoke damage). As long, after all, as knowledge of these benefits and costs is absent, we would argue, such questions are hardly relevant. We would ask, on the other hand, what transactions currently not being entered into would be completed (and what current transactions would *not* be completed) were the various market participants aware of one another's attitudes. Once we raise the question why the factory owners and the householders do not make a deal, it becomes difficult to *avoid* seeing the possible reasons why the factory owner does not offer to reduce the smoke damage for a price (or why the householders do not offer such a price). A coordination approach directs our attention to the important social questions relating to externalities — questions that all too often are not raised in orthodox analysis. These questions should surely concern the likelihood that external effects *may not be noticed at all* (or if they are noticed, that the possibility of avoiding them through rearranging activities is not noticed). But this raises those questions of entrepreneurship (whether in the market economy or the centrally planned economy) which are simply not considered in welfare economics.

THE "WASTES" OF COMPETITION

The normative approach adopted in this chapter requires that we dissent from certain judgments frequently passed on the efficiency of the competitive process. One is often confronted with references to the wastefulness of competition (referring of course not to perfect competition, but to the rivalrous character of real-world competition). It is pointed out that there is wasteful duplication under competition,[18] that the process of achieving competitive equilibrium involves temporary positions in which resources are "monopolistically" misallocated,[19] and that the way the process corrects imperfections in knowledge is wasteful because the correction comes only after the mistakes have been made.[20] Such statements are often accompanied by remarks recognizing that these "misallocations" or "wastes" are unavoidable; or even that they may involve less inefficiency than alternative (nonmarket) equilibrating mechanisms. What I wish to point out here is that such statements asserting the

18. See, e.g., J. Backman, *Advertising and Competition* (New York: New York University Press, 1967), p. 32.

19. K. Arrow, "Toward a Theory of Price Adjustment," in *The Allocation of Economic Resources*, ed. Abramovitz et al. (Stanford: Stanford University Press, 1959), p. 50.

20. K. Rothschild, "The Wastes of Competition," in *Monopoly and Competition and Their Regulation*, ed. E. H. Chamberlin (London: Macmillan, 1954), p. 307.

inefficiency of the competitive process display the fundamental weakness of the orthodox welfare approach.

During the competitive process through which the market approaches equilibrium there is imperfection of knowledge, which the process steadily moves toward eliminating. From the point of view of an *omniscient* observer the market indeed displays waste and misallocation at every stage. On the other hand, each step in the process improves the coordination of existing information and eliminates some of the discordant decisions made earlier. And, perhaps even more pertinent, at each step in this process no perceived opportunity for improving the allocation of resources is left ungrasped. Thus one is surely entitled to question the appropriateness of labeling *inefficient* an allocation of resources whose inefficiency no one, including the welfare theorist, has been able to discover. The notion of a misallocated resource rests on the existence of a potential use for a given resource that is superior to its present use. Where in 1920 a resource was being employed in the best use currently known for it, one is inclined to raise eyebrows at a charge that it was inefficiently allocated merely because, from the point of view of 1970 technology, a still better use could have been found. Surely the notion of inefficiency implies that an available, superior course of action that *might have* been taken was ignored. If the notion is to be valid for condemning any given allocation of resources, one should surely confine its use to cases where these available alternative courses of action were not simply overlooked, but were deliberately rejected.

Once the spotlight is focused not on the degree of conformity to the ideal allocation as seen from the perspective of omniscience, but on the degree to which currently known information is being optimally deployed, one is compelled to appraise the efficiency of the competitive process in a way drastically different from the views cited earlier. Not only will one refrain from efficiency judgments based on an irrelevant yardstick of omniscience, but one will recognize that decisions currently being made reflect the most up-to-date intelligence gathered by alert, profit-motivated entrepreneurs and that these decisions will in turn effectively communicate this information to others.

Suppose there is a single producer of a given product. A new competitor enters the industry, "duplicating" the production facilities already used. It is surely misleading to describe this as a misuse of resources (even if one hastens to concede that this misuse may in the end be justified by the advantages achieved through competition). The truth is that until the newly competing entrepreneur has tested his hunch about the lowest cost at which he can produce, we simply do not know what organization of the industry is "best." To describe the competitive process as wasteful because it corrects mistakes only after they occur [21] seems similar to ascribing the ailment to the medicine which heals it, or even to blaming the diagnostic procedure for the disease it identifies. What appears from the viewpoint of omniscience to be waste springs from precisely that imperfection of knowledge which it is the role of the competitive process to locate and eliminate.[22]

LONG-RUN AND SHORT-RUN EVALUATIONS

In concluding this chapter it is necessary to notice that the very same set of actions in an economy may be judged, equally validly, in several quite different ways. As this circumstance seems not to have received emphasis in the literature, and is in addition closely related to the analysis of chapter 5, it seems worthwhile to discuss it carefully.

In chapter 5 extensive attention was devoted to the insight that the positive character of a sequence of market events de-

21. Ibid.
22. For a highly refreshing critique of the myth of the wastefulness of competition see D. Dewey, The Theory of Imperfect Competition: A Radical Reconstruction (New York: Columbia University Press, 1969), chap. 7. See also above, pp. 129–31, for comments on the Schumpeter-Galbraith thesis that only in the absence of perfectly competitive conditions can there be incentive for economic progress.

pends crucially upon the time perspective from which these events are interpreted. We saw, for example, that such familiar aspects of production as costs and profitability may appear quite different when related to (and measured from the perspective of) decisions made in the more distant past than they appear when related only to decisions made in the recent past. A process of production which appears in the short-run view (defined by recent decisions) as costless and profitable may, when interpreted in the long-run view (identified by decisions made further in the past), appear to have been costly and unprofitable. Similarly, a market process which from a short-run view appears to reflect resource monopoly may, we found, in a longer-run view display a wholly competitive face. Here I wish to draw attention to the parallel possibility in normative analysis. One's evaluation of a sequence of market events will depend upon whether it is being undertaken from a long-run or a short-run perspective. This insight can be helpful in a number of ways.

Consider a firm engaged in a line of production, say shoe manufacturing, which is profitable when viewed from the short-run perspective but unprofitable in the longer view. From the perspective of the date in the past when the decision was made to erect a factory for this line of production, the venture seems clearly to have been a losing one: it should never have been started. All the resources poured into the venture, the steel employed in the plant construction as well as the leather used each month in its operation, should never have been applied to these purposes. However, from the shorter-run view, from the perspective of a date well after the plant was unfortunately constructed, the decision to keep operating the plant is seen to have been profitable. The resources employed to keep up shoe production are seen now to have been well used in this employment. It is fortunate that they were not snapped up and put to work in other industries. Whatever the normative yardstick employed in evaluation (whether the orthodox allocation-of-social-resources standard, or the coordination-of-knowledge-and-actions standard recommended here), it turns out that a judgment on the desirability of the firm's current operations depends entirely upon whether we undertake a long- or short-run assessment. The decision to build the factory was badly coordinated with the decisions of potential customers in later years; but once the factory had been built, rightly or wrongly, the decision to operate it was eminently coordinated with consumer decisions.[23]

Consider now the cases discussed in chapter 5, where short-run monopoly positions were acquired through earlier entrepreneurial alertness (e.g., buying up the entire supply of a resource) in competitive markets open to all. We saw that the actions of the producer (who is now in the favored monopoly position) must be described as monopolistic in the short run, but as competitive from the longer-run view. Let us appraise such a sequence of events from the normative viewpoint.

We may recall from chapter 3 that our view on the nature of monopoly led us to an understanding of the harmfulness of monopoly that differs from the orthodox position. For us the harmfulness of monopoly does not lie in the bare fact of a divergence between the price of output and its marginal cost (and, moreover, the mere presence of a downward-sloping demand curve facing a firm does not, for us, spell monopoly). We saw the possible harmfulness of monopoly (in relation to the interests of consumers) as arising because monopoly ownership of a resource motivates its owner to avoid using a scarce resource as fully as consumers' tastes demand. Even the most complete coordination of available information would fail to enlist the monopolized resource for the fullest service to con-

23. The long-run–short-run dichotomy used here is that developed in chapter 5. The welfare literature offers examples of the distinction between long-run welfare analysis and short-run analysis that depends on the duration of time being considered (short-run welfare judgments being those which take into account only the effects that are visible within a short period of time).

sumers.[24] The interest of the monopolist is not necessarily best served (as the interest of a resource owner without monopoly *is* served) by placing his resource at the complete service of consumers. "The monopolist does not employ the monopolized good according to the wishes of the consumers." [25]

Where a monopoly position has been acquired through competitive entrepreneurial alertness and is being subsequently exploited through underutilization of the monopolized resource, one's appraisal of the situation must depend on the "length of run" of the perspective adopted. From the short-run view one sees simply a monopoly situation. A resource owner holds a monopoly position and is able to exploit it by failing to use the monopolized resource as fully as consumers wish. The monopolist's interests run counter to those of the consumers.

From the longer-run perspective, however, the monopolist's activity is perceived as the completion of an entrepreneurial plan which began when he acquired the scarce resource. That plan (of which an integral part was exploiting the resource monopoly) was possible and profitable only because other producers had failed to realize the potential of this resource. Their failure to realize this profit potential may reflect either of two possibilities. It is, first of all, possible that other producers fully perceived the value consumers place upon the employment of the resource in this particular use (i.e., the use to which the monopolist puts it.) Thus, in the absence of the entrepreneurial act of the would-be monopolist, there would have been a more or less rapid tendency toward the fullest employment of the resource in line with consumer wishes. What the other producers failed to see, in this case, was only the potential profit from acquiring monopoly control over this resource. For this possibility, it is clear, the long-run normative

24. Thus the important conclusion emerges that this notion of underutilization of a monopolized resource does not depend on perfect knowledge as a norm.

25. L. Mises, *Human Action* (New Haven: Yale University Press, 1949), p. 676.

view of the situation does not differ significantly from the short-run view. The potential for monopolistic restriction has diverted long-run entrepreneurial alertness into channels which "deprive" consumers of some of the productivity of an available resource.[26]

In the second possibility, however, the entrepreneurial alertness of the would-be entrepreneur may impinge on a market in which the other producers have not yet perceived at all the importance consumers attach to this product (into which the resource is directed by the monopolist). Thus, in the absence of the entrepreneurship of the would-be monopolist there would have been delay in harnessing the resource to make this product. The long-run interests of the consumers have, in this case, been well served by the would-be monopolist. At the time when he acquired sole control over the resource, every part of the entrepreneurial plan (even his planned restricted use of the resource) meant an improvement in resource allocation, as viewed by consumers, over the alternative entrepreneurial plans then being attempted.

Normative economic analysis is undertaken, in part, to formulate economic policy. The discussions in this chapter do not of themselves yield unambiguous policy prescriptions. But they do help direct attention to the questions that need to be answered before reasoned policy can be formulated. Where monopolistic restriction of resource use occurs, it might appear to be in the consumers' interests to press for a policy that would dissolve the monopolist's unique control over the resource. The discussions have revealed that such a policy, although indeed suggested by the short-run normative view of the case, may *not* be supported by the long-run view.

A long-run view may, we have seen, reveal that the consumer's interests have been furthered by the creation of monopoly. To be sure, it will be argued that, although the entrepreneurship which originally created the resource monopoly

26. See further above, chap. 5, n. 7.

and directed it into its present use certainly improved the coordination between resource availability and consumer tastes, nonetheless this should not affect the desirability of breaking the monopoly *now*. It is true that the entrepreneur who carved out the monopoly niche for himself (and in so doing ensured that the monopolized resource would be assigned to this, rather than to less important branches of output) did so only in anticipation of high profits from monopolistically restricted use of the resource. But if consumers are to act in what is clearly their interest *now* (now that the resource has been successfully steered away from less important uses), then they should surely take advantage of the original act of entrepreneurship while depriving the entrepreneur of the monopoly profits which motivated that act. Tempting as this line of argument may appear, however, there seems reason to suggest that this may be an unwise attitude. And because the market process, as discussed in this essay, is likely to inspire this attitude rather frequently, it is worthwhile to point out its shortcomings. Let us restate the problem before us.

The market process is likely to offer cases in which profitable opportunities depend upon the completion of a series of transactions. The interests of consumers are in these cases unquestionably furthered by the earlier steps. Once these first steps have been taken, however, it is in the immediate interest of consumers that the subsequent steps be different from those the prospect of which originally inspired entrepreneurs. Is it now in the interest of consumers [27] to seek to abrogate the entrepreneurs' right to proceed to the transactions originally planned for?

That such abrogation may be unwise may be shown by recognizing the cost abrogation entails. Although the immediate consequences of such abrogation seem desirable for consumers, there are likely to be attendant disadvantages not immediately

27. We abstract here from the ethical question of the *justice* of such abrogation under the stated circumstances.

apparent. Abrogating the rights of the monopolist cannot, it is true, nullify the advantages which have already accrued to consumers from the earlier transactions completed by the would-be monopolist. But a social policy which arbitrarily confiscates from entrepreneurs the profitably secure positions their entrepreneurial alertness has achieved cannot fail to discourage such alertness in the future. And since such alertness, even when it leads to monopoly positions, may very well improve the extent to which consumer tastes are satisfied, any discouragement of it must be deplored.

Index

243

Index

Corporate firm, the, 55–57, 62–65
Costs: long-run and short-run, 189–97; sunk, 191–95. *See also* Production costs; Selling costs; Transaction costs
Cournot, Augustin, 90
"Creative destruction," 91–92, 125–31

De Alessi, L., 190n
Demand curve, relevance of for defining monopoly, 103–4
Demsetz, Harold, 89n, 117n, 175, 177, 186n, 204n, 205n, 226n, 228, 231
Dewey, Donald, 93n, 112n, 117n, 186n, 202n, 236n
Disequilibrium. *See* Entrepreneurship, and market process; Ignorance
Doyle, P., 153n, 162n

Economic progress, 130
Economizing, 31–32; contrasted with human action, 33, 86; not competitive, 94–96, 108–9; as pure Robbinsian decision-making, 32–33, 94, 147
Edwards, H. R., 89n, 117n, 118n, 139n, 165, 189n
Entrepreneurial process, as process of coordination, 218–25
Entrepreneurial profits. *See* Profits
Entrepreneurship, 30–87; and competition, 7, 94–101; distinguished from factors of production, 66; as equilibrating force, 74, 81; in individual action, 39, 85; and knowledge, 65–69; and market process, 13–17, 37–43, 69–75, 218–25; nature of, 30–32; not requiring ownership of assets,

16, 40, 99–100; performed by producers for consumer, 136, 146–51; pure, 39–41; Schumpeter's view of, 72, 79–81, 126–29; seen as "control," 57, 83; separate from capitalist role, 49; as source of monopoly position, 22–23, 131–34; 199–211; and speculation, 86; as "ultimate hiring," 69
Entry, role of freedom of, 97–100, 103, 210
Equilibrium: as cessation of competitive process, 13; emphasis on in contemporary theory, 1, 4–5
Excess capacity, doctrine of, 117, 177n, 185–86
Expectations, 71
Externalities, 233–34

Firm, theory of, in contemporary economics, 27, 46, 52–54, 84, 101–2, 229. *See also* Monopoly
Fraser, L. M., 86n
Freedom of entry. *See* Entry, role of freedom of
Friedman, Milton, 82n, 192n

Galbraith, John K., 171–72, 174–75, 177
Georgescu-Roegen, N., 90n, 183n
Gordon, Kermit, 142n
Gordon, R., 56, 83

Hahn, F. A., 177n
Hayek, F. A., 71n, 74n, 91, 93, 119, 129n, 175, 213–15, 217, 218, 230–31
Heflebower, R. B., 152n, 185n, 206
Heiser, R., 178n
Hennipman, P., 89n

244

Index

Hicks, J. R., 154, 161, 189n
Hirshleifer, J., 190
Human action, as Misesian decision-making, 33, 86–87
Hutt, W. H., 167n

Ignorance: as cause for disequilibrium, 10, 12, 69–70; as cause for profit opportunities, 14, 216; as preventing coordination, 217–25
Impediments to entry. See Entry, role of freedom of
Industry, notion of the, 102, 105–6, 119–25
Inefficiency, 216
Information, economics of, 66, 151–63

Kaldor, N., 142, 146n, 151, 164, 169–70, 171n
Kirzner, Israel M., 35n, 72n, 75n, 183n, 192n
Knight, Frank H., 69n, 75n, 81–84, 211n
Knowledge, 215–18. See also Entrepreneurship
Koplin, H. T., 45n, 63n
Kuenne, R. E., 105n, 112n, 120–23

Leibenstein, H., 46n, 223n
Lever, E. A., 151n
Lewis, A., 104n, 133
Long run, and short run, 187–211. See also Costs; Monopoly; Profits
Lucas, R. E., 190n

McCord Wright, D., 93n
McFarland, D., 101n, 105n, 106n, 121–24
Machlup, F., 66n, 93n, 98n, 99, 101n, 141, 142n, 189n, 190, 202n

McNulty, P. J., 89n, 90n
Manne, Henry G., 63n
Market process, 1, 9–11. See also Entrepreneurship
Markham, J. W., 126n
Marshall, Alfred, 91, 151n, 165, 170, 188
Mason, Edward S., 125n
Maximization of profits, 27, 46, 84
Misallocation, 111, 225–31
Mises, L., 33, 39n, 84–87, 107n, 119, 129n, 142n, 188n, 239n
Misesian human action, 33
Modigliani, F., 98n
Monopoly, 19–23, 101–12; consistent with competitive market process, 21; does not relate to theory of firm, 108; harmfulness of, 109–11, 238–41; short-run, 205–11; source of in entrepreneurship, 22–23, 131–34, 199–211; source of in resource ownership, 20; temporary, 133–34, 203, 208–9; in a theory of market process, 102–3, 101–12
Monopolistic competition, 91–93, 112–19

Nutter, W., 183n

Olson, M., 101n, 105n, 106n, 121–24
Ownership, not a source of entrepreneurial profits, 50

Papandreou, A. G., 52
Pareto-optimality, 217n
Peterson, Shorey, 56n, 91, 112n
Pigou, A. C., 151n, 164, 165, 170
Price-takers, as Robbinsian economizers, 42

245